PENGUIN

THE ART OF HAPPINESS

EPICURUS (341–271 B.C.) founded one of antiquity's most influential philosophical schools, which
focused on the pursuit of happiness. Born on the
Greek island of Samos, he operated the Garden,
devoted to philosophy and communal living, outside of Athens.

GEORGE K. STRODACH (1905–1971) taught at
Lafayette College, in Easton, Pennsylvania—first
in the language department and then in the philosophy department—for more than thirty-five years.

DANIEL KLEIN is the author of *Travels with Epicurus* and, with Thomas Cathcart, of the interna-
tional bestseller *Plato and a Platypus Walk into a
Bar*. A graduate of Harvard, in philosophy, he is
the author or coauthor of twenty-five other books.
He lives in western Massachusetts with his wife,
Freke Vuijst.

EPICURUS

The Art of Happiness

*Translated with an Introduction
and Commentary by*
GEORGE K. STRODACH

Foreword by
DANIEL KLEIN

PENGUIN BOOKS

PENGUIN BOOKS

Published by the Penguin Group
Penguin Group (USA) Inc., 375 Hudson Street,
New York, New York 10014, USA

USA | Canada | UK | Ireland | Australia | New Zealand | India | South Africa | China
Penguin Books Ltd, Registered Offices: 80 Strand, London WC2R 0RL, England
For more information about the Penguin Group visit penguin.com

First published in the United States of America as *The Philosophy of
Epicurus: Letters, Doctrines, and Parallel Passages from Lucretius*
by Northwestern University Press 1963
This edition with a foreword by Daniel Klein published
in Penguin Books 2012

LIBRARY OF CONGRESS CATALOGING-IN-PUBLICATION DATA
Epicurus.
[Selections. English. 2013]
The art of happiness / Epicurus : translated with and introduction and
commentary by George K. Strodach ; foreword by Daniel Klein.
p. cm.
Includes bibliographical references and index.
ISBN 978-0-14-310721-7
1. Epicureans (Greek philosophy) 2. Philosophy, Ancient.
3. Epicurus—Correspondence. I. Strodach, George K. II. Title.
B570.E5S8 2013
187—dc23   2012040886

Printed in the United States of America
25 27 29 30 28 26

Contents

Foreword

In Athens in the third century B.C., everyday consciousness reached an unprecedented level of wonder. Athenian minds were animated with questions: What is the nature of the universe? What is real? How does man fit into the cosmos? What is a good life? What is a happy life? Are those two— "good" and "happy"—in harmony or at odds with each other? And what role do the gods play in all this?

Philosophical discourse had become the gossip of the realm. Out on the south slope of the acropolis, where the Theater of Dionysius was producing a new comedy by Menander, the audience remained buzzing long after the play was over as they discussed the moral implications of the drama. Are extramarital affairs ever justifiable? Does bad behavior necessarily lead to personal unhappiness? Aristotle's *Nicomachean Ethics* was invoked, as were the moral arguments of Plato.

Later, as members of the audience walked back through the agora, they may have encountered Zeno of Citium in the colonnade lecturing students on the tenets of stoicism, turned east and passed the Lyceum, where Aristotelian philosophy was being taught, then cut back toward the Academy, where Platonic philosophy was the subject at hand. And then, farther up a hill overlooking the metropolis, they would have reached a garden gate that bore these words:

Stranger, here you will do well to tarry; here our highest good is pleasure. The caretaker of that abode, a

kindly host, will be ready for you; he will welcome you
with bread, and serve you water also in abundance, with
these words: "Have you not been well entertained? This
garden does not whet your appetite, but quenches it."

They had arrived at Epicurus's Garden, home of the Master's boarding school. Here, at the long outdoor table, non-
stop philosophical discussion reached its zenith, and fine
dining, as one can tell from the host's offered menu, reached
its nadir. (No pseudo-Epicurean "foodies" at this table.) Unlike at the Academy or the Lyceum, women, some of them
concubines and mistresses, as well as a few slaves, joined the
conversation; further, many of the students here had arrived
without academic credentials in mathematics or music, de
rigueur for entry to the other Athenian schools of higher
learning. Everyone in the Garden radiated earnestness and
good cheer. The subject under discussion was happiness.

#   #   #

Epicurus's notion of happiness has a decidedly Buddhist
quality. Happiness is tranquility, and tranquility comes principally from putting aside worldly "hankerings"—ambitions
for power, status, involvement in government, the pursuit of
voluptuous sensory experiences, and the accumulation of
material goods. Two of Epicurus's most quoted maxims distill this idea: "Not what we have, but what we enjoy, constitutes our abundance" and, in its more admonitory form,
"Nothing is enough for the man to whom enough is too
little."

Remarkably, Epicurus's ideas about *ataraxia*—the freedom from mental anguish and disturbance that is required
for true happiness—were more directly influenced by Buddhist thought than a twenty-first-century reader might imagine for a Greek philosopher of that epoch. Two of Epicurus's
early influences, Democritus and Pyrrho, had actually jour-

neyed all the way to what is now India, where they had encountered Buddhism in the schools of the gymnosophists
(naked teachers).

A parallel requirement for Epicurean happiness is freedom from fear of nature and from punitive gods. In his
magnificent opus inspired by the philosophy of Epicurus,
The Nature of Things, the Roman poet Lucretius reserved
some of his highest praise for Epicurus's brave resistance to
religious tradition and its superstitious interpretations of
natural phenomena. Epicurus was among the first of his
time to make such a clean and decisive break with what he
considered religious hocus-pocus. Interestingly, in Epicurus's
youth on the island of Samos, he often accompanied his
mother, Chaerestrata, on her visits to peasants in her role as
fortune-teller and faith healer. Apparently, Epicurus eventually saw more harm than benefit in his mother's occupation.

Epicurus defined happiness as the absence of pain, both
physical and mental, and this raises some fascinating questions for the philosophically minded of every era. One could
argue that the absence of pain brings a person up to only
zero on the happiness scale; to push the meter into the positive zone, more is required, say a plate of roast lamb with all
the trimmings. But Epicurus would shoot back that the
pleasure of eating lamb has all kinds of future pains attached to it, like a bloated stomach or, worse in the long
run, a hankering for more lamb or lamblike delicacies, putting a person back in the position of the perpetually frus-
trated individual for whom enough is always too little.
These calculations—which pleasures lead to future pain and
which pains lead to future pleasure—comprised a good deal
of the discussions around that table in Epicurus's Garden.

The deliberations could get particularly tricky when they
touched on questions of the relativity of measurement. What
if a man in physical pain is administered tincture of poppy—
opium—and subsequently reports that not only is his pain
gone but he is also experiencing more pleasure than he ever

did before? From this the man might conclude that in his ordinary, non-opium life he has all manner of pains that he was not fully aware of until they were removed; only now does he truly "feel no pain." Of course, Epicurus would warn him that the life of an opium user is one of always hankering for the next "fix," hence not pleasant in the long term at all. Nonetheless the question raised by the opium user who says that he finally feels no pain makes the idea of happiness as the absence of pain more slippery than it at first appears.

On the other hand, looking at Epicurus's philosophy of happiness from a less analytic point of view, there may be a spiritual/psychological dimension to the idea that the absence of all pain should be the goal of life. Perhaps without both physical pain and mental disturbances in the form of fears, frustrations, and anxieties, a person may be able to participate fully in simply "being." That is not zero; it is the best it gets. Such a man can revel in his sheer existence. He can achieve that summit of human experience sometimes known as "being here now." Reading Epicurus, one may find himself returning again and again to that blissful idea.

#   #   #

To be sure, the question of how to lead the happiest life is only one aspect of Epicurus's comprehensive philosophy. His cosmology that described, with astonishing prescience, all matter as consisting of minute atoms guided by laws of cause and effect, and its theory of "swerves," which exempts human volition from these deterministic laws, constitute much of his opus, especially as restated by Lucretius; yet the question of the best way to live always remained Epicurus's fundamental consideration. His theories about the composition of matter, causation, perception, truth, and knowledge are all in service of this ultimate concern. The primary importance of his atomization of the physical world is in what it reveals about the pain we needlessly inflict upon ourselves due to ignorance and superstition, as well as what it tells us about the mechanics of human nature and therefore how we can satisfy that nature.

Reading Epicurus now, with a twenty-first-century mind-set, it may be hard to resist reflexively viewing his teachings about the nature of things as naive science riddled with logical fallacies and unjustified leaps of reason. But if we return to his prescientific world while willfully suspending our attachment to the scientific method, we are able to read Epicurus's philosophy as life-enhancing poetry rather than as testable theory. And what compelling poetry it is.

#   #   #

At the table in Epicurus's Garden, the men and women are listening attentively to the Master. They all agree that Epicurus is the best teacher they could have. He has thought about his philosophy long and hard, honing it in his discussions with others. He is welcoming of his students' questions, patient with their misunderstandings, tolerant of opposing views. In spite of his obvious physical infirmities, his joy in simply being alive is palpable and infectious. People feel good about life and themselves merely by being in his company. In short, Epicurus has all the makings of what in contemporary terms we would call a charismatic self-help guru.

For a moment, the twenty-first-century mind might recoil at the idea of a self-anointed pundit proclaiming to his students— and to us—exactly how to live. But I, for one, read on for the simple reason that I suspect Epicurus may, in fact, have gotten it right.

DANIEL KLEIN

Preface

Epicurus is a neglected philosopher. No complete translation of his extant works has appeared in English since Cyril Bailey published his Oxford edition in 1926. Bailey's work was intended primarily for scholars in the field of Epicurean studies and for university students with an extensive knowledge of the Greek language. The present edition is intended primarily for American undergraduates (most of whom today have little Latin and less Greek) who are taking courses in ethics, the history of ideas, or the history of science, in any one of which fields Epicurus will find his rightful place. In place of Bailey's overly literal and sometimes unintelligible renderings I have substituted what I hope is a modern and readable English, which still remains quite close to the original text. In addition, the flat and pedantic style of Epicurus has been enriched by the inclusion of numerous parallel passages from the philosophical epic of Lucretius, who was Epicurus' most devoted and gifted Roman follower.

The public image of Epicurus has come down to us gravely flawed. The educated layman has picked up various stereotypes to the effect that he was an epicure, an atheist, a pleasure-monger, and an ethical materialist. The introduction and commentary of this book attempt to correct these grievous and unnecessary errors by defining terms and by setting forth the leading concepts of the Epicurean school in full context. In addition to clearing the ground of misconceptions, care has been taken to show the substantial con-

tributions of Epicurus to the Western tradition: his popularization of the atomic theory of Democritus and the implications of this theory for human happiness, his propaganda
against antiscientific superstition and popular religion, his
revolt against Platonic rationalism and insistence on empirical methods of verification, and his new "peace of mind"
gospel for the troubled intelligentsia of the Hellenistic period.

It is a pleasant duty to acknowledge here with gratitude
and humility the debt I owe to others in this enterprise. My
greatest debt is to Bailey himself, but among the living I
wish to single out Professor Norman W. DeWitt of the University of Toronto for his admirable and unorthodox study
of Epicurus (1954) and, nearer to hand, my friendly critics
of the Lafayette College faculty, Professors W. Edward
Brown, George A. Clark, Charles C. Cole, and William W.
Watt, who are specialists, respectively, in the fields of Greek,
philosophy, history, and English. All of the last named have
read the manuscript in part or in whole and have made numerous constructive suggestions, some of which I have eagerly adopted, others of which I have had the temerity to
disregard. Professor Clark is in a real sense the book's "onlie
begetter," for without his initial stimulus and encouragement
it would never have been written. Lastly, my warm thanks
go to Mrs. Wilma Benka, whose patience and skill in typing
the manuscript from hand-written copy have been indispensable.

G. K. S.

Easton, Pennsylvania

June 1962

The Art of Happiness

Introduction

I. DEVELOPMENT OF THE ATOMIC CONCEPT

Many of the characteristic positions which Western philosophy has developed in its long history of twenty-five centuries are already clearly represented or at least adumbrated by Greek thinkers of classical antiquity.[1] One of the best known of these ancient schools of thought is the point of view traditionally known as materialism, the theory that all reality is reducible to matter or matter-in-motion. Ancient materialism has a number of representatives, but chief among them are the Greek philosopher Epicurus (c. 342–270 B.C.) and the Roman poet-philosopher Lucretius (94–55 B.C.), and it is with these two figures that this book is principally concerned.

If we are to consider materialism, we must first consider matter itself, and if we discuss matter we cannot avoid talking about the Greek conception of the atom, the irreducible unit of matter and the foundation of all reality—physical, psychological, biological, moral, social, and historical. Neither Epicurus nor Lucretius had originated the atomic theory, though they both had much to do with propagating its doctrines. When Lucretius came to versify in hexameters for Roman readers of the Ciceronian and Caesarian period, he utilized one of the longer, more popular digests of atomism (the so-called "Major Epitome") composed by Epicurus two centuries earlier. And Epicurus in turn had relied heavily, especially for his physics and metaphysics, on the works of the Greek atomist Democritus, of the fifth century B.C. Between Democritus and the first beginnings of Greek thought there is an expanse of over 150 years, during which the initial crudities were enlarged upon, contradicted, compromised, and at last refined into the first statement of atomism. Let us see briefly how this came about.

A perennial question in Greek philosophy, early and late, is the metaphysical problem of the One and the Many. This may be put in the form of a question: Is it possible to penetrate the veil of the senses, which reveal the world as multiple and diversified, and to discover some underlying unity from which the many may be derived? In other words, is it possible to reconcile the multifarious world of sensory experience with ultimate reality? Or what is the nature of the "real" world that lies behind the ordinary everyday world? The Greeks attacked these speculative questions with zest and great ingenuity and were by no means discouraged when they found themselves unable to obtain a final, definitive answer. The earliest speculators, three members of the Ionian or so-called Milesian school, Thales, Anaximander, and Anaximenes (*c.* 600 B.C.), were frank materialists who postulated primary stuffs such as water or fiery air as the underlying real from which the entire world of physical objects is derived. At the same time they assumed this primary stuff to be living in itself and, if living, to be capable of all possible change. The actual mechanics of change they explained by two principles, condensation and rarefaction. Thus water, for example, is rarefied into vapor or steam or compacted into ice, rock, bone, tissue, etc.

But this first attempt to explain natural change did not pass muster with the more sophisticated thinkers who came later. So the successor of the Milesians, Heraclitus of Ephesus (*c.* 500 B.C.), concentrated on the problem of change, so much so that he made change itself the metaphysical real. The world has no underlying unity except flux, which is the denial of unity. Heraclitus pictured the world of things dia-

lectically as an unstable and temporary harmony of opposing cosmic forces. On the one hand, he believed, there is a
force that compounds the four Greek elements—earth, air,
fire, and water—into "things"; simultaneously the opposing
cosmic force is at work decompounding them, so that per-
manence, stability, and self-identity are written off as illu-
sions of the senses. "It is impossible to step into the same
river twice," Heraclitus said, but he might just as well have
said, "It is impossible to step into the same river once," because "same" is a mere linguistic convenience which falsifies
the nature of things. The cosmic process is poetically sym-
bolized as Fire (for Heraclitus, like all the early cosmologists,
philosophized in poetry) and is called "god," but it would be
a mistake to suppose that he conceived reality as being either
of these exclusively. Reality is all things simultaneously, or,
in the Greek phrase, it is a process of "becoming" in which
even apparently clear-cut opposites lose identity and merge
into each other. Thus, "Good and evil are one" and "It is the
same thing in us that is alive and dead, awake and asleep,
young and old; the former are shifted and become the latter,
and the latter in turn are shifted and become the former."
Heraclitus' position is well summed up in the two words
panta rei ("All things are in flux"), and of all the pre-
Socratic thinkers he is perhaps the most congenial to us today
because he is the distant forerunner of all modern thinkers
who represent the world as dynamic process—thinkers such
as Spencer, Bergson, Whitehead, and Dewey.

Now if we have one thinker who finds that ultimate reality is flux, it is dialectically possible, indeed necessary, to
have another thinker who finds that reality is nonflux, i.e.,
complete immutability and immovability. And that is precisely what happened in the Greek development. Parmenides
(*c.* 470 B.C.) contradicts his predecessor Heraclitus at all
points. Parmenides first points out that nothingness is inconceivable or, as we say, contradictory, since if you attempt
to conceive of nothing you conceive of something. Further-

more, he argues, if nothingness is inconceivable, then nothingness is likewise nonexistent; there is no such thing as nothing. If nothingness is nonexistent, empty space is likewise nonexistent. That leaves only one alternative: namely, that only "what is"—or being, or full space—exists. How shall we describe this "what is" of Parmenides? In his own words: (1) "There are very many tokens that what is is uncreated and indestructible; for it is complete, immovable, and without end. Nor was it ever, nor will it be; for it is now, all at once, a continuous one. . . . I shall not let you say or think that it came from what is not; for it can neither be thought nor uttered that anything is not" (i.e., reality can neither be created from nor destroyed into nothingness, since nothingness is nonexistent; and if reality is both uncreated and indestructible, that is the same as saying it is eternal). (2) "Nor is it divisible . . . , for what is is in contact with what is" (i.e., reality is a plenum, absolutely full space; if it were divisible, it would contain interstices of nothingness, which is inconceivable). (3) "Moreover, it is immovable. . . . It is the same, and it rests in the selfsame place, abiding in itself" (i.e., motion and its correlative, change, are both ruled out; if a thing changes, something that is passes into nonexistence, and something that is not comes into being from nonexistence, both of which are impossible). And (4) "since . . . it has a furthest limit, it is complete on every side, like the mass of a rounded sphere, equally poised from the center in every direction . . . for the point from which it is equal in every direction tends equally to the limits."

Reality, then, according to Parmenides, is a single and undifferentiated sphere—material in nature, eternal, absolutely continuous, and without motion or change. Furthermore, it is finite, and, if finite, it must be bounded—by what? Not by empty space or nothingness, because these are both nonexistent![2] Thus we see that not only Heraclitus lied but our senses lie to us daily when they tell us that the world is multiple and full of motion and change. Such an extreme denial of the senses is rare among the Greeks, who often doubted the evidence of the senses without writing them off altogether. But Parmenides was a doctrinaire rationalist, one who believed that truth is attainable by logic and by logic alone.[3]

It is obvious that we have now reached an apparent impasse in the Greek development, where two major thinkers and their respective principles contradict each other. Parmenides contradicts Heraclitus, and the principle of stasis contradicts the principle of flux. But this is by no means the end, because the Greek genius now proceeds to the final stage of the dialectic, which is a synthesis of the two contradictories, a synthesis that reconciles both and thereby saves parts of both. This saving compromise is known as pluralism. The Parmenidean real is still retained in principle but is now fragmented into minute particles, each particle being eternal, completely solid, without motion or change. Empty space is at first denied, and extraneous forces, or prime movers, such as Love and Strife (attraction and repulsion), are imported in order to energize the inert particles of matter, to assemble them into the configurations we call "things," and to shift them about in orderly processes. Thus change and motion are allowed but are interpreted as wholly relative. They pertain to phenomena only, things as they appear to us through the senses; but in the ultimate particles themselves there is neither change nor motion. By a feat of imagination the Parmenidean real has now been converted into a tiny miniature of itself, and at one stroke we have moved from the macrocosm to a microcosm that is almost atomic. This is clearly a sensible reconciliation of two ways of knowing—the way of logic, or rationalism, and the way of the senses, or empiricism; and it is essentially the same outlook that animates science today.

The earlier pluralists, like Empedocles and Anaxagoras (c. 450 B.C.), presented certain crudities that were later refined in the atomism of Democritus. For example, Empedocles broke down the Parmenidean real into a host of earth-particles, water-particles, fire-particles, and air-particles, each particle being unmixed, eternal, and inert. Under the action of Love and Strife these are shuffled and reshuffled into changing individual things that have no peculiar substance of their own. Things "are only a mingling and interchange of what has been mingled. Substance is but a name given to these things by men." The particles of Anaxagoras, on the other hand, are far more elaborately conceived. There are, to be sure, particles, or "seeds," that are predominantly earth or water, hot or cold, sweet or bitter, rough or smooth, hair or bone or flesh; but each of these, being infinitely subdivisible, contains also subparticles of every other natural quality, but not in large amounts. Everything is "in everything; nor is it possible for them to be apart, but all things have a portion of everything." In this way Anaxagoras aimed to explain the infinite variety of the natural world and the countless changes that occur in it.

This qualitative hodgepodge in the ultimate particles of matter is radically revised by Democritus (c. 425 B.C.), who along with his little-known predecessor Leucippus represents the last refinement in ancient particle theory. Democritus' "seeds," now also known as "atoms," apparently for the first time, are denuded of all qualities except size, shape, and inherent motion. Natural qualities such as colors, tastes, sounds, etc., are explained in quantitative and kinetic terms, an explanation still valid in principle today. Odors, for example, are subjective responses in us to atomic films impinging from without. We smell different odors because the films differ in structure, complexity, type and velocity of atoms, etc. In addition, Democritus held that the atom, though mathematically divisible, was physically indivisible.[4] Each atom was homogeneous throughout, without parts or empty space—in other words, a tiny Parmenidean world. He furthermore introduced two revolutionary changes in the pluralistic theory, which still labored under the dead weight of

Parmenides' logic: (1) He postulated the real existence of nothingness or empty space, primarily in order to provide a medium for free atomic movements of all sorts. His predecessors had ruled out empty space as a logical impossibility and had been content to work a miracle by having their particles move about in a plenum under the action of omnipotent cosmic forces. (2) He endowed each atom with eternal motion as an inherent trait, thereby reducing the cosmic processes to kinetic mechanisms and obviating the introduction of such concepts as divine creation, providence, and cosmic purpose, which are always an embarrassment to any materialistic system. But his predecessors had consistently clung to Parmenides' view that self-motion is a contradiction and that the real cannot move without ceasing to be itself.

At this point we might do well to compliment the Greeks, especially the Atomists, for having gone thus far in the direction of what we today call science. But then we should immediately ask, Why was the progress of science stalemated for so many centuries? To this there are several answers: First, the Greeks neither understood nor employed experimental method to any significant extent. In certain cases they erected brilliant hypotheses, such as the atomic theory, and then dogmatically asserted the truth of such hypotheses without rigorous testing. An untested hypothesis is scientifically valueless except as a starting point for verification; so we should not give the Greeks too much credit for the atomic theory, especially in view of the fact that the Modern conception of the atom is radically different from theirs.[5] In fact, perhaps the only noteworthy similarity between the ancient and modern theories is the name itself. On the other hand, science without hypothesis is dead; so we must credit the Atomists at least with speculative depth, with vision into the finer structure of matter. Second, the Greeks never applied mathematics to physical nature so as to obtain precise quantitative measurements, as is done constantly in science today. Although the ancient Pythagoreans were expert mathematicians and the Atomists good physicists, there was never any fruitful union of the two schools. Third, it must be remembered that in the ancient and medieval worlds materialism was always a poor competitor of transcendentalism of various sorts. The prosaic truths and morally repugnant (to many, at least) values of materialism simply could not compete on an equal footing with the soaring poetries of Platonism and a Platonized Christianity. In addition, the new theory of mechanistic causation did not fall on sympathetic ears. The majority of men were not prepared either intellectually or psychologically to believe that everything that happens in nature, including the nature of man himself, occurs through blind and impersonal causes involving the movements of unseen atoms. They were much more inclined to explain events in terms of the will of anthropomorphic gods or a benign Providence whose ways they could not hope to understand. Hence for more than fifteen centuries there was a severe dislocation of human interest in the natural world, and the scientific attitude all but perished. Atomism itself was not resurrected until the time of Gassendi, a seventeenth-century Jesuit who was a contemporary of Descartes.

II. FIRST PRINCIPLES OF ATOMISM
AND THEIR IMPLICATIONS

The following sections are constructed primarily from the writings of the later Atomists, Epicurus and Lucretius, inasmuch as the works of Democritus, once voluminous in extent, are now unfortunately almost entirely lost.

1. NOTHING ARISES FROM NOTHING. "Nothing is generated from the nonexistent," Epicurus tells us. "This is so because otherwise anything could be generated from anything and not require seminal particles."[6] In other words, if things

were created out of nothing, either with or without divine agency, there would be no fixed order of happenings in nature, and things would occur at random. We should be inclined today to restate this in positive form as the principle of universal causation: every event whatsoever has a prior cause, whether known or not. The whole structure of modern science (at least insofar as it concerns itself with gross aggregates of particles) still rests on this assumption, and the principle, though strictly unprovable, has the highest possible pragmatic value. In the Atomists such principles usually have two aspects, scientific and ethical, and the scientific is regularly subordinate to the ethical. Thus Lucretius uses the "nothing from nothing" principle to explain and illustrate the regularities of nature, the fixity of species, and so on. But in his hands it is also a powerful weapon in the Epicurean war against superstition, fear, and popular religion. To know the causes of things and to know that these are wholly natural is to banish groundless fears of a god or gods who work in unsearchable ways; and the conquest of such fear represents a marked diminution of human pain and suffering and hence is an essential ingredient of the good life. If we want to bring this point home in modern terms, we can remind ourselves that there are plenty of people throughout the world today who attribute cancer and other diseases, hurricanes, droughts, floods, and other natural disasters to the machinations of an inscrutable god who has his own plans for us miserable men. Such people, and they are counted in the millions, lead lives of fear and propagate a vulgar religion of fear. The Epicurean devil, of course, was (and is) popular religion with its massive ignorance and superstition. The Epicurean savior today would be the humanitarian scientist, who would tell us that cancer is not divinely sent but naturally caused, even though he does not yet know its precise cause. With the Epicureans it was never science for the sake of science but always science for the sake of human happiness.

2. NOTHING PASSES AWAY INTO NOTHINGNESS. "If an object that passes from our view were completely annihilated," says Epicurus, "everything in the world would have perished, since that into which things were dissipated would be the nonexistent."[7] This is formulated today as the principle of the indestructibility of matter. And from the premise that basic atomic matter is eternal Epicurus is able to derive a corollary: "The totality of things was always just as it is at present and will always remain the same because there is nothing into which it can change, inasmuch as there is nothing outside the totality that could intrude and effect change."[8] In other words, the universe as a whole is eternal, although individual worlds within the system are born and die; and if the universe is eternal it must be self-sustaining and require no divine assistance for its maintenance.

> When we gaze upon the heavenly tracts of the great
> cosmos above, and at ether set with its glittering stars,
> and we bethink us of the courses of sun and moon, a
> vexing question then begins to waken and rear its head
> in hearts already burdened with other cares: Is there per-
> haps a measureless power of gods over us, a power that
> wheels the dazzling constellations on their various courses?
> And an impoverished reason assails the mind with fur-
> ther doubts: Was there a beginning of the world, a gene-
> sis? And will there be an end? Until then will the
> ramparts of the world be able to endure this toil of
> ceaseless motion, or are they divinely endowed with ever-
> lasting health and the power to contemn the stout rigors
> of eternity as they slip along the endless current of time?
> [Lucr. 5.1204–17]

The indestructibility principle has application on the human level also. Although "all that is of mortal frame" must die, it is only the configuration of atoms we call the soul that is forever broken up and disbanded into space; the component atoms of the psyche are indestructible. Atomic immortality may be cold comfort, but the Epicureans attached the greatest importance to this stark reality. Death and the hell of myth are totally without meaning for us, and human happiness can only be enhanced if we accept this fact as a dogmatic truth.

> Since the soul's substance is seen to be mortal, death is nothing to us, nor does it concern us in the least. In times long past we knew no ill when the Carthaginian assembled from every side for the fight; when the whole earth, shaken by the tumult and alarms of war, quailed in fright beneath heaven's high strand and it was unknown which side was destined to bear the rule over humankind on land and sea. Just so, when we shall no longer be, after the divorcing of body and soul, of which twain we are fitly joined, nothing whatsoever will have the power to affect us, since we shall not then be; nothing be able to move our senses—no, not if earth shall be confounded with sea and sea with sky. [Lucr. 3.830–42]

3. ATOMS EXIST. "The components [of compound bodies] are irreducible and immutable atoms . . . , particles completely solid in nature and incapable of decomposition in any manner whatsoever. Thus the primal entities are necessarily indivisible corporeal atoms."[9] Epicurus says we arrive at this truth empirically, i.e., by inference from our sensory experience of compound bodies; and Lucretius proceeds to add a number of commonplace examples that lead us to believe that matter is composed of tiny bodies, e.g., the slow wearing away of rings by use or of statues' hands by touching and kissing, the hollowing out of stones by dripping water, the wearing away of paving stones by feet or by vehicles, etc. "The fact of sensation itself universally attests that there are bodies, and it is by reference to sensation that we must rationally infer the existence of imperceptible bodies."[10]

4. ATOMS AND SPACE ARE THE SOLE EXISTENTS. "The totality consists of bodies and space. . . . If what we call 'the void' or 'space' or 'impalpable being' were nonexistent, bodies would not have anywhere to exist, nor would they have a medium through which to move, as they manifestly do. In addition to these two entities it is impossible to think of anything else . . . as being a complete and independent entity and not, rather, a property or accident of body and space."[11] If there are two and only two basic realities, matter-in-motion and empty space, then everything in the world of sensory experience is either a combination of these (such as physical objects) or emergent from these (such as life, mind, values, human cultures, complex social and historical events).

On the basis of his previous demonstrations Lucretius argues that atom and void are mutually opposed and exclusive, like a pair of logical contradictories."[12] Where matter is, there is no void, and where void is, there is no matter; there is no middle ground, no third substance. "Thus besides empty space and material body there remains no autonomous third entity in the catalogue of nature, nothing that is ever subject to our perception, nothing that the mind's reasoning can apprehend." [1.445–48] This is logically sound if we accept his assumptions regarding the absolute solidity and indivisibility of the atom, and yet somehow we want to demur. Consider, for example, such primary phenomena as things. What is a physical thing? The Atomist tells us that any physical object is a combination of atoms of varying sizes, shapes, and velocities. But surely a thing is more than a mere collection or aggregation of atoms. A thing is an intricate *structure* of atoms bonded together in a system of relationships. What is the status of these relationships? It is very difficult, if not impossible, for any materialistic theory to deal with anything as nonmaterial as a system of relationships of material bodies in space. This is one of the fundamental errors of oversimplification characteristic of atomism; it is corrected in both Platonism and Aristotelianism, where the material principle always has its complement in form or structure.

Even more puzzling is the exact status of life, sensation, and consciousness. It is clear that they cannot have been superimposed from outside by some external agent, for the gods are impassive and never engage in creative activity. They must, then, be continuous with nature and be the product of atoms that in themselves have neither life nor sensation nor consciousness. The atoms that produce life and sensation are said to be specialized, very fine in texture, very rapid in their movements, and consequently able to set up an intricate system of vibrations when they interact with the coarser atoms of the body. Life and mind, then, seem to be by-products of a system of specialized atomic relationships. This again raises the question of the material status of structure and organization, but the atomic theory at this stage is clearly not refined enough to deal successfully with this problem. The metaphysical postulate that there are two and only two basic reals—matter-in-motion and empty space—raises more questions than it answers. Is life real? Is sensation real? If so, in what sense?

5. SPACE AND ATOMS ARE INFINITE. As for space, "the totality of things is unlimited, because anything limited has an end point and this end point is seen against something else. But the totality, having no end point, has no limit and, having no limit, it must be infinite and without boundaries."[13] This argument is reduced to imagery by Lucretius: Suppose an imaginary javelin is hurled outward at the edge of an imaginary finite universe—what happens? Either something blocks its flight and prevents it from completing its trajectory, or "it is borne outward." In the first case that which blocks it must be something in space *beyond* the supposed end of space, and in the second case it obviously moves into outer space. And the experiment may be repeated indefinitely "wherever you place the outer bounds."

Assuming that all existing space is constituted finite, if one were to run out and out to its furthest edge and cast a speeding javelin, would you say that, if whirled with all one's might, this javelin would go whither it is sent and speed into the far distance, or do you think that something would hold it back and oppose it? For you must assume and admit that one or the other would happen. But in either case your escape is blocked, and you are driven to concede that the universe lies open, immune to limit. For whether there is something that holds it back and prevents it from moving whither it was hurled and reaching its goal or whether it is borne outward into space, it did not start at the world's end. In this wise I shall continue, and wherever you place the outer bounds I shall ask, "What then becomes of the javelin?" It will be the case that the world's end can nowhere be established, and the possibility of the javelin's flight only extends its escape into space. [Lucr. 1.968–83]

As for the number of atoms in infinite space, "the totality is infinite both in the quantity of atomic bodies and in spatial magnitude, because . . . if space were infinite but the atomic bodies finite in number, the atoms would not remain in any position but would be borne about and dispersed throughout infinite space, not having supporting bodies to stabilize them in their recoil from other atoms."[14]

Given infinite space and an infinitude of atoms, a corollary follows: "In addition, there are infinite worlds—worlds like and unlike our own—because the atoms, being infinite in number, as was just now shown, are in motion extremely far out in space; and atoms of the sort from which a single world could be generated . . . have not been used up on one world or on a finite number of worlds."[15]

If each of these worlds is a replica of our own local system, some interesting questions suggest themselves: Are these worlds inhabited? If so, are these manlike beings unhappy like us? Do they experience more pain than pleasure because of their ignorance of nature? Are they, like us, burdened by archaic and irrational religious fears? And so on. The possibilities of propagating the true gospel of Epicureanism thus become tremendous, but Epicurus as a sensible humanist confines himself to the task of reducing human unhappiness locally and never raises such questions.

III. THE MOTION OF ATOMS

1. MOTION IS ETERNAL, i.e., atomic motion has neither beginning nor end.[16] This proposition is obviously not empirically derived but is a bold metaphysical postulate first made by Democritus (and adopted unchanged by Epicurus and Lucretius) when he declared his independence from the stultifying principles of Parmenides. By this postulate Democritus was able, without evidence or argument, to answer the awkward question, How do atoms happen to be in motion?

2. MEANING OF "BODY." A physical body or object is a complex structure of atoms of various shapes, sizes, and velocities. Such bodies become perceptible to us because of their internal atomic collisions, which have the effect of reducing normal atomic speeds to the range of human perceptions. Atoms in a compound body are analogous to free atoms in space. Within the limited internal space of the object they too move at a uniform rate of speed unless temporarily checked by collisions with other atoms in their aggregate. A "slow" body is different from a "fast" body because of the higher rate of internal collisions.[17]

3. THE TWO KINDS OF MOTION. There are two kinds of motion in the world, both real—one, atomic motion unseen by us; the other, the observed motion of sensible bodies. A moving object that we observe is "the sensory counterpart" or "appearance"[18] of all the internal atomic motions which we do not observe. Its motion is its own; it is real and not

illusory, because the object is a sensed entity in its own right and not merely the sum total of its component motions. What is true of the observed motion of bodies is not true of the subempirical motion of atoms, because the truth of the senses is different from truth that is logically inferred or "mentally apprehended,"[19] even though the latter must be verified or at least not contradicted by empirical evidence. Thus our senses tell us that one subject (e.g., a car or a ball) is moving faster than another, but we cannot infer that the atoms of the faster object are therefore moving faster than the atoms of the slower object. Atomic speed is one thing (i.e., a construct, or inference), and the speed of atomic aggregates is another (i.e., a datum of sensation).

One further point: If it is true that "atoms and space are the sole existents," or realities (II, 4, above), is it not a contradiction to say, as we said above, that the sensed motion of anything is real and not illusory? Strictly yes, but the strong empirical bias of Epicurus in both the *Letter to Herodotus* and the *Letter to Pythocles*, and his insistence that "if a person fights the clear evidence of his senses he will never be able to share in genuine tranquillity" (*Letter to Pythocles* 96) would seem to indicate that both *real* and *true* were ambiguous, two-level words for him. And in the last analysis the Epicurean is ethically "saved" not by metaphysics but by "the clear evidence of his senses."[20]

4. THE ATOMIC SWERVE. Democritus not only postulated eternal motion for the atoms but apparently represented them as flying about every which way in space—colliding, coalescing, and separating as "necessity" dictated. Into this picture of original chaos Epicurus later introduced a startling and gratuitous innovation, one of his few major departures from Democritus' theory. On the analogy of falling terrestrial bodies he pictures the atoms as "falling" eternally in parallel lines through infinite space; since they fall in a complete vacuum, their velocities are equal,[21] and there is no opportunity for heavier atoms to overtake lighter ones or

to collide and combine with them. In order to provide for such collisions and combinations, which were necessary, of course, for the production of objects and whole worlds, Epicurus then postulated his notorious atomic swerve, according to which certain atoms deviate ever so slightly from their perpendicular fall and, continuing in this erratic path, collide with other atoms. The initial collisions set up a "chain reaction," with the result that multiple collisions occur and atomic aggregates, small and large, are formed.

> In this context I also desire you to recognize that when the atomic bodies are borne straight down through the void of their own weight, they deviate a bit from the perpendicular at quite unpredictable times and places, but only enough for one to say that their course of motion has been altered. If they were not in the habit of swerving thus, they would all keep raining down through the vastness of the void like water drops, and no occasion would present itself for them to collide and strike together—with the result that nature would have wrought nothing. [Lucr. 2.216–24]

The postulate of the swerve occasions a difficult logical dilemma, and we must critically take note of it. The swerve is either caused or uncaused. If it is uncaused, then the principle of "nothing arises from nothing" is violated; if it is caused, it must be caused by something—but by what? Epicurus and Lucretius do not tell us, and Lucretius' phrase "at quite unpredictable times and places" is more than a hint that such swerves are random, uncaused events.

Although an uncaused event in a tight deterministic system such as atomism is an absurdity, Epicurus had an overwhelmingly good reason (as he thought) to entertain such a notion. His reason was ethical rather than physical, although the swerve was also very serviceable in explaining cosmic origins. Epicurus, and Lucretius after him, wished to free man from tyranny—not only the tyranny of unpredictable gods but also the tyranny of matter itself. If man is *nothing but* a material mechanism and part of the world mechanism, then his choices of good and evil are mechanically determined, and he cannot be said to be an autonomous and responsible ethical being. Thus if materialism is to save moral responsibility and at the same time save determinism, it must represent man as partially determined (in his organic functions) and partially free (in his ethical capacity). Freedom is introduced into the human machine by postulating tiny swerves in the soul atoms. "It is this slight deviation of the primal bodies, at indeterminate times and places, which keeps the mind as such from experiencing an inner compulsion in doing everything it does and from being forced to endure and suffer like a captive in chains." [Lucr. 2.289–93][22] Ethical choices, then, are the result of random atomic events occurring in the psyche and brought to consciousness in "the will," rather than the outcome of determinate antecedent conditions, both psychological and environmental, brought to focus in the psyche. In other words, my act of "free will" is not an act caused by *myself*, by my settled character, independently of external force or coercion, but by purely accidental atomic irregularities that happen to operate in my will. This is not what we ordinarily mean by "moral freedom," nor would most people consider themselves morally responsible for acts of this sort. On both counts the doctrine of the swerve is a complete failure and a blot on ancient materialism.[23] It is scientific nonsense and ethical folly, and is destructive of the very values that Epicurus sought to protect.

IV. SENSATION AND PERCEPTION

1. Sensation a Product of the Interaction of Soul and Body Atoms. "You must bear in mind that the soul plays the most important role in causing sensation but would never have achieved sensation unless it were somehow incorporated in the rest of the organism. The latter in turn, after providing the soul with this ground for sensation, has itself come to participate in the same function, thanks to the soul, but not in all the functions that the soul has. . . . [The latter,] by actualizing its own potentiality through motion, at once achieved the function of sensation for itself and imparted it to the body also as a result of its proximity and congruence with the latter."[24] Thus a nexus of vibrating, nonsentient atoms somehow produces a totally new phenomenon in nature which we call sensation. This event bears witness to the truth that Lucretius points out, that nature is "creative," but "creative" does not really explain the emergence of sensation from an aggregation of atoms, however specialized, any more than does Epicurus' question-begging phrase, "by actualizing its own potentiality." We have previously discussed (II, 4 above) the puzzling status of sensation in a universe where there are only two basic realities, atoms and space, and if we wished to press home the point we could seriously question the reality of our whole sensory experience, as Democritus candidly did.[25] But Epicurus never did, because too much in his system, especially human happiness, depended on the life of the senses.

2. SENSATION IMPOSSIBLE IN DEATH. This corollary follows immediately once we accept the postulate that sensation is the product of the interaction of soul and body atoms. "On the dissolution of the entire organism the soul is scattered abroad and no longer has its usual functions, nor does it undergo motion, with the result that it does not have sensation either. It is impossible to think of it as sentient if it is not present in a composite whole and if it does not enjoy its usual movements at such times as its housing and environment are not the same as the present environment in which it carries out these movements."[26]

The ethical implications of this are vast. Far from being

depressing, this materialistic truth can only serve to enhance human welfare and happiness. At one stroke two of man's greatest prospective miseries are nullified—death and a hellish afterlife. Once a man has purged away "the terror in the soul" by acknowledging that death "is nothing to us" and hell simply a psychological projection of present torments and frustrations,[27] he is ready for the happy life—pleasure (properly interpreted), a minimum of pain, freedom from neurotic fears, and spiritual composure. This is a cardinal example of how the physical aspects of atomism were never allowed to remain purely theoretical but were always directed to humane and human ends.

3. PERCEPTION DEPENDENT ON ATOMIC FILMS FLOWING OFF OBJECTS. Granted that we have sensations, how do we come to perceive objects in the external world about us? Democritus first devised the ingenious theory (although one would never know it from reading Epicurus) that out beyond the periphery of our bodies there are innumerable aggregations of moving atoms which emit thin films, or replicas of themselves (known as *eidola* in Greek). These atomic films are constantly impinging in a steady stream on our various sense organs, which are likewise collections of moving atoms, and there they excite complicated patterns of vibration which we *experience* as whole "things" with all their natural colors, odors, shapes, and so on. In other words, there are no "things" in the external world, only collections of atoms; furthermore, there are no colors, odors, etc., in outer nature, only atoms having velocities, quantitative dimensions, and organizations. "Things" with natural qualities exist only in our sensory experience as the "appearances" or "phenomena" of outer realities. Thus Democritus reduced subjective qualities to objective quantities, one of the most striking feats of ancient materialistic thinking. (This picture is somewhat similar to that of the seventeenth-century empiricist John Locke, although Locke held that certain properties such as size and shape are also

external, "out there," and not purely subjective. His successor in the eighteenth century, Bishop Berkeley, more consistently reduced *all* qualities to subjective status, which at first glance seems to be exactly the view of Democritus but isn't at all because Berkeley categorically denied the existence of matter. Empirical evidence shows that we know only the subjective world of our own experience, which is wholly mental. How, then, can the mind, our world of experience, be derived from an unexperienced X called "matter," which is obviously not-mind? "Matter," then, is a totally useless and misleading postulate, and any honest "common-sense" empiricist can and must dispense with it!)

Democritus' brilliant theory of films, or *eidola*, was later altered by Epicurus, gratuitously and for the worse. He has it that experienced qualities such as color are mechanically *transferred* to us by the films that already have them from the external objects themselves. Thus we see a green leaf, for example, because a green configuration of atoms emanating from a green object in nature has impinged on the retina of the eye and there registered its own true quality. Thus greenness and all other natural qualities exist not only in us as private receptors but also in the public domain of atomic configurations called nature. Epicurus, of course, never held that individual atoms are green but only that objective collections of atoms take on greenness and so on. Once again we must ask the question, If only atoms and space are really real, is objective greenness in nature—not to mention the sensation of greenness in us—real in any sense? Epicurus never honestly confronted this embarrassing question.

After curtly criticizing the views of his predecessors regarding perception, and without even mentioning the name or the theory of Democritus, Epicurus continues: "These theories are less credible than my own hypothesis that certain atomic films having the same colors and shapes as their objects impinge on us, entering either the eye or the mind, depending on the relative sizes of their atoms; that these films have a rapid course of movement and for this reason present the phenomenon of a unitary and continuously existent object; and that they preserve the qualitative changes of the underlying physical object in their uniform impact on us from that source, which results from the atomic pulsations deep within the physical object."[28]

Granted the fact of human perception, how do we know that these films actually exist? They are subempirical, as invisible as atoms themselves. We do not experience *them*, only the result of their impact on our sense organs. To establish the existence of the films Epicurus must resort to a process of inference or deductive logic, just as he does in establishing the existence of the basic atoms themselves.[29] "The correspondence between the perceptions that we take as representations [of objects] . . . and what we call real existent objects could never arise unless certain entities of this sort were making their impact on us."[30] Bishop Berkeley might have called this dogmatic statement a capital piece of question-begging. From our own experience how do we know there are "real existent objects" in an external world? And even supposing there are, how can we assume a "correspondence" between them and our own perceptions, when all we know or can know is our own perceptions? Any Greek materialist would have been dismayed at the startling turn that empiricism later took, especially in the hands of Berkeley and Hume. The whole world of things which seem so indubitably material and external disappears into the subjective world of our own experience, a world that is wholly real but also wholly mental. But neither Democritus nor Epicurus had the faintest inkling that the material could thus become the immaterial.

4. TRUTH AND FALSITY IN PERCEPTION. Any discussion of perception inevitably, sooner or later, raises the question of truth. Do our senses give us a true picture of the world? Do they ever deceive us? If so, under what conditions? It was most important for Epicurus to give clear, dogmatic

answers to these questions, particularly since he was bitterly opposed to the contemporary school of the Skeptics, who had called in question the evidence of the senses and even the powers of the mind to gain any sort of reliable knowledge about the world. To all who would undermine the senses, the very foundations of knowledge, as well as to his own disciples he makes the following technical and carefully worded statement: "Any perception of shape or qualities that we receive by atomic impingement on the mind or sense organs represents the true shape or quality of the physical object and is generated by the unbroken series of films or its residues, whereas falsity and error always consist of the element of belief superimposed on a percept which awaits verification or noncontradiction and which is then not verified or is contradicted."[31] In other words, the senses themselves never deceive us. It is the element of interpretation that we immediately add to the sensory data from our own background or funded experience that frequently misleads us. But the senses mechanically report what the films bring to them, and the films by definition are facsimiles of their original objects, though sometimes in transit they become altered or mutilated so that only "residues" reach us.

This Epicurean statement of what we today call the verification principle may perhaps be best explained by a concrete illustration: Suppose I am a Roman Epicurean and am in the habit of walking frequently into the country along the Appian Way. One day I see in the distance, perhaps less than a mile away, what appears to be a round tower. As an Epicurean I know that I always see what I see but that I may be misled in my beliefs by some unconscious interpretation ("the element of belief superimposed on a percept"). So partly from curiosity and partly to verify my perception, I walk closer and closer and find to my satisfaction that the object is indeed a tower and that it is round. I have now verified my original percept and have found it to be not contradicted by the close-up view of the object; and, moreover, interpretation has played no distorting role in this case at all. I repeat this walk every week for several months and form a deep impression of many objects, including the tower. But then for the sake of variety I leave the Appian Way one day and strike off across country. It is coming up to rain, and I can't go too far. And then I see what appears to be another round tower. Strange, way off here. But I decide not to investigate that day and turn back. The following week I decide to check on this "percept that awaits verification" to see whether my impression of the week before was right or wrong. It was wrong. The object turns out to be the sole remaining pier of a ruined aqueduct! Did my eyes deceive me? No, the films flowing off the pier may possibly have been altered by passing through those low-lying rain clouds, but the main trouble was "the element of belief," i.e., I unconsciously interpreted what I saw in the light of my many experiences of seeing the real tower on the Appian Way.

In this way Epicurus sought to counter the corrosive criticism of the Skeptics, who held that the senses themselves frequently deceive us and are therefore *never* to be trusted. Such a position in Epicurus' eyes was tantamount to destroying *all* possibility of knowledge, since even reason becomes impotent if the evidence of the senses is called in question.[32]

In his *Leading Doctrines*, a collection of sayings and aphorisms circulated among students and laymen, Epicurus gives us another careful statement on sensation, which is even more pointedly directed against the Skeptics: "If you summarily rule out any single sensation and do not make a distinction between the element of belief that is superimposed on a percept that awaits verification and what is actually present in sensation or in the feelings or some percept of the mind itself, you will cast doubt on all other sensations by your unfounded interpretation and consequently abandon all the criteria of truth. On the other hand, in cases of interpreted data, if you accept as true those that need verification as well as those that do not, you will still be in error, since the whole question at issue in every judgment of what is true or not true will be left intact."[33] In other words, uncritical rejection of any given sensation through failure to distinguish between sensation and its interpretation (as in the case of seeing a mirage) may lead one eventually to reject the veracity of *all* sensations (as the Skeptics do) and consequently the means for determining truth. Contrariwise, blind acceptance of all interpreted sensations as correct is equally unjustified, since "the whole question at issue"—the superimposed interpretation—is ignored. The only safe procedure is to distinguish between the percept as such and its interpretation.

This epistemological discussion has an unexpected application in the field of ethics also. If we follow the Skeptics and come to distrust our senses as the means to truth, we may likewise come to distrust our feelings of pleasure and pain as the criteria of what is right and wrong in conduct. Although Epicurus, like most Greek thinkers, believed in the power of reason to guide and control, he held that the feelings were even more fundamental and natural guides to the good life than reason itself. This important point will be treated at length in a later section (VII) of this Introduction devoted to ethics.

V. THEORY OF KNOWLEDGE

The theory of knowledge, also known technically as epistemology, is that aspect of philosophy which is interested in a special group of questions centering around human knowing. Typical questions are, What do we know and how do we know it? What are the limitations of knowledge? What is truth and what standards are available for determining truth and its opposite, falsity? What role does language play in human knowing? And so on.

The Epicureans had a fairly well-developed theory of knowledge as a result of their rivalry and opposition to other schools of thought such as the Platonists, the Skeptics, and the "mythologizers," or adherents of traditional popular religion. This body of theory exists piecemeal and is not to be found entire in any extant Epicurean work; consequently it must be assembled from whatever sources and documents are still left to us. The Epicureans have often been accused of dogmatism by detractors and friends alike, and it is in their epistemology that this trait becomes quite evident. Although dogmatism is philosophically indefensible, there are at least good historical reasons to account for its existence in this case. The Epicureans were thoroughly alarmed that the whole basis of knowledge of the natural world was being undermined by contemporary trends: (1) by the Platonists, who had shifted attention from natural phenomena and the world of flux in general to an immutable transcendental world of ideal objects called forms (e.g., tree-ness, cat-ness, triangularity, justice *per se*, etc.) whose very existence Epicurus found "inconceivable," i.e., contradictory to his own empirical canons; (2) by the Skeptics, whose criticism of sensory knowledge was powerful and corrosive, as we noted in the previous section; and (3) by reactionary adherents of astral and popular religion, whose numbers were large and on the increase during the Hellenistic period.[34] The strong stand taken by the Epicureans against all these tendencies was taken not in the name of science and human knowledge alone but in the name of human happiness, on the reasonable assumption that if men know the true nature of reality (which in this case is decidedly physical and material!) they are more likely to be happy than if they do not. Hence the happy and the good life presupposes knowing and knowing how to know.

1. PURPOSE OF KNOWLEDGE. The purpose of all knowledge, metaphysical as well as scientific, is to achieve what Epicurus called *ataraxia*, freedom from irrational fears

and anxieties of all sorts—in brief, peace of mind. If this goal seems a bit strange to us today, we must remember that the Hellenistic period was a time of turmoil and great uncertainties and that Epicureanism was devised specifically as a "salvation" philosophy, a positive way of escape from a most unpleasant social and political environment. So it became imperative, in a positive sense, for the Epicureans to imitate the perfect serenity and self-sufficiency of their own idealized gods, who were actually a psychological projection of the kind of beings they themselves wanted to be. As a means to this end it was necessary for the Epicurean to acquire a large body of "scientific" knowledge that was entirely free from the taints of popular superstition and religiosity, particularly knowledge about the natural causes of celestial phenomena. For the heavenly bodies were widely regarded as divine and as having unpredictable powers to influence human fortunes for better or worse, and such beliefs could only assist in the formation of mass phobias and neuroses. To neutralize these sources of popular anxiety and unhappiness by the antidote of knowledge was therefore one of the chief goals of Epicurean humanitarianism. Consider the following typical pronouncements: "First of all, then, we must assume that no other end is served by the study of celestial phenomena, whether considered by themselves or in some larger context, than mental composure and a sturdy self-reliance, just as in the case of the other disciplines."[35] And "We must consider that it is the task of natural science to determine with precision the causes of the most important phenomena and that our happiness is bound up with causal knowledge of the heavenly bodies, i.e., with the understanding of the nature of celestial phenomena, and everything else that is germane to scientific knowledge relating to human happiness."[36]

2. EPICUREAN EMPIRICISM. Both Epicurus and Lucretius held that the stock of our general ideas is derived from experience rather than from innate *a priori* concepts and that

our judgments and beliefs are true or false insofar as they correspond or do not correspond to our sensations, feelings, and general conceptions. To attach the modern label "empiricist" to both these thinkers seems, then, wholly justifiable, although it has been called in question on technical grounds.[37] This is not to deny that they likewise made ample use of the complementary method of rationalism or deductive logic in order to arrive at some of their basic principles, such as the existence of atoms, infinite space, and infinite worlds; for the latter are all "imperceptibles," i.e., truths not open to empirical investigation or confirmation.

The hard empirical core of Epicureanism emerges clearly in the criteria or tests for truth, which are either three or four in number, depending on whether some or all are listed in the various pertinent passages. For example, we read in the authoritative *Letter to Herodotus* that "we must keep all our judgments in line with our sensations (specifically our immediate perceptions, either of the mind or of any particular sense organ) and also in line with our actual feelings of pleasure and pain, in order to have the means with which to interpret a sense datum awaiting verification or a problem involving imperceptibles."[38] Here only three of the tests are listed: sensations, direct perceptions of the mind, and the feelings. Let us now discuss each of these and add a fourth test from other sources.

a. *Sensations.* All sense data are what they are, and they are infallible, being mechanically transmitted to us by atomic images from the outer world. They may be overlaid with misleading interpretations and lead to "false opinions,"[39] but they are true if confirmed by close inspection or if they are not contradicted. There is nothing more basic or irrefutable than the testimony of the senses, and furthermore the whole superstructure of reason rests upon them.

What should we consider as having greater validity than sensation? Will reasoning that takes its rise from "false" sensation have power to contradict the senses when it originates wholly from them? If they are not true, all reasoning likewise becomes false. [Lucr. 4.482–85][40]

Most important of all, from the Epicurean point of view, our spiritual health depends upon our acceptance of our senses and their testimony: "If a person fights the clear evidence of his senses he will never be able to share in genuine tranquillity."[41] In other words, a person who doubts his senses will either lose contact with the reality of the surrounding world, like the Skeptics, and become psychologically isolated and insecure, or he will fall prey, as do the religionists, to theological explanations which do not allay anxiety but foment it.

b. *Direct perceptions of the mind.* These are supersensations, as it were, that do not originate in the ordinary organs of sense but are generated in the mind-atoms themselves by direct impingement of images from space. They are in general of two sorts, and they have the same validity or truth-value as ordinary sensations: (1) Free-floating images enter the mind singly or in combination when we are asleep and produce the often incredible experiences we call dreams. But all such visions are "true," since they are atomically caused. If we allow for the long persistence and intermingling of certain films in space, there is no occasion for skepticism about the reality of dreams! (2) "The gods do indeed exist, since our knowledge of them is a matter of clear and distinct perception."[42] Far from being a materialistic atheist, Epicurus accepted the gods of Greece in highly idealized form and claimed that the conception of them as "indestructible and blessed beings" was universal to all mankind. How to account for this universal conception? Men have "seen" the gods in their dream images, but in cases where this is not so, images of them have been transmitted from interstellar space directly to the minds of men.

The men of old, when waking and yet more in sleep,
were wont to see the wondrous countenances of gods
and their bodies of surpassing size. To these shapes they
ascribed sensation because they were seen to move their
limbs and to give out noble words that accorded with
their splendid mien and copious powers. They also endowed them with eternal life because their presence was
ever manifested and their form remained unchanged;
above all because they believed that beings so enlarged
with powers could not easily be overcome by any force.
And they thought them eminently blessed because not
one was harried by the fear of death and likewise because in sleep they saw them work many marvels and
suffer naught from the toil thereof. [Lucr. 5.1169–82]

c. *The feelings* are definitive criteria of truth, especially in
the area of the moral life, though they have application
elsewhere too. In general, an act that in the long term tends
to produce an excess of pleasure over pain or neutralizes
pain and tends to produce a state of psychological well-
being and spiritual serenity is to be considered morally good
and right. This principle has extremely wide application in
literally thousands of cases, both for personal living and for
living in society in relation to others. Two examples must
here suffice as illustrations: (1) the enjoyment of sex in the
married state as against illicit sex in adultery; (2) quitting a
hectic, "two-ulcer" job in the city that pays $20,000 a year
in favor of a more relaxed job in a country town that pays
only $10,000. The second case would not ordinarily, at least
not in our society, be considered a matter of morals at all,
but by Epicurean standards it is very obviously a case in
point, since our own feelings make it incumbent upon us to
avoid pain and to seek pleasure or at least a neutral comfort. Conversely, any act that in the long term tends to produce more pain than pleasure is to be considered morally
wrong or bad; for example, overindulgence in any typical

human activity—eating, drinking, sex, "socializing," status-seeking, and so on.

Epicurus as a moral empiricist felt that our immediate feelings are far more cogent and authoritative guides to the good life than abstract maxims, verbal indoctrination, or even the voice of reason itself. Hence he based his ethics on nature, not on convention or on reason.

d. *General conceptions* or universals such as "horse," "ox," "man," etc., are likewise common criteria of truth, since they are all distillations or residues of repeated sensory experience, particularly in their original meanings. Without these general ideas, or "package" concepts, there could be no ordering of experience, no learning process or education, and no scientific investigation of nature.

In the second century A.D. the Greek biographer Diogenes Laertius wrote an excellent *Life of Epicurus* in which he included some interesting remarks on our general conceptions. In the first quotation that follows he gives us a primitive statement of a thesis that was richly elaborated many centuries later by John Locke in his famous *Essay Concerning Human Understanding* (1690): "All ideas take their rise from sensations through processes of coincidence, analogy, resemblance, and combination, with reflection contributing something also."

No examples are given, but Locke will readily supply us with a few. Thus "resemblance" might account for the idea of *unity*, which is produced when the mind compares the many different objects that it has experienced individually as one thing. By "combination" we might derive the idea of *beauty*, which according to Locke consists of "a certain composition of color and figure causing delight in the beholder." And "reflection," or reason, might produce the idea of *power*, when we reflect on our own ability to move the various parts of the body and consider the effects that physical objects have on each other.

The second quotation is more informative and also illustrates how concepts are used when we wish to establish the truth of something.

By "concept" the Epicureans mean "comprehension," "correct opinion," "a thought" or "universal idea" deposited in the mind—in other words, a remembering of something frequently given in sensation from the external world. For example, take the expression "X is a man." As soon as "man" is uttered, we immediately think of a typical human being in line with the concept formed from antecedent sensory data. Hence the original meaning assigned to any word is clear and distinct evidence of truth. Furthermore, we could not look into what we want to investigate if we did not have prior knowledge of it. For example, the question "Is that thing in the distance a horse or an ox?" implies that one must have some conceptual knowledge of the appearance of a horse or an ox. We could not even have named anything without having first learned of its appearance through the concept. Hence concepts are clear and distinct evidences of truth.[43]

3. The Principle of Noncontradiction. We have seen that a judgment or a belief is true if it is confirmed by one or more of the criteria discussed above. The negative aspect of this principle is also very important in the Epicurean theory of knowledge. If it is impossible to verify a given judgment positively, such a judgment is still true if it is not contradicted by anything "in our experience." This escape clause made it possible for the Epicureans to give plausible (but to us unscientific) explanations of "imperceptibles," i.e., atomic phenomena lying below the range of the senses and also celestial phenomena that are too remote to be observed closely. An example from each category will illustrate the principle:

> *It is not impossible that* such atomic discharges [i.e., films] should be generated in the environment of objects, *nor that* suitable circumstances for the production of these hollow, thin films should exist, *nor that* these emanations should maintain the successive positions and structure that the particles had in the solid external bodies.[44]

Notice the negative emphasis running throughout this quotation: *It is not impossible that, . . . nor that, . . . nor that. . . .* In other words, nothing in our experience runs counter to any of these statements, and therefore they may be assumed dogmatically to be true.

> The risings and settings of the sun, the moon, and the other heavenly bodies may come about from the lighting up and quenching of their fires . . . ; for nothing in our sensory experience runs counter to this hypothesis. Or the said effects may be caused by the emergence of these bodies from a point above the earth and again by the earth's position in front of them; for nothing in our sensory experience is against this.[45]

Here two alternative explanations of "risings and settings" are offered; both are of equal value and equally true, since neither is contradicted by anything in our experience. On the contrary, we have all seen fires die down from lack of fuel, and lights obscured or blacked out by objects coming in front of them.

This promiscuous hospitality to any and every explanation which is not contradicted by empirical data is a serious flaw in the science of the Epicureans and makes their theory of natural causation practically worthless, as we shall see. The student should note the striking similarity of the noncontradiction principle to the *ad ignorantiam* fallacy in logic, according to which a proposition is supposedly true if it cannot be proved false. For example, it does not follow logically that the proposition "God exists" is true simply because it cannot be proved false. Nor by the same token can we infer that the setting of the sun is caused by the temporary extinguishing of the solar fires, on the ground that this explanation is not contradicted by anything analogous in our experience on earth. In neither case is lack of conclusive evidence against something the same as evidence in favor of it.

The Epicureans were on somewhat firmer ground when they ruled out explanations that "run counter to our experience," i.e., are positively contradicted by some analogous occurrence here on earth. Thus both Epicurus and Lucretius rule out the unlimited growth or expansion of worlds on the ground that this is contradicted by the limited growth of organisms that we can observe.[46]

4. USE OF ANALOGIES AS MEANS TO SCIENTIFIC INFERENCES. The principle of noncontradiction made it possible for the Epicureans to explain "imperceptibles" (occurrences lying below or beyond the range of sensory perception) by the copious and uncritical use of analogies drawn from "our own experience" and so to remain safely within the bounds of empirical method, as they interpreted it. Thus Epicurus lays it down as a cardinal rule of procedure that "we should investigate the causes of all celestial and nonperceptible phenomena by making a comparison of these with the various ways in which an analogous phenomenon takes place in our own experience."[47] For example, if we wish to explain solar and lunar eclipses we should first observe the various ways in which light may be partially or totally obscured here on earth, and then proceed to frame our hypotheses in such a way that they are not contradicted by earthly phenomena. Having done this we can feel confident, in the light of the principle of noncontradiction, that these explanations (which may be two, three, or even four in number in specific cases) are equally possible or probable. This analogical method led to a huge proliferation of causal hypotheses,[48] most of which would not pass muster today, but once again

there were good historical reasons why the Epicureans were forced into this untenable scientific position, as we shall see in the next section on causation.[49]

5. CAUSATION.

I shall recount how men's minds oftentimes hang fearfully in the balance at the sight of what comes to pass on earth and in the sky. Their spirits are demeaned by dread of the gods and crushed drooping to the dust because their ignorance of natural causes forces them to ascribe all to divine rule and to concede the reign of gods. [Lucr. 6.50–55]

The Epicureans with good reason saw a direct correlation between religious superstition and ignorance of natural processes, and in their humanitarian zeal to purge away "the terror in the souls of men" they struck to the heart of the matter with their most powerful weapon, an elaborate theory of causation. To know the causes of things and to know that they are wholly natural is to banish the groundless fears that arise from "the antique notions of religion." The conquest of fear, especially fear of unaccountable divine beings who meddle in nature at will, means a reduction in the sum total of human pain and suffering and opens the door to the calm acceptance of a new picture of the world—a world in which nature is autonomous and where there are ideal beings who never meddle.

If you recognize and cling to these truths, you will see that Nature is freed forthwith and delivered from her haughty overlords and that she does all of her own will without divine action. By the holy godheads who pass the placid eternity of their serene lives in tranquil peace! Who is able to rule the boundless all? Who has the power to hold in his hand the stout checkreins of the abyss? Who can make all the skies to revolve together? Who can

warm all fruitful lands with ether's fires? *Who* has the
power to be omnipresent at all times? [Lucr. 2.1090–99]

a. *The "one cause" principle versus multiple causation.*
The Epicureans employed either a single causal explanation
or a plurality of theories, depending on the nature of the
phenomena involved and also on who their opponents were.
The "one cause" principle was legitimate, indeed mandatory,
in the field of terrestrial physics, metaphysics, and ethics,[50]
where their opponents were non-Atomists such as the Platonists and the Skeptics. But it was dogmatically ruled out in
favor of multiple causation in the field of celestial phenomena, where their opponents were religionists who stubbornly
held to the single "divine causation" theory. This unhappy
and confusing bifurcation in causal theory is clearly illustrated by the following extracts from the *Letter to Pythocles*, a treatise on astronomy and meteorology with a
strong bias in favor of naturalistic explanations and an
equally strong opposition to theological "explanations."

We must not force an impossible [i.e., theological] explanation on these [celestial] phenomena or make our
treatment similar in all respects to an ethical discourse or
to an explication of the problems of noncelestial physics—
as seen, for example, in the statements "The universe
consists of bodies and an intangible substance" or "Atoms are indivisible" and in all other such cases where
there is but a single explanation that is consistent with
phenomena. This is not the case with the heavenly bodies. Their origins have more than one cause, and there is
more than one set of predications relating to their nature
that is compatible with our sensory experience.

The phases of the moon may occur in any of the ways
in which events in our own experience prompt us to give
an account of this lunar phenomenon, provided we do

not become overly fond of the "one cause" principle and irresponsibly reject other explanations without first considering what can and what cannot be observed, and consequently end up desiring to observe the impossible.[51]

The "single explanation that is consistent with phenomena" is, of course, the atomic theory, and it is uniformly used throughout the *Letter to Herodotus* (the sole surviving treatise on physics and metaphysics from Epicurus' own hand), to the exclusion of any competing theories offered by predecessors or members of rival schools. A wide range of phenomena is there accounted for by the orthodox "one cause" atomic method, e.g., perception via atomic films, natural change in the external world, the nature of the soul and sensation, other worlds and their genesis.[52]

In the *Letter to Pythocles*, on the other hand, the method of multiple causation and explanation is the rule, and all theories that were found to be consistent with earthly phenomena or confirmed by analogy were welcomed. In this letter the "one cause" method is constantly under attack, for the obvious reason that it is no longer the same as the orthodox theory of atomism but is now the discredited theological principle of divine causation and control. This latter principle was a focal point of sectarian attack, not only for humanitarian reasons, as explained earlier in this section, but also on purely logical grounds. The gods by definition were absolutely "blessed" and impassive beings who were incapable of any kind of motion or activity. Their whole existence consisted in the highest form of happiness: contemplation of perfection, their own perfection. It was, therefore, a contradiction to picture them simultaneously as "blessed" and as intervening in nature, as did those who still held to traditional anthropomorphic religion.[53] Hence readers of the *Letter to Pythocles* are frequently reminded that preoccupation with this outmoded "one cause" method of popular theology, to the exclusion of empirical observation and theory, is destructive of true causal theory and at the same time of human happiness, which is deeply involved in the correct understanding of the heavens. And at the same time they are exhorted to hold to the method of "the possible" (i.e., natural causation) and reject "the impossible" (i.e., belief in divine creation and control).[54]

Thus for a variety of reasons—sectarian, humanitarian, practical, and logical—the Epicureans decided to adopt the principle of multiple causation in dealing with the phenomena of the heavens, and as a result we have in the *Letter to Pythocles* a grab bag of ill-assorted and sometimes fantastic theories.[55] For example, thunder is explained in four ways, lightning in six ways, earthquakes in two, snow in three, the rainbow in two, comets in three, and so on.[56] Although the *Letter to Pythocles* adds little or nothing to our scientific knowledge of the heavens, its historical importance is nonetheless great and lies, from our point of view, primarily in its advancing of the theory of knowledge, specifically in promoting naturalistic principles of explanation as against theological. For the hand of the gods (or God) is not traceable in nature, and theological explanations cannot be shown to be either true or false and hence are scientifically worthless. Only naturalistic hypotheses admit of empirical testing, of confirmation or disconfirmation. And that is the virtue of this Epicurean treatise. The empirical method is there in the germ, awaiting the instruments and techniques of later centuries.

Now, none of these theories or theories related to these are incompatible with our clear and distinct perceptions of things, provided we hold to the possible in these matters and are able to refer each theory to some phenomenal counterpart. . . . The divine nature, once more, should never be brought into these events. Let us exempt it from such responsibilities and keep it in the full state of blessedness. If we fail to do this, our whole causal theory regarding celestial phenomena will be meaningless, as it has already be-

come for those who have not availed themselves of the
method of possibility.[57]

VI. RELIGION AND THEOLOGY

1. EXISTENCE OF THE GODS KNOWN THROUGH PERCEP-
TION. "The gods do indeed exist, since our knowledge of
them is a matter of clear and distinct perception."[58] According to the Epicurean theory of knowledge, every thought is
traceable, directly or indirectly, to a physical counterpart
external to us, and before we can think about anything we
must perceive it either by one of the ordinary sense organs
or directly by the atomic activity of the mind itself. In the
case of the gods Epicurus did not claim that we see them as
physical objects but rather that we perceive films or images
of the gods which have traveled from remote interstellar
space where they reside and which have impinged directly
on the atoms of the mind.[59] Thus, he claims, our knowledge
of the gods is real empirical knowledge because it is based
on a kind of "seeing." (Epicurus conceived of thinking in
imagistic terms, and many of the verbs he used for the mental processes have the root meaning of "see.")

A mechanistic materialism such as Epicureanism could
apparently dispense with any kind of deity and suffer nothing
therefrom except the stigma of atheism. Nature is an eternal
system, uncreated, self-regulating, and self-maintaining.
What need is there for gods? Are they not superfluous and
absurd in such a system, an archaic remnant of the folk imagination or a cowardly concession to popular prejudice?
Despite all that can be said on philosophical grounds
against their inclusion in a materialist system, there remains
one function, and a most important one, that the gods per-
form. This function is ethical; they are the paragons of the
good life, exemplifying in their own existence the highest
Epicurean ideals—serenity, detachment, unadulterated hap-

piness, all summed up in the one word *ataraxia*. For an Epicurean to achieve personal *ataraxia* was therefore not only happiness in a human sense but an *imitatio Dei*, a becoming godlike. The motivation underlying the pursuit of the good life was thus deeply religious in part, a fact usually overlooked by the critics of Epicureanism.

2. EPICURUS' THEOLOGY. To use the term "theology" in connection with Epicureanism seems at first blush a ridiculous contradiction, but, as we have just pointed out, Epicurus himself held lofty conceptions of the gods and their function in the scheme of things. We know from his biographer Diogenes Laertius that he wrote a separate treatise *On the Gods*. This is now unfortunately lost, and furthermore Lucretius never lived to climax his poem *On the Nature of Things* with a seventh book on the gods, as he apparently intended to do. Our knowledge of the Epicurean theology, therefore, exists only in broad outline and suffers from lack of detail.

a. *Nature of the gods*. Voltaire once maliciously remarked that "God is the noblest work of man," but, as is well known, the gods of classical Greek religion were ignoble projections of the human imagination. They were lechers, intriguers, haters, fighters, avengers—all in superhuman style. Not so the gods of Epicurus. These beings are completely nonanthropomorphic; they have been stripped of all human frailties and "cleaned up" beyond recognition. They do not walk the earth and have bastard children, nor do they reside on Mount Olympus and pursue their personal feuds and infighting. Epicurus has transported them to remote interstellar space, where they become beautiful symbols of calm and repose, absorbed in contemplating their own unalloyed perfection and unable to receive human worship or listen to human supplications.

As soon as the voice of reason rises from your [Epicurus'] godlike mind to enunciate the nature of things, the

terror in the soul dissolves, the walls of the world fall
back, and I see what comes to pass throughout the void.
The holy godheads are manifested, and their tranquil
thrones; the winds do not buffet them or clouds bestrew
them with storms, nor snow, clotted by piercing frost,
profane them with falling hoar. An ever cloudless ether
arches them over, smiling with its amplitude of light. Nature supplies all their wants, nor does anything vex their
peace of mind at any season. [Lucr. 3.14–24]

So quiet and exalted have the gods become in Epicurus'
hands that they appear to us non-Epicureans as faceless abstractions, mere ideals without form or body—in a word,
psychological projections of what every good Epicurean
wanted himself to be. From certain key passages in Epicurus
and Lucretius we can infer various characterizing attributes
that seem to describe these beings. They were perfect, self-
sufficient, impassive, and self-contemplating, somewhat in
the manner of Aristotle's Unmoved Mover, who had preceded
them chronologically in the list of philosophical godheads.
Their perfection and self-involvement absolved them from
doing anything—from motion and activity of any sort and
from the duties and responsibilities that deities normally
have, such as the creation and supervision of the world. The
latter activities would have been an invasion of their holy
privacy and perfect bliss and, furthermore, utterly contrary
to their real nature. It was (logically) impossible for these
beings either to create or to show providential concern, first
because they were immobile and could not participate in
motion without contradicting their own natures, and second
because they were perfect and therefore needed nothing to
fulfill themselves.[60]
Hence it would be blasphemous to attribute control of
nature (e.g., the heavenly bodies) to the deities, and any religious reactionary who made the mistake of doing so was
bound to suffer "the gravest spiritual disturbances" in the

form of those irrational fears which this naïve view of the world generated.

We should not regard the courses and revolutions of the heavenly bodies, their eclipses, risings and settings, and the like, as the operations of some deity who dutifully performs these functions, who decrees or did decree them, and who simultaneously enjoys absolute blessedness as well as immortality. . . . Nor, on the other hand, should one imagine that these bodies, which are actually aggregations of fiery matter, enjoy divine blessedness themselves and take on these motions by an act of will. On the contrary, we must preserve the full dignity of the divine in all expressions we use in connection with ideas such as these, in order that notions contradictory to the divine majesty may not arise from this source; otherwise this very contradictoriness will produce the gravest spiritual disturbances.

Those who have rightly learned that the gods lead lives of unconcern may yet marvel at times how things take place, particularly those occurrences that we observe overhead in the spaces of heaven; and they may again lapse into the antique notions of religion by acknowledging gods as the fierce lords of nature; and in their piteous ignorance of what can and what cannot be they may believe them omnipotent, not understanding the manner in which each thing's natural power is hedged by a limit set deep within. . . . Unless you cast such notions out of your mind and cease altogether to think thoughts unbecoming to the gods and alien to their tranquillity, the holy godheads that you have yourself impaired may ofttimes work you harm—not that you could profane the gods' high estate or that they would wrathfully thirst for hot vengeance but that you in your own mind would picture these serene beings, in their utter calm, rolling up great tides of wrath against you and would come to their shrines with unquiet heart and have neither strength nor peace of mind sufficient to receive those messengers of deity, the images which flow from their holy bodies into the minds of men.[61]

Thus a relapse into "the old-time religion" of a god-controlled universe has very serious consequences: It cuts the worshiper off from the gods' images—that is, alienates him from the divine communion—and it plunges the naïve believer once more into the ancient fears that Epicurus seeks to allay: namely, that the gods will avenge themselves on wicked men by causing natural disasters, political upheavals, and finally the torments of death and hell.

But Epicurus was no reckless destroyer of religion. If he attacked popular religion it was for the good and sufficient reason that it destroyed *ataraxia*. In its place he proposed to substitute a new religion that was ethically emancipating and elevating: the religion of contemplation, not of worship. For conventional worship was both absurd and futile. The gods did not need men's adoration, nor did they hear their prayers, and if they did they would take no steps to answer them.

> It is not true religion to be seen turning with veiled head ever and anon toward an image of stone, or drawing nigh to every god's altar, or prostrating oneself on the ground with suppliant hands before the holy shrines; nor is it piety to wet the altars with the abundant blood of beasts and to twine vow with vow. True religion is rather the power to contemplate nature with a mind set at peace. [Lucr. 5.1198–1203]

b. *The world is nonpurposeful (ateleology).* An idea often associated with traditional religion is that the world exhibits purpose both in its parts and as a whole. On the assumption that an intelligent and benevolent being or beings has or have designed and created the cosmos, the idea of cosmic purpose is a most natural and logical inference, even though it is frequently twisted to serve some narrow anthropocentric interpretation. But since Epicurus rejected this assumption and held instead that the world is "a fortuitous concourse of atoms," the view of the world as nonpurposeful was the only one that was consistent with his materialism and theology. He conceded only that an idea of the purpose of eyes, hands, legs, etc., developed *after* the natural formation of these organs, not that any idea of purpose preceded and caused their formation. If ideas of purpose were prior, they must have existed in nature or in the minds of the gods. But nature is not a cosmic mind; it is a nonintelligent system of atoms that incidentally and accidentally produced minds. And the gods, as we have seen, were immobile and impassive, engaging in no activities of creation or benevolent planning. Hence it would have been a contradiction for Epicurus to hold that purpose preceded natural formations or, in general, that nature was purposeful.

> How was the model for creating things and the idea of mankind itself first implanted in the gods, so that they could know and envisage what they wanted to do, or in what manner did they ever become cognizant of the power of the primal bodies and of what they could bring about by interchanging their positions, if it was not Nature herself that provided the exemplar of creation? [Lucr. 5.181–86][62]

In the following passage Lucretius states the argument against purpose, or teleology, in a different and much weaker form. He claims, without evidence, that use or function (e.g., seeing, talking, hearing) developed much later than the corresponding organ (eye, tongue, ear) and that therefore use or function could not have determined the natural formation of the organ. His argument is supposedly empirical, but since he offers no evidence, it is unsupported and unconvincing.

You must guard carefully against the error of thinking that those bright luminaries, our eyes, were created in order that we might look out through them or that the extremities of calves and thighs were rooted in the feet and made to bend, to the end that we should take long steps forward, or again that forearm was joined to sturdy upper arm and ministering hands provided on either side in order that we could do what was requisite for life. Other instances of this sort, whatever their claims, are all absurdly reasoned and put the matter backwards, because nothing in our bodies came into being to the end that we might use it; on the contrary, what has come into being begets its own usefulness. Seeing did not exist before the birth of the luminous eye, nor speaking with words sooner than the tongue was formed. Rather is it the case that the origin of the tongue long preceded speech and ears were created much before sound was heard. In short, I take it, all the organs and members existed before there was a use for them. Hence they could not have developed by reason of their utility. . . . All these things were first formed, and only later did they yield the conception of their own usefulness; and we observe that the principal members of this category are the senses and the limbs. [Lucr. 4.824–42, 853–55]

3. THE ATTACK ON POPULAR RELIGION. *Tanturn religio potuit suadere malorum.* The criticism of popular Greek religion is found in all the Epicurean documents that are still extant and is directed toward a single glaring defect of such religion: namely, that it is fear-producing and hence destructive of *ataraxia*, or true happiness. Under no circumstances could the traditional beliefs of Greece be allowed to stand in

the way of human welfare. The language of criticism in the *Letter to Herodotus* and *Letter to Menoeceus* is moderate and controlled, but the writer of the *Letter to Pythocles* (probably not Epicurus himself) engages in frequent blasts of propaganda and sometimes descends into outright contemptuous language for the benefit of "mythologizers," "astrologers," and other hacks.[63] By the time we reach the later tradition represented by Lucretius in the first century B.C. the contemptuous tone is noticeably more passionate. It is heightened, of course, by the poetry itself and also by the fact that Epicurus himself has now become a culture hero, indeed a savior of the race, the first mortal to have lifted mankind from its religious debasement and to have brought it into the light of truth.

When humankind lay prostrate and unseemly to the eye, ground to earth by the burden of religion, which reared its head from the quarters of the sky, frowning on us men with baleful mien, it was the Greek Epicurus who first dared to lift mortal eyes and take a stand confronting her. The gods' repute did not stay him, nor their bolts, nor heaven's threatening mutter. Rather, his trenchant mind was provoked the more to be the first to burst the tight-drawn bolts of Nature's gates. And so his quickening powers of mind won through, and he advanced far beyond the flaming bastions of the world and wandered in spirit through the limitless cosmos. Returning thence a conqueror, he comes to tell us what can and what cannot come to pass and how each thing's natural power is hedged by a limit set deep within. Thus religion in its turn lies prostrate, ground beneath our feet, and his victory exalts us to the skies.

Here I fear lest you perhaps suppose that you are being initiated into the rudiments of ungodly reason and are treading the path of evil. Quite the contrary! More often than not it is this religion which has spawned misdeeds both wicked and ungodly. Consider how at Aulis those worthies, the chosen captains of the Greeks, did brutally defile the altar of the virgin Diana with the blood of Iphigenia. The fillet encircling her virgin locks flowed evenly from both her cheeks, and her sorrowing father stood facing the altar. As she beheld the attendants hard by, cloaking their steel, and her townspeople shedding tears at sight of her, she became mute with terror and fell on her knees to the ground. Unhappy girl, it did not profit her at such a time that she had been the first to give the name "father" to King Agamemnon. For she was raised by men's hands and led quivering to the altar, not to be attended by Hymen's clarion song after the solemn rites of sacrifice but to fall foully to her murderous father, a victim unfouled at the very moment of wedlock—and all to provide a happy and prosperous departure for the fleet! So suasive of evil hath religion ever been! [Lucr. 1.62–101][64]

a. *Death and hell.* We have already seen in other connections (II.2 and IV.2, above) that death is a word and not a possible experience. The complete breakdown and dispersal of the soul atoms at death forestall any future sensation and life and at the same time cancel out the prospect of a hideous existence after death. Mankind's two greatest foes and phobias are swept from the board together by the atomic theory—truly the most humane act ever performed by any philosophy, materialist or otherwise![65]

If a man is perhaps to be wretched and in pain in the future, he must of course be existent at that time, if evil is to befall him. Now, since death does away with life and cancels the existence of everyone to whom such afflictions might accrue, we may infer that there is nothing in death for us to fear and that we cannot be wretched if we are nonexistent. In fact, when once the death that

knows no death has done away with our mortal existence, it is no different than if we had never been born at
all! [Lucr. 3.861–69]

b. *A sermon by a modern Epicurean on the evils of religion.* Religion is usually considered a "good" word, especially by the majority of middle-class Americans today who
are caught in the midst of the cold war being waged by
Christian-capitalist America and atheistic Russian Communism. But to a majority of materialists, both Marxist and
non-Marxist, religion has been a distinctly evil word. To the
Marxist it has meant the exploitation of the "have-nots," the
working classes, by a power- and money-hungry institution
that offers the proletariat "pie in the sky" in place of the
solid goods of this earth and makes them pay through the
nose for it. To Victorian materialists like Huxley, Darwin's
"bulldog," religion meant medieval ignorance and obscu-
rantism making a last ditch fight against an enlightened science that represented the wave of the future. To Epicurus,
Lucretius, and all good Epicureans it meant a set of archaic
and erroneous beliefs that generated irrational fears and
destroyed the possibility of human happiness, and was
therefore to be fought to the death by the new knowledge
called atomism.

The fight against the "popular" religion[66] so detested by
all materialists is far from won today, even in officially atheist Russia, where the Orthodox Church is reliably reported
to be increasing in numbers. Since most of us uncritically
accept religion as a "good" word and the effects of religion
as generally good, it might be well to put the Epicurean
point of view in sharply modern terms and imagine some
jaundiced devil's advocate preaching a lay sermon on the
evils of religion. He could well take as his text the famous
line in Lucretius, "So suasive of evil hath religion ever been"
(1.101), and then proceed as follows:

"In the twenty centuries that have passed since Lucretius

wrote, the evidence against popular religion has grown to massive proportions, and it is overwhelmingly unfavorable. Furthermore, such evidence now exists on a world-wide scale, as it did not for him. Wherever it is found, popular religion is uniformly retrograde, a burden upon the nations, and a major detriment to human advance and happiness. Such religion is still the home of sanctified ignorance, Bronze Age cosmologies, preposterous hopes, and impossible moralities. It has embalmed its prescientific myths and fobbed them off as 'revealed truth.' It has been notoriously antagonistic to the growth of genuine knowledge and to social changes based on such knowledge. It has tormented countless millions with feelings of unexpiated guilt and fears of hellish punishment at the hands of a kindly God. It has espoused high-flown ethical creeds that bear little relation to the facts of human nature, such as the promotion of universal love and brotherhood, and has succeeded instead in promoting universal hypocrisy, self-righteousness, fanaticism, contentiousness, division, and even violence among men.

"Consider the case of India with her seven major sects—how pitifully religious she is and how socially wretched! If we had no other evidence than that of India, the case against popular religion would still be conclusive. As recently as 1948 hundreds of thousands of Moslems and Hindus killed each other off during the great migrations of populations that occurred when the British raj departed and the country divided itself into two halves. After three thousand years of social evolution the caste system is still intact and doing its vicious work. The moral prestige of Gandhi succeeded in winning a drastic change in the status of the untouchables, but the change is largely legal, 'on the books,' and unenforced. How many Gandhis can India count on? Those who pin their faith on holy men or on social evolution may wait in vain. As the devil's advocate, do I dare to say that India probably needs the radical remedy of atheistic Communism to lift forever the curse of her pernicious religiosity? Education and industrialization will continue to improve the lot of the Indian masses bit by bit, but so long as the endemic disease of popular religion remains, India's fundamental situation will continue unchanged.

"Or, again, consider the case of the Moslem countries of the Near East and the twenty-one Catholic republics of South America. In both areas we find stagnant and petrified cultures that are profoundly religious and also profoundly benighted and unprogressive. In both areas these cultures are linked with exploiting feudal oligarchies, which do all they can to promote popular religion in the hope that the masses will continue to accept their poverty and ignorance fatalistically as the natural order of things ordained by God.

"The social record of the Roman Church in South America is poor indeed, but by no means untypical. Throughout its long history Catholicism has pretty consistently been interested in power and self-aggrandizement, not in humanity and humanitarianism. In the face of the menacing upsurge of population all over the world Catholicism still holds dogmatically to its 'party line'—no intercourse without issue. The future welfare of humanity must be subordinated to so-called natural law as ordained by God and implemented by the Church. The old men of the Vatican do not themselves propagate offspring, but neither do they leave its musty corridors to visit the teeming rabbit warrens of Naples and Rome, Bordeaux and Santiago. They stand convicted of the invincible ignorance that they accuse others of.

"There has been a perennial failure of the Christian churches to educate as well as to edify, and here the Protestant sects are just as culpable as others. What does one hear from the pulpits on Main Street about the great issues of the day—peace, racial integration, anti-Semitism, the population explosion? These issues are played down as controversial, and instead one gets the same dry pabulum about personal morality and salvation, the same banalities and clichés Sunday after Sunday. Where is the united Chris-

tian front for peace? It should be massive and powerful today when we stand on the brink of nuclear incineration instead of old-fashioned hell-fire. It should be demanding, in
the name of Christ, the only possible Christian solution to
the cold war—unilateral and total disarmament. But what
do we hear? A few courageous voices crying in the wilder-
ness of Christian apathy and conformism, and that is all.

"There is another aspect of popular religion that continues to trouble many observers, both within the churches and
outside them. This is the moral laxness, the bigotry, in-
grained prejudice, and insensitivity that often go hand in
hand with respectable church membership. I am not sure
that there is a causal relationship here in all cases, but at
least it seems plain that religion has done nothing to mend
these faults. The often repeated argument that we need religion in order to guarantee moral values seems trivial in view
of the evidence. The ethical effects of religion seem to be nil
in the majority of cases. It is the prevailing mores of society
that mold people's behavior, and historically religion has
usually accommodated itself to these mores. Thus the pious
Catholic may sin royally during the week, even attend por-
nographic movies, so long as he has the magic of the confes-
sional to fall back on. Or the Protestant who is an elder and
a pillar of the church may be notoriously sharp and fraudu-
lent in his business practices. And the dear old lady who
hasn't missed church in forty years may be bitterly anti-
Semitic and anti-Negro. What Christian of your acquaintance
loves our enemies, the Russians? How many of them would
favor a holy war with Russia right now, to stamp out atheistic Communism for ever? What Christian nation dropped
the first two atom bombs? If it were not our own, we would
call that nation pagan and barbarous.

"Without being overly prejudiced, I think it can fairly be
said that some persons who voluntarily stand *outside* the
church or who have renounced institutional religion often
exhibit higher standards of ethical belief and practice than

THE ART OF HAPPINESS

those who remain within the pale. The point is this: Religion, through its powerlessness to change people, has to acquiesce in current beliefs and practices, thereby involuntarily helping to perpetuate immorality. In many cases it is only by separating oneself from this whole impotent system and the groups that stumble along blindly within it that one can achieve any moral progress. And this statement is by no means refuted by the tiny handful of people who are true examples of the Christian life and who deserve our highest respect. These persons are the saving remnant that historically has failed to save.

" 'He that sitteth in the heavens shall laugh; He shall hold them in derision.' Or, as Lucretius would put it in less truculent fashion, the gods go right on about their business, taking no notice whatsoever of the unholy mess men have got themselves into with their holy religions. The Epicurean gods were true Olympians, above the battle at all times. But what about *us* meantime? What about the human predicament? Some sort of Lucretian answer is still pertinent today. To know the causes of things and to know that they are wholly natural, not supernatural—this is the mark of the free mind, the mind free from ignorance, superstition, and the major liabilities of religion. Religion explains nothing except in terms of myth and symbol; it does not tell us about the causes of things; it does not help us control disease and poverty but calls them 'acts of God;' it does not promote men's happiness and welfare on earth but claims that happiness and man's true good come only after death. To know the causes of things and to know that they are wholly natural—this is the heart of Lucretius' gospel, and it is essentially what we mean by scientific knowledge today.

"But whereas Lucretius' attitude toward such knowledge was idolatrous, ours in the twentieth century must be much more cautious and restrained. Science is not a good in itself, nor is it evil; it is ethically neutral. Science is simply a means to moral ends that lie outside science proper. The moral ends which science serves are based on human desires, and these desires are both rational and irrational, humane and barbarous. If we wish to control disease and poverty, science will provide effective means; if we desire suicide for the human species, science is now well equipped to that end also. Science has no conscience; it tells us nothing about good and evil. Nor is science a panacea for human ills, as Lucretius believed; it is a terrible two-edged sword. In fact, there are no human panaceas. The long history of religions shows plainly that religion has worked more evil than good; the much shorter history of science shows that its whole value is ambiguous, especially at the present time. The cry heard in many quarters today, 'Back to religion!' is childish and obscurantist, an evasion of our present predicament. Our best hope today, twenty centuries after Lucretius, is still scientific knowledge, but it is indeed a tenuous hope."

4. EPICUREANISM AS A SECULAR RELIGION.

a. *Veneration of Epicurus.* A philosophy that attempts to destroy religion must supply a viable substitute with both intellectual content and with emotive or affective values that provide a dynamic of belief or "faith" but do not appeal directly to the mind. In the case of Epicureanism the traditional view of the world as god-created and god-governed was not only displaced as intellectually untenable; its displacement was more than adequately compensated for by the new system of knowledge called atomism. But this was not enough, as the later history of the school shows. Distinctively religious values began to cluster around the person and writings of Epicurus at least by the time of Lucretius, two hundred years after the master's death, and probably long before.[67] The adulation of Epicurus that is so marked in the Latin poet stands out like an unaccountable blemish on a first reading. But not all this emotional tone can be written off as Roman rhetoric. A good part of it is sincere religious feeling directed to the godlike "ornament of Greece" who had dethroned the gods and led mankind toward the good life. The element of feeling that is so needed to make any world view or ideology personally meaningful and that was conspicuously lacking in atomism, with its stark scientific framework and its bleak abstractions called "the gods," is here supplied in some measure in the saintly person of the Greek master and his writings, which have now attained the rank of scriptures.[68]

> You who were the first to lift so bright a light in a night so deep and to illumine the good things of life, I follow after you, O Epicurus, ornament of Greece, and pliantly set my feet in the tracks you have already printed—not from desire to vie with you but because I thirst with love to imitate you. Can the swallow contend with the swan? Can the young goat with its timorous limbs rival the doughty horse in the race? You are our father; you impart to us a father's precepts, O revealer of nature! Like as the bee sips in flowery dells, so we from your illustrious pages do cull the golden words—all golden they are and worthy of a life everlasting. As soon as the voice of reason rises from your godlike mind to enunciate the nature of things, the terror in the soul dissolves, the walls of the world fall back, and I see what comes to pass throughout the void. The holy godheads are manifested, and their tranquil thrones. . . . In all this the tracts of hell are nowhere seen; yet earth does not bar the sight of aught that comes to pass in the void below. At this a kind of godly joy and chill transfix me, that nature is thus manifested by your power, made plain and evident in every part. [Lucr. 3.1–30]

b. *Epicureanism as a spiritual therapy.* Both Epicurus and Lucretius were agreed that the spiritual ills of men are caused by the unnatural values they pursue—money, power, position—and by their ignorance of nature and the ethical goals that nature prescribes—a life of simplicity free from mental and bodily pain. Since human anxieties and fears are fairly general in all times and places, Epicurus regarded them as symptoms of an endemic spiritual disease that called for a universal therapy. Like other Greeks (pre-Freudians all) he pinned his faith on reason. Reason can "cleanse" man of his animal ignorance about the world, thereby emancipating him from his childish dread of the supernatural and a horrible afterlife; it can also "purify" his irrational desires by showing him that true happiness rests on the basic mechanisms of pleasure and pain. Epicureanism by Lucretius' time had taken on the added religious signifi-cance of a therapeutic cult;[69] and Epicurus had become the spiritual healer who showed the convert how to imitate the ideal blessedness of the gods by a twofold procedure—moral catharsis and "revealed" knowledge.

The student should note in the second of the following two passages certain expressions which have a decided cult flavor, e.g., the comparison of the human being to a cracked and ill-smelling vessel that taints everything put into it; the "cleansing" of this vessel with words of truth; the "narrow way" that leads to ethical salvation; the "darkling terror in the mind" as a description of the average man's spiritual condition.

> If the heart is not cleansed, what struggles, what trials we then thrust upon ourselves, and by no will of our own! What sharp pains of desire harrow the unquiet man, and equally what fears! Self-esteem, lechery, shame-lessness, pomp, indolence—how they lay a man in ruins! He, then, who has vanquished all these and driven them from our hearts by words, not force of arms—may we not rightly deem such a man fit to be numbered with the gods? [Lucr. 5.43–51]
>
> He [Epicurus] saw that men had on hand almost all that was needful for their living, that their lives were se-cured in so far as this was possible, that many flourished

in conditions of wealth, preferment, and repute or were
noted for the goodly name of their children. And yet pri-
vately their hearts were not the less troubled. By no will
of their own they bedeviled themselves without ceasing,
being compelled to vent their ugly moods in violent re-
sentments. He then understood that it was the human
vessel itself which created the evil and that everything
gathered into it from without, even good things, was de-
filed by the vessel's own imperfection. This he inferred in
part because he saw that it was a damaged and leaky
thing, so much so that it could never in any wise be filled,
and in part because it infected with its own foul flavor all
that it took within. He therefore cleansed our hearts with
words that speak true. He set limits to our desires and
fears; he showed us the highest good toward which we all
tend, and pointed out the narrow way by which we may
pursue it straightly. He revealed to us what there is of evil
in the affairs of men everywhere, how it ranges about in
divers forms, how it is generated by chance or by Nature's powers (since she has so arranged things), and what
avenues it is best to follow in confronting it. And he
showed that men have stirred up tides of grief and woe in
their own hearts, usually to no avail. Just as children
quail in the blinding dark and are fearful of all, so we in
the light of day are often terrified by things which are no
more to be feared than what children tremble at in the
dark and think is going to happen. This darkling terror in
the mind must then be routed not by the sun's rays, not
by the bright shafts of day, but by the observation and rational inspection of Nature. [Lucr. 6.9–41]

VII. ETHICS AND THE GOOD LIFE

The Epicurean theory of the good life—that is, the life
that is simultaneously satisfying and moral—had two as-

pects, one negative and the other positive. Before one can enjoy the fruits of living, one must free oneself of certain crippling liabilities. These liabilities, specifically, are the fear of gods, the fear of death, and the fear of the torments of hell. Both Epicurus and Lucretius took great pains to neutralize these fears and to show that they were utterly groundless. Epicurus devoted the first third of his *Letter to Menoeceus* to this task,[70] and we have already seen how the atomic philosophy was able to lay these ancient ghosts without difficulty (II.2, IV.2, VI.2, above). Lucretius wrote more than four hundred lines and adduced more than twenty-five arguments to show that the soul is mortal and therefore unable to experience any sort of life after death.[71] He put the fear of death in a special ethical context of its own by attempting to show that it is the root cause of many typical human vices such as greed, murder, envy, self-pity, suicide, treason, and betrayal.

The blind avarice and lust for office which drive poor wretches to transgress the bounds of right and oftentimes to become partners and abettors of crime whilst they toil night and day with consummate effort to reach the peak of power—these cancers of the moral life are fed in no small part by the dread of death. For ugly rejection and bitter poverty are commonly viewed as far removed from the pleasant life of station—a sojourning, as it were, before the doors of death. In their desire to shun these ills and keep them far away, men are driven by this spurious fear to inflate their means through civil strife and to compound murder with murder whilst they avidly triple their wealth. They take savage pleasure in a brother's mournful death. They detest and dread the kinsman's banquet. In the same way and often from the same fear, they pine with envy that he who walks abroad in the dignity of his office is a powerful man esteemed by all, and they wail that they themselves wallow in the mud

and murk. And some give up their lives for the sake of
statues and a name! And often from the fear of death
men are so seized by hatred of life and the light of day
that they decree their own deaths in despondency of
heart, forgetting that it is this fear which is the fount of
their ills, this fear that plagues their self-respect, ruptures
the bonds of affection, and casts duty from her high seat.
Heretofore men have often betrayed fatherland and be-
loved parents as they sought to escape hell's domain.
[Lucr. 3.59–86]

1. EPICURUS' HEDONISM. The positive aspect of Epicurus'
ethical teaching is known as hedonism, from the Greek
noun for "pleasure." His hedonism has two basic assumptions, both materialistic in character: (a) that moral good is
the same as pleasure, either physical or mental, since the
experienceable range of pleasure is very wide and extends to
more than one level; and (b) that moral evil is the same as
pain, whether physical or mental. Both pleasure and pain
can be analyzed further into configurations of atoms in motion, so that our moral experience is just as material as anything else in the world. Moral acts involve deliberate
"choices" of possible concrete pleasures and "aversions,"
i.e., the deliberate avoidance of prospective pain.[72] An act is
moral if in the long run, all things considered, it produces in
the agent a surplus of pleasure over pain; otherwise it is
immoral. This working principle is applicable in literally
thousands of cases of individual "choice and aversion" and
can readily be illustrated by examples from our life today:

1. A student decides to cheat in a college exam in order
to pull up his grade. Is this act moral by Epicurus' standards? (We will forget, for the time being, all other possible
standards.) Suppose the student "gets away with it" this
time. His "pleasure" is increased, but at the same time he is
a little worried that he may have aroused the instructor's
suspicions. Pleasure and pain are more or less evenly bal-

anced, and it is impossible to tell in this instance whether the act is moral or immoral. Encouraged by his previous success, the same student decides to make a habit of cheating. Several alternatives are now possible: (a) The student may finally be detected and thrown out of college, in which case pain outweighs pleasure and the act is immoral. (b) The student may be clever and consistently avoid detection but at the same time experience a nagging anxiety, in which case pain probably is greater than pleasure and the act immoral. Or (c) he may consistently avoid detection and feel no qualms or anxiety whatever (and there seems to be plenty of this kind of student in the colleges today). In this case Epicurus would be forced to admit that the act is completely moral, since only pleasure is produced by it! However, the habit of successful cheating in college may well be carried over later into cheating in marriage and dishonesty in business, where the consequences may turn out to be more painful than pleasurable. The long-term effects of our habits are always pertinent to judgments of moral and immoral.

2. A convivial drinker who loves martinis may consume ten or more at a party and stay on his feet. Is this act moral by Epicurus' standards? We have to take into account not only the short-term effects (our friend enjoys himself hugely for two hours) but all the consequences. If he suffers no ill effects during the night or the next morning, the act is wholly pleasurable and therefore wholly moral; otherwise it is probably immoral, depending on the intensity of his hangover. (It was this sort of example that gave Epicureanism a "black eye." Epicurus himself would have frowned on it, since he disapproved, on principle, of sensuality, raw pleasure, and overindulgence. Nevertheless it is characteristic of "epicures" in every age and is certainly pertinent to modern living.)

3. A young couple deeply in love are unable to marry because of financial obstacles. They decide nevertheless to enjoy premarital intercourse the two- or three-year period before they marry. Is this act moral or immoral? Again there

are alternatives: (a) The couple may wish to enjoy each other sexually but be severely inhibited by feelings of guilt traceable in the one case to a frigid mother and in the other to a tyrannical father. Their pleasure has a deep overlay of pain, and the act consequently is immoral. (b) The couple may have no feelings of guilt, and their sex pleasure may be unadulterated; furthermore, their tensions are successfully relieved by this periodic indulgence. They later marry and live happily ever after. In this case the act is clearly moral. (c) If, however, this couple does not marry, because they tire of each other after two or three years, their later sex life may be rendered unstable and promiscuous, with the result that each may have two marriages and two divorces. These later painful consequences may be traceable to the early affair. Once again the long-term effects must be viewed before any ethical judgment can be arrived at.

In the light of these examples the student may work out answers to still bigger problems: Is marriage moral? Is it ever immoral? Is adultery ever moral? Is war moral? Racial discrimination? And so on.

This basic description of hedonism still needs certain important qualifications in order to fit Epicurus' own meaning of the term, but for the time being it is obvious that: (1) The pleasure-pain principle is extremely flexible and can be used to uphold both conventional and unconventional moral values. (2) Hedonism proceeds to judge an act as moral or immoral not by the act itself, nor by any hard and fast rules of behavior, nor by the dictates of reason, but by the experience it produces, specifically the feelings of pleasure and pain resulting from the act. For Epicurus believed that these feelings were the only true and natural foundation for an empirical ethics. "Every pleasure is a good by reason of its having a nature akin to our own, but not every pleasure is desirable. In like manner every state of pain is an evil, but not all pains are uniformly to be rejected.[73] (3) The ethics of hedonism is relative and not absolute, and the morality of many acts is ambiguous, since the value of a given act does not depend on the *a priori* character of the act itself but on its psychological consequences, which of course differ from person to person and from time to time.

a. *Pleasure is neutral or negative in meaning.* The doctrine that pleasure is the highest ethical good lends itself immediately to serious misunderstanding because of the unfortunate ambiguity of the key term "pleasure." The Epicureans have been purposely misrepresented as sensualists and "high livers" by their rivals and detractors, both ancient and modern; for "pleasure" has been a "dirty word" in the eyes of many moralists and laymen in all periods of history. Actually the strict Epicurean sectarian was rather ascetic and even puritanical, both in teaching and in practice, and this fact is borne in on anyone who reads the surviving texts sympathetically. Epicurus regarded "pleasure" as the logical opposite of "pain"; in other words, for him pleasure meant nonpain, or the relative absence of pain in mind and body, i.e., both physical comfort or well-being and peace of mind. The good life, then, is quite simply one that daily and yearly conduces to these ends. It is emphatically *not* a life of sensual enjoyments, excitement, competition, social prestige, and monetary success—all of which we in this country tend to believe constitute the good life, or what we call the "American way of life."

> When I say that pleasure is the goal of living I do not mean the pleasures of libertines or the pleasures inherent in positive enjoyment, as is supposed by certain persons who are ignorant of our doctrine or who are not in agreement with it or who interpret it perversely. I mean, on the contrary, the pleasure that consists in freedom from bodily pain and mental agitation. The pleasant life is not the product of one drinking party after another or of sexual intercourse with women and boys or of the sea food and other delicacies afforded by a luxurious table. . . .[74]

The good life for the Epicurean involves disciplining of the appetites, curtailment of desires and needs to the absolute minimum necessary for healthy living, detachment from most of the goals and values that are most highly regarded, and withdrawal from active participation in the life of the community, in the company of a few select friends—in a word, plain living and high thinking.

It will be seen from this that the Epicurean ideal is hardly what we mean by a life of pleasure or even a pleasant life. The conception of pleasure is wholly negative—the minimizing of all the pains of living, great and small, and of the three besetting fears, and the maximizing of inner peace, serenity, and well-being. The ideal, then, in its strict interpretation is practically Oriental—the achieving of a Buddha-like tranquillity—with the difference, of course, that the Epicurean asserted the full reality of the physical world and did not seek to be absorbed into a mystical nirvana.

But there were Epicureans and Epicureans. That is to say, there were strict sectarians leading the secluded life, on the one hand, and Epicureans-in-the-world, on the other. The latter group are represented by the examples used earlier, especially by the imbiber of martinis and the young couple in love. It will be seen immediately that these people are all degenerate Epicureans, since what they seek from life is a maximum of positive pleasure with a minimum of unpleasant consequences. This is perfectly natural and human, but it is not according to Epicurean Hoyle. Nevertheless from a purely pragmatic and nondogmatic point of view there is no reason why a person cannot live a successful, even a sophisticated life by applying the pleasure-pain principle in this unorthodox manner. For every true Epicurean there have been thousands of pseudo-Epicureans in every age, just as for every Jesus there have been hundreds of thousands of pseudo-Christians. Where ideals are too high and austere, they are bound to be diluted and corrupted by that coarse breed, man-in-the-world. It was the switch from negative to positive pleasure in lay practice that destroyed the credit of "straight" Epicureanism and eventually gave "epicure" the meaning of a connoisseur of fine foods and wines. And the mere presence of the word "pleasure" at the heart of the ethical teachings was enough to condemn it in the eyes of those who never looked deeper or didn't wish to look at all. In the same way the disciplined and demanding ethics of Jesus has been almost entirely discredited by the practice of the undisciplined and the spiritually shallow. In each case the pearl of great price has been trampled by the herd.

The negative attitude toward pleasure and the minimizing of all the worldling's chief values are perfectly illustrated by the life of Epicurus himself, who was a master practitioner of his own doctrines. First, he withdrew from active participation in the social and political life of Athens and secluded himself with friends, both men and women, in a walled Garden. He followed his own precept *lathe biosas* ("Live the obscure life"). Second, he lived a simple life, especially as regards diet. He ate no meat, drank no wine, and once in a letter to a friend he naïvely asked for a potted cheese as a special luxury. Third, he spent his time in unworldly pursuits—study, writing, teaching, conversation, contemplation. Fourth, like Jesus, he avoided sexual contacts but at the same time laid himself open to scurrilous jibes by surrounding himself with female disciples, both free and slave. Epicurus and all true Epicureans took a dim view of man's most intense and sometimes most painful pleasure, sexual love: "The sophisticated man will not fall in love," and "Sex never benefited any man, and it's a marvel if it hasn't injured him!"[75] Epicurus would have approved the complete wisdom of a recent professorial pronouncement: "I would rather spend an hour in bed with Dickens than with any woman."

b. *Rational selection of pleasures and pains.* Although every pleasure is a natural good in itself and every pain a natural evil, not every pleasure is desirable, nor is every pain to be avoided. At this point a kind of prudential process of calculation enters in, to prescribe the necessary conditions for a mature hedonism. Reasoning overlays the naiveté of nature with wisdom and tries to guide it aright. Thus if one knows beforehand that ten martinis will result in a hangover, it is the part of wisdom to take only five. By the same token if surgery is indicated, it should be undergone for the sake of future comfort and safety. And if the typical American boy wants to "succeed" today, he must be sensible and undergo the pains of four years of a college education. His present discomforts will pay handsome dividends in the future. (These are again examples drawn from the layman's Epicureanism.)

> Because of the very fact that pleasure is our primary and congenital good we do not select every pleasure; there are times when we forgo certain pleasures, particularly when they are followed by too much unpleasantness. Furthermore, we regard certain states of pain as preferable to pleasures, particularly when greater satisfaction results from our having submitted to discomforts for a long period of time. . . . It is our duty to judge all such cases by measuring pleasures against pains, with a view to their respective assets and liabilities, inasmuch as we do experience the good as being bad at times and, contrariwise, the bad as being good.[76]

For example, if confronted with a choice between a simple and a luxurious diet, between obscurity and fame, between a life of contemplation and a life in politics, the strict Epicurean would always choose the less obvious value—simple diet, obscurity, and contemplation. He would much prefer to be a Thoreau or a Frost than board chairman of U.S. Steel or President of the United States. And indeed to choose the simple life has a certain wisdom, though from the American point of view it looks like sheer inertia, defeatism, or stupidity. It means choosing the way that very probably presents the fewest pains and disappointments rather than the way that seems to promise the largest number of positive satisfactions but contains many hidden frustrations, not to mention ulcers. The defensive and negative attitude to life was wisdom distilled from an age of troubles, when it did not pay to be either optimistic or enterprising.[77]

> Accordingly we have need of pleasure only when we feel pain because of the absence of pleasure, but whenever we do not feel pain we no longer stand in need of pleasure. . . . In addition, we consider limitation of the appetites a major good, and we recommend this practice not for the purpose of enjoying just a few things and no more but rather for the purpose of enjoying those few in case we do not have much. We are firmly convinced that those who need expensive fare least are the ones who relish it most keenly and that a natural way of life is easily procured, while trivialities are hard to come by. Plain foods afford pleasure equivalent to that of a sumptuous diet, provided that the pains of penury are wholly eliminated. Barley bread and water yield the peak of pleasure whenever a person who needs them sets them in front of himself.

> How unhappy are the lives of men! How purblind their hearts! In what black ignorance and dark peril their small lives are spent! They do not see how little Nature cries out for. She demands only the secession of pain from the body; she requires only that the mind be secluded from anxiety and dread and enjoy feelings of pleasure. We see, then, that few things, all told, are necessary for the body's well-being—in fact, only those that shut out pain.[78]

c. *Hedonism deficient as a social ethic.* The self-protective and individualistic attitude of Epicurus' hedonism prevented it from turning outward toward society at large and developing into a mature social ethic. True, it did emphasize friendship and the practice of gentleness and loving-kindness among its members, and it did show considerable human concern, in fact actual religious fervor, in spreading the gospel of atomism as a counterirritant to the phobias generated by popular religion.[79] But these are not the same as a comprehensive theory for the welfare of society as a whole, such as John Stuart Mill developed in Victorian England from a hedonistic base. The altruistic spirit of Mill's "greatest good for the greatest number" (which, incidentally, included the British working classes) was far different from Epicurus' introverted escapism: "Withdraw from the world; avoid the pains and dangers of involvement; seek your own security and serenity."

The difference between a constructive altruism and an egocentric happiness theory is quite obvious from Epicurus' scattered dicta on justice (and injustice), which is perhaps the most important of social values:

> The just man is the least disturbed by passion, the unjust man the most highly disturbed. [*L.D.* 17]
>
> The most important consequence of just dealing is inner serenity. [*Frag.* 80]
>
> Justice was never an entity in itself. It is a kind of agreement not to harm or be harmed, made when men associate with each other at any time and in communities of any size whatsoever. [*L.D.* 33]
>
> Injustice is not an evil in itself. Its evil lies in the anxious fear that you will not elude those who have authority to punish such misdeeds. [*L.D.* 34]

In other words, justice is not a transcendental Platonic Form but a social contract empirically arrived at. But it is not a contract to insure the general happiness, the peace and prosperity of the whole community, as the seventeenth-century materialist, Thomas Hobbes, pictured it in *Leviathan*. Rather, it is a contract somewhat in the sense that an insurance policy is a contract—a device to insure *me* against private pain and the inroads of the world on my personal security and happiness. This is all quite consistent with the outlook of an egocentric hedonism, but it is also lamentably shortsighted. Justice and injustice are viewed purely in terms of their psychological effects on *me* in my capacity as the agent, not in terms of the happiness or unhappiness of the recipient whom my acts affect, and least of all in terms of their objective social consequences. Justice on my part is a good solely because it is conducive to serenity, the supreme Epicurean value. If I do not impair the happiness of others by acting unjustly, experience shows, generally speaking, that I may have the calm assurance that they will not impair my happiness. In the same way injustice is bad not in its effects on others but because *I*, the wrongdoer, must live in fear of being caught and punished by the authorities!

This may be worldly wisdom for hard times, but somehow one misses the more comprehensive social realism of Hobbes and the generosity and largeness of spirit of Mill in this narrow egoism. Given the trying and dangerous conditions of the Hellenistic period, the Epicurean, with a little imagination, could easily have enlarged the concept of pain experienced by *myself* to include the pains experienced by *others* as a result of personal or social injustice. This would have been a first negative step in the direction of Mill's Greatest Happiness Principle, but it was never taken. Pain and pleasure were always conceived as my pain and pleasure, and as a result the Epicurean ethic remained a feasible way of life for individuals and little more. Paradoxically this narrow spirit stands in strong contrast to the real altruism that the school exhibited in its war on the evils of religion and in its zeal to save men from superstitious ignorance. The polemical passion of the Epicureans spent itself entirely in that warfare, so that when they came to the field of morality proper they were exhausted and, like their gods, had to make a virtue of impassivity and unconcern. (This imbalance between expansion and contraction of interest in human welfare is somewhat paralleled by the overriding concern of the Christian churches for the salvation of souls and their frequent unconcern for the social evils in their midst, such as poverty, slavery, and racial discrimination.)

From the egocentric question, What acts are likely to bring *me* pain or pleasure? it seems not too huge a step to the altruistic questions, What acts of mine are likely to bring pain or pleasure to *others*? Do I have a duty to increase the happiness of others as well as my own happiness? Can I be happy myself if I ignore the unhappiness of others around me? Am I ever to suppress and sacrifice my own pleasure for the good of others, including at times the community? A modern hedonist, with his social conscience enlarged by the impact of Mill and others, would be bound to seek answers to these questions and then go on to apply a new version of the pleasure-pain principle to pressing current problems such as anti-Semitism, racial discrimination, world over-population, thermonuclear war, the growth of Communism, and others. The student should let his mind play over the whole range of these social and political problems, consider their vast implications for human happiness and unhappiness, and then finally ask himself whether Epicurus' advice— "Seek your own security and peace of mind"—is adequate for our own age of troubles.

2. DETERMINISM AND FREE WILL.

The good Epicurean believes that certain events occur deterministically, that others are chance events, and that still others are in our own hands. He sees also that necessity cannot be held morally responsible and that chance is an unpredictable thing, but that what is in our own hands, since it has no master, is naturally associated with blame-worthiness and the opposite. (Actually it would be better to subscribe to the popular mythology than to become a slave by accepting the determinism of the natural philosophers, because popular religion underwrites the hope of supplicating the gods by offerings but determinism contains an element of necessity, which is inexorable.)[80]

We have already seen in another connection (III.4, above) that Epicurus was just as concerned with freeing man from the tyranny of matter as he was with liberating him from the rule of gods and that this was one of the chief reasons why he postulated the atomic swerve. In his ethical choices man enjoys freedom from atomic compulsion, or "necessity," by reason of the tiny swervings of his soul atoms. Since these swerves are not mechanically caused by antecedent motions but occur spontaneously, man's ethical choices are likewise uncaused by what has gone before—that is, they are "free" from mechanical necessity—and man as an ethical being is an exception to natural determinism. The Epicurean argument for moral freedom follows the pattern of the familiar *reductio ad absurdum*: If man were not free, he would be a moral automaton, and he would not have the feeling of being free to "move where the mind listeth"; all his actions would be completely predictable and inevitable; and he could not be held responsible for anything he did. But since he does feel quite free to choose as he wills, since his actions are neither predictable nor inevitable, and since he is held morally responsible for what he does, it follows validly that man is indeed a free moral agent. And if man is free, the swerve theory is the most likely hypothesis to account for his freedom.

If every motion of atoms is always continuous with another, if new motion always originates from old in determinate sequence, and if it is the case that the primal bodies do not swerve and at least begin to break the bonds of determinism, thus preventing cause from following cause in perpetuity, then why do living creatures throughout the world have freedom of the will, this freedom torn from necessity that allows each of us to go where his pleasure bids? Why are our motions unpredictable in both time and direction? Why do we move where the mind listeth? It is past doubting that our wills initiate motion in all such cases and that movement is channeled from this source throughout the frame. . . . Thus it is this slight deviation of the primal bodies, at indeterminate times and places, that keeps the mind as such from experiencing an inner compulsion in doing everything it does and from being forced to endure and suffer like a captive in chains. [Lucr. 2.251–62 and 289–93]

In evaluating this argument for moral freedom we cannot criticize the *reductio ad absurdum* itself, since it is a variant of a valid argument form (known in logic as "denying the consequent"), but we may legitimately attack the assumption that atomic swerves provide a basis for such freedom. On the swerve theory an act of will is causally free if we grant the assumption that the swerves that make it possible are uncaused. But, at the same time, the will is not free from the tyranny of matter, or from mechanism, as Epicurus wished it to be. It is free only from the normal, regular atomic mechanisms but is now subject to freak mechanisms over which it has no control whatever. Even though these are localized in the will, the will itself is not an autonomous agent in its own right, operating independently of the swerves. Being an atomic configuration itself, the will which chooses A rather than B is simply giving expression to random and irregular atomic events occurring within itself. The swerve theory thus has the effect of reducing man to a moral freak. It does not provide him with a settled or determinate character to act from but allows him only choices that are totally unpredictable, since they have no causal roots in his own past but rest upon pure chance. On this theory man cannot be a moral agent in his own right; he is a mere robot who expresses the occasional vagaries of nature. This is clearly not what we ordinarily mean by "moral freedom," nor would most people consider themselves morally responsible for "free" acts of this sort. Freedom, responsibility, and the caprices of atomic behavior do not make moral sense when brought together.[81]

It so happens that the swerve theory has a perfect modern analogue in the Heisenberg Uncertainty Principle (1927) of modern physics. According to this principle there is a basic uncertainty (sometimes interpreted as a-causality) at the very heart of matter. The behavior of subatomic particles is not uniform or wholly predictable, even under identical conditions of experimentation. It is only in the case of gross aggregates of such particles ("things," or "objects") that these irregularities cancel out statistically and that we can still speak of nature as uniform and predictable. The physicist may not be able to predict the behavior of a given particle, but the astronomer can still predict a solar eclipse with complete accuracy. Needless to say, interested parties, from theologians on down to moralists, have seized on the Heisenberg Principle as a final support for the tottering doctrine of the freedom of the will. But here again mere random behavior of subatomic particles cannot form a basis for human freedom and responsibility, any more than in the case of Epicurus' swerve. In a word, the Heisenberg Principle is irrelevant to ethical questions, particularly the question of human freedom.[82]

3. EVALUATIONS OF EPICUREAN HEDONISM.

a. *Psychological and ethical hedonism.* Although the life of pleasure, or the pleasant life—either in the raw, impulsive sense of "doing what comes naturally" or in the sophisticated and selective meaning used by the civilized person—has appealed to countless numbers of acknowledged and unacknowledged hedonists in every age, there are good technical reasons why pleasure or happiness cannot be regarded as the highest ethical good or hedonism proved as an ethical principle. One of the earliest critics of hedonism was Plato himself. In the Platonic dialogue named *Protagoras* after the great Sophist of that name, Socrates has no difficulty in getting Protagoras to admit that if one is to choose successfully between competing pleasures or between prospective pleasures and pains there must be an "art of measuring" these against each other. Since the measuring principle or criterion can be none other than knowledge or reason, it is immediately obvious that pleasure is dependent on a principle other than itself and therefore cannot be regarded as the highest good.[83] Epicurus admits the need for such a criterion, but, since he was an anti-Platonist, he does not draw the conclusion that knowledge is superior to pleasure: "It is our duty to judge all such cases by measuring pleasures against pains, with a view to their respective assets and liabilities."[84]

The modern hedonist believes that the case for hedonism is perfectly obvious and easily proved. He argues as follows: It is a plain fact of human nature that each of us is consistently motivated by our individual desire for our own pleasure or happiness and that we always act in such a way as to attempt to achieve a balance of pleasure over pain. This statement, he claims, is a true description of human motivation and behavior and may justly be called an empirical generalization, since it rests on the experience of countless generations of observers of human nature. This solid factual basis is the stage of the argument called *psychological hedonism*. It is pre-ethical, since it simply reports a salient fact about human nature without telling us how we should ideally act if we are to be moral beings. Now since ethics is concerned only with the ideal *should* or *ought*—in other words, with obligations rather than facts—the hedonist must make the transition from the factual *is* of human behavior to the ethical *ought*. This second and final stage of the argument is known as *ethical hedonism*. The transition from *is* to *ought*, from empirical fact to ethical ideal, is made with the greatest of ease: If people actually do act for their own happiness, what is more logical than that they *should* act for their own happiness—in other words, that individual happiness should be our moral goal? To conclude otherwise would be queer and downright absurd.[85]

The critic immediately objects that sweeping generalizations about human nature are unsafe; there are always negative instances that show the generalization to be faulty. It is simply not true, he argues, that everyone at all times seeks his own happiness to the exclusion of all other values. What about the company commander who throws himself on a hand grenade in order to save the lives of the men behind him? What about the parents who scrimp and sacrifice for eight years to put their two sons through college? Or the Freedom Riders who voluntarily faced mob violence and prison terms in order to break down the color bar in Southern bus terminals? The hedonist immediately turns these examples to his own advantage by interpreting them as *disguised* instances of a generalization that has no exceptions. The company leader is a fanatic who seeks to immortalize himself in his community by his act of bravery beyond the call of duty; in seeking death he is finding his true happiness. The Freedom Riders are masochists who find intense pleasure in physical pain and humiliation. And as for the parents, being uneducated themselves they have a vicarious happiness in seeing their sons happily educated. And so on, and so on. Every exception is twisted so as to reinforce a rule that has no exceptions, and the psychological hedonist ends up refuting himself by his own perverse dogmatism.

Hedonism can thus be attacked at the psychological stage.[86] But even more devastating is the criticism that can be leveled at the ethical stage. Even granting that psychological hedonism represents a sound generalization about human motivation, which it does not, it would still be impossible to derive ethical hedonism from it by logical processes. For if every act that *is* actually motivated by pleasure *ought* to be so motivated, then (1) there is no difference between *is* and *ought*, no difference between a natural fact and a moral obligation, *is* and *ought* are tautologous or logically identical, and ethics disappears into mere fact; (2) the hedonist surrenders the right to evaluate human conduct as moral or immoral, because if every act is what it ought to be and ought to be what it is (which is what the tautology *is* = *ought* entails), then there are no grounds for either praise or blame, and the ethical life is reduced to the level of amoral animal behavior.

Actually every hedonist is both a self-critic and a critic of others; that is, he does have some outside standard of "measuring" (as Plato said) pains against pleasures and of deciding between the relative merits of different acts. In other words, the good life is not so completely "natural" or grounded solely in our feelings as Epicurus made out. Nature (the feelings) must be supplemented by reason and "good judgment."[87] But since it was Plato who exalted reason at the expense of nature, Epicurus as an anti-Platonist swung strongly in the opposite direction.[88]

The plain fact of the matter is that hedonism cannot be logically demonstrated, and the same can be said for any other ethical principle as well. Jesus' *agapé* principle, Mill's Greatest Happiness Principle, Nietzsche's master morality—all are unprovable; and yet each provides a viable existence for certain people. If egoistic hedonism is accepted, it must be accepted as a way of life and *lived*; one cannot subscribe to it intellectually as though it were a political program or an abstract confession of faith. And as a way of life it is adopted (1) instinctively, i.e., on an amoral, animal-like basis, or (2) pragmatically, i.e., because it "works out well" and pays good dividends in happy living, either in the strict sectarian sense or in the looser "man of the world" meaning, or (3) existentially, i.e., as an act of personal commitment and "faith," in the manner of the committed Christian or the committed Communist. Much can be said pragmatically for strict Epicureanism as a method of simplifying and enriching life at one and the same time. This type of existence is obviously not for everyone, and the saintly and affectionate Epicurus is far and away the best example. It is sometimes claimed that the worst possible advertisement for lay Epicureanism is the behavior of millions of Americans on Saturday night, when half the population of the nation tears loose, burns up the roads, kills a few hundred citizens, swills beer, gin, or whiskey, and then has a lot of fun between the sheets afterwards. Obviously this is a barbarous corruption of what the fastidious Epicurus intended, and can be linked with his name only by malice aforethought. (The Greeks had a name for the pleasure drives of the immature and half-civilized: "Cyrenaicism.") The chief trouble with a mature and serious Epicureanism is the long-term effect of such a way of life. Not only may the hedonist miscalculate the delicate balance of pleasures and pains and end up an unhappy man, but his life is too self-protective and introverted, and it runs the risk of becoming increasingly indifferent to social values and to the happiness and unhappiness of other persons. The egoist of this type is an enriched and highly cultivated moral pygmy. "By their fruits ye shall know them."

b. *Summary and evaluation.* Since Epicureanism has come down to us in the Western tradition in grossly garbled form ("Eat, drink, and be merry"), it may be well to take stock at this point and see what may be said for and against it:

First, we should note the distinctive way of life of the sectarian Epicureans. Though based on the pleasure-pain principle it was not what we would ordinarily call a pleasant life. In Nietzsche's terms, it did not say *yea* to life but *nay*. It was largely negative, escapist, self-protective, and therapeutic. By withdrawing from the active concerns and responsibilities of the citizen, it remained socially and politically immature. These are the traits summed up by Gilbert Murray in his brilliant phrase, "the failure of nerve."

At the same time, despite their civic irresponsibility, the Epicureans had a strong sense of social mission to alleviate human unhappiness, particularly the neurotic fears that seemed to abound in the Hellenistic age. By skillful use of the atomic theory and by purging the Olympian gods of their anthropomorphic dross, they forged a new religion for the intelligentsia of the time. This religion, which was more of a peace-of-mind technique than a religion in the ordinary sense, was at least as effective as the esthetic religion which has attracted thousands of intellectuals to Anglo-Catholicism in our own time. Epicureanism numbered among its converts Atticus, the millionaire friend of Cicero. Cicero himself and the Augustan poet Horace were part-time Epicureans. The most fanatical and disturbed of all Epicureans was the great Lucretius himself, who is said to have committed suicide after completing the *De Rerum Natura*. Epicurus the founder remains the chief saint of the sect.

Third, and perhaps most important of all in the long view, is the linkage of Epicureanism with atomic science and the wholesale substituting of naturalistic explanations for the traditional superstitions. With the Epicureans it was never science for the sake of science, however, but always science for the sake of human happiness. Consequently their science was not an open-end experimental science but a closed body of dogmatic truth to which they anticipated no additions or amendments. For better or worse, this materialistic aspect of Epicureanism proved so unpalatable to the ancient and medieval worlds that atomism as a theory of reality disappeared from view and was not revived until the seventeenth century, when it was resurrected by the Jesuit priest Pierre Gassendi, a contemporary of Descartes.

A Note on the Translation

Epicurus was a prolific writer of treatises, both technical and semipopular. Of his vast output the chief extant remains are the three letters, or essays, contained in this book. His masterpiece was a work on the physics and metaphysics of atomism, *Peri Physeos* (*On Nature*), in 37 rolls, or "books." This is now entirely lost except for a number of fragments from the 28th roll discovered a generation ago on papyri recovered at Herculaneum.[1] These are for the most part so mutilated and conjectural in form that it did not seem worthwhile to include them in a book of this kind, which is intended for undergraduate students rather than for experts in the field, and I have consequently omitted them altogether. In addition, we are told by his biographer Diogenes Laertius that Epicurus wrote many shorter and in some cases semi-popular essays, e.g., *On Love*, *On the Gods*, *On Religion*, *On Fate*, *On Music*, and *On Atomic Films* as well as many letters to his friends. He also made two condensations of his entire system, one called *The Major Epitome*, intended for beginners and for popular dissemination, and the other *The Minor Epitome*, intended for advanced students. The latter, which also carried the title *Letter to Herodotus* (the first of the three essays in this book), is by far the most important of the remaining Epicurean documents left to us. *The Major* (or popular) *Epitome* was probably the source book from which Lucretius, two hundred years after Epicurus' death, constructed his great philosophical poem in Latin hexameters, *De Rerum Natura* (*On Nature*), which apart from its literary magnificence contains a multitude of details and illustrations not found in the *Letter to Herodotus*. The second of the extant essays, *Letter to Pythocles*, is probably not by Epicurus himself but by a second- or third-generation member of the school, whose name is unknown. It is a treatise on astronomy and meteorology and has an unexpected importance as a propaganda document in the Epicurean campaign against popular religion and astrology.

The Greek style of Epicurus, as we have it, is a scholar's style. It is dry, precise, technical, uninteresting, and nonliterary by intention. (The only exception to this dismal repertory of adjectives is the *Letter to Menoeceus* on ethics, which makes a few concessions to a more flowing and literary expressiveness.) It is a poor style by the best Greek prose standards, worse even than Aristotle's, and is apparently the result of a persistent attempt on Epicurus' part to write in a jargon peculiar to himself alone—a conjecture borne out by the fact that he nowhere acknowledges any debt to any of his predecessors and also by the fact that he uses terms used by no other Greek writer as well as standard terms in senses peculiar to himself. Since it is the task of the translator to "carry over" what he reads into another language and not to embellish or to rewrite, I have reproduced Epicurus' style faithfully in a dry, precise, technical, uninteresting, and nonliterary manner. My only departure from this has been to introduce clarity where there was little or none in the original, for a translation must above all make sense. Lack of clarity was a failure of the last complete English translation of Epicurus' letters, made in 1926 by Cyril Bailey, a British scholar eminent in the field of Epicurean studies. In spite of my great debt to Bailey, as regards both the text itself and the elucidation of the text, I have seen fit to depart completely from his slavishly literal and sometimes unintelligible rendering of the Greek.[2] The result is a version that is still fairly close to the original, faithfully dull, and one that makes approximately the same sense (I hope) to the modern reader as the original did to the ancient reader, which must be the aim of any good translation.

In reading the parallel passages from Lucretius the student will notice immediately the enormous difference between the styles of Epicurus and the Roman poet. From the translator's point of view this is unavoidable and even desirable. It represents the difference between a third-rate prose style and a first-rate poetic style, or, to put the matter differently, it represents two literary phases of a long tradition that are separated from each other by two hundred years in time. Because of the seriousness of his theme, Lucretius chose to model his hexameters on the epic style of Ennius, who had written a hundred years earlier. As a result his lines have a rough vigor and an old-fashioned tone, especially when compared with the "modern" verse style of Vergil and Ovid, who followed him a generation later. What Lucretius' poem lacks in polish and sophistication, however, is amply redeemed by the sweep of its design and by the abundant beauty and power of expression that are to be found on almost every page.[3]

The translator of Lucretius should himself be a poet. This unfortunately has seldom been the case. Beginning with H. A. J. Munro in England a century ago, most translators have had to be content with a poetic prose into which they injected varying amounts of archaic flavoring. Cyril Bailey, the editor of Epicurus, was also a distinguished editor of Lucretius. He lavished a translator's love on the De Rerum Natura,[4] but the result, admirable though it is in many details, seems today a bit fussy, overly archaic, and sometimes merely quaint. Too much of these refinements detracts from the clarity of Lucretius' arguments and saps the vigor and robustness of his verses. The transition to a more modern and readable style suitable for our own generation was attempted by Ronald Latham a decade ago.[5] The success of this translation is uneven, in my judgment. Mr. Latham has eliminated all Bailey's archaic flavor (which, of course, is

also a distortion of Lucretius himself) and has thereby clarified the structure of the argument considerably. He has retained here and there the richness of the poetic texture, but
he has unforgivably descended into tasteless, prosaic para-
phrases of whole passages, which are far removed from the
text and the spirit of the original. As for my own translations in this book, I am unable to judge them properly, since
I cannot see them objectively. My intention, however, has
been (1) to avoid some of the flaws of Bailey and Latham as
well as their actual language; (2) to keep the lines of the argument clear, where argument is present, without lapsing
into paraphrase or flat prose; and (3) to preserve the characteristic poetic values of Lucretius, including some of his archaic tone. *Judicet ipse lector!*

Excerpts from the Life of Epicurus
by Diogenes Laertius[1]

The Stoic Diotimus, who bore Epicurus ill will, (3
slandered him most cruelly by publishing fifty las-
civious letters under his name, and so did the person
who compiled the love letters that are supposedly
Epicurus' but are traceable to Chrysippus, not to
mention Posidonius the Stoic and his followers. . . .
They claimed that he went around to houses with
his mother, reading off chants of purification, and (4
that he taught grammar school with his father for a
miserable fee; also that one of his brothers was a
pimp and had relations with the hetaera Leontion,
and that Epicurus passed off theory as his own. . . .

In his letters to Pythocles,[2] who was then in the
bloom of his youth, he wrote, "I shall sit down and (5
await your beauteous, godlike advent." . . . And
they claim that he wrote to many other hetaerae,
especially Leontion, of whom Metrodorus was also (6
enamored. And in the essay *The Purpose of Life* he
supposedly wrote, "As far as I am concerned, I do
not know how I can think of the good if I subtract
the pleasures of taste and the pleasures of sex,
sound, and form." In a letter to Pythocles he said,
"Hoist sail, happy youth, and speed far from all
book learning."

Epictetus,[3] too, called him a "foul-mouthed bastard" and abused him savagely. And even Timocrates, the brother of Metrodorus and a student of

Epicurus' who later quit the school, says in a book entitled *The Amenities* that Epicurus vomited twice a day because of his high living, and he explains that he himself hardly had the strength to escape those nightly colloquia on philosophy and the mystic brotherhood. Also that Epicurus was ignorant in many ways about his subject and even more about life; that his body was in pitiable condition, so that for many years he was unable to get out of his sedan chair; also that he spent a mina[4] every day on his table, as he himself mentioned in a letter to Leontion . . . , and that there were other hetaerae living with him and Metrodorus, named Mammarion, Hedeia, Erotion,[5] and Nicidion. . . .

7)

.   .   .   .   .   .

9)   But these critics are all crazy. The man Epicurus has plenty of witnesses to his unparalleled benevolence toward all: his country, which honored him with bronze statues; his friends, so many in number that they could not even be counted by whole cities; his intimates, all of whom remained bound to him by the siren call of his teachings. . . .[6] Then there is the continuity of the school, which lasted on and on after almost all the others had ceased to exist and which produced countless leaders, chosen one after another from among the "friends."[7] And there is his gratefulness to his parents, his generosity to his brothers, and his kindness to his house slaves, as is evident from the provisions of his will and from the fact that they participated in the discussions on philosophy. The outstanding example is Mys, previously mentioned.[8] We have, in short, his humanity toward all. It is impossible to describe his attitude of reverence for the gods[9] and his love of country; it

10)

was because of his excessive reasonableness that he did not engage in politics. And though very difficult conditions prevailed in Greece at that time, he lived out his life there and crossed over to Ionia only two or three times to see his friends in various places. But they came to him from everywhere and lived with him in the Garden (as Apollodorus[10] tells us) on a very frugal and plain diet. In fact, they were (11 satisfied with a half pint of cheap wine and usually drank water. Epicurus did not think it right for them to deposit their property in a common fund, as did Pythagoras (who had said, "The property of friends is common property"), because this was the way of people who distrust each other, and if people are distrustful they are not friends. Epicurus himself remarked in his letters that he was satisfied with just water and plain bread. "Send me a small pot of cheese," he wrote, "so that I can have a costly meal whenever I like." This was the man who gave it as his opinion that pleasure is life's goal. . . .

Apollodorus tells us in his *Annals* that Epicurus was born in the third year of the 109th Olympiad in (14 the magistracy of Sosigenes[11] . . . , seven years after Plato's death. At the age of thirty-two he first established a school at Mitylene and Lampsacus[12] and (15 ran it for five years; after that he moved over to Athens. There he died at the age of seventy-two, in the second year of the 127th Olympiad in the magistracy of Pytharatus. Hermarchus of Mitylene, son of Agemortus, took over the school. Epicurus died of a stone that blocked his urine, as Hermarchus also tells us in his letters, after an illness of fourteen days. Hermippus relates that he got into a bronze tub filled with hot water, called for straight wine, and swallowed it. He then exhorted his friends to (16 remember his teachings and passed away. . . .

22)   As he was dying he wrote the following letter to Idomeneus: "On this happy day, which is also the last day of my life, I write the following words to you. The symptoms of my strangury and dysentery are continuing and have not lost their extreme seriousness. But offsetting all this is the joy in my heart at the recollection of the conversations we have had. Take charge of the children of Metrodorus,[13] as behooves one who from boyhood on has been attached to me and to philosophy."

· · · · · · ·

26)   Epicurus was an extremely productive writer and surpassed all other philosophers in the number of his works, of which there are upwards of 300 rolls. There is not one reference in these to outside authorities—nothing but Epicurus' own words. . . .[14]

27) The best of his works are the following: *On Nature*, 37 rolls; *Atoms and Space*; *On Love*; . . . *Problems*; *Leading Doctrines*; *On Choice and Aversion*; *The Purpose of Life*; *The Criterion, or Canon*; . . . *On the Gods*; *Religion*; . . . *Lives*, 4 books; . . . *Sympo-*

28) *sium*; . . . *On Vision*; . . . *Atomic Films*; *Perception*; . . . *On Music*; *Justice and the Other Virtues*; . . . *Letters*.

     I shall now attempt to set forth the teachings contained in these works by laying before you three of his letters,[15] in which he provided a summary of

29) his entire philosophy; . . . but I shall first say a few words about the divisions of his philosophy.

30)   It is divided into three parts—the normative, the physical, and the ethical. The normative contains the methodology of the system and is found in the single work entitled *The Canon*.[16] The physics contains his whole theory of nature and is found in the 37

books of *On Nature* and, in elementary form, in his letters.[17] The ethical part has to do with acts of choice and aversion and is found in the treatises entitled *Lives* and *The Purpose of Life* and also in his letters.[18] The Epicureans, however, ordinarily group the normative part with the physical, claiming that it deals with fundamental criteria and the elements of the system. Physics, on the other hand, has to do with the generation and destruction of worlds and with nature as a whole; ethics, with things to be chosen or avoided, with different ways of life, and with the purpose of life.

They reject dialectic as deceptive, because (they say) it is enough for the natural philosopher to proceed according to the names of things.[19] In *The Canon* Epicurus says that sensations, concepts, and feelings are the criteria of truth, and his followers add direct perceptions of the mind.[20] [Epicurus says as much in the *Letter to Herodotus*[21] and in *Leading Doctrines*.] (31

1. Sensation is completely irrational and incapable of memory; it is not activated by itself, nor when activated by something else can it add anything or subtract anything.[22]

2. Nor is there anything capable of refuting sensations, because a sensation of one class cannot refute another of the same class, since they are of equal authority; nor can sensations of different classes refute each other, since they do not pass judgment on the same objects.[23] (32

3. Nor, again, can reason refute sensation, since it is wholly dependent on the sensations.[24]

4. Nor can one sensation refute another, since we give our attention to them all.

5. Furthermore, the existence of our apperceptions is a guarantee of the truth of the sensations.[25]

6. Our seeing and hearing are actualities, just as much as our experience of pain.

7. Thus it is necessary to draw inferences from phenomena regarding things that are not perceived.[26]

8. All ideas take their rise from sensations through processes of coincidence, analogy, resemblance, and combination, with reflection contributing something also.[27]

9. The mental images of madmen and dream images are realities, since they activate the mind, whereas the nonexistent does not thus activate it.[28]

33)   10. By "concept" the Epicureans mean "an apprehending," "correct opinion," "a thought" or "universal idea" deposited in the mind—in other words, a remembering of something frequently given in sensation from the external world. For example, take the expression, "X is a man." As soon as "man" is pronounced, we immediately think of a typical human being in line with the concept formed from antecedent sensory data. Hence the original meaning assigned to any word is clear and distinct evidence of truth. Furthermore, we could not look into what we want to investigate if we did not have prior knowledge of it. For example, the question "Is that thing in the distance a horse or an ox?" implies that we must have some conceptual knowledge of the appearance of a horse or an ox. We could not even have named anything without having first learned of its appearance through the concept. Hence concepts are clear and distinct evidences of truth.[29]

11. In addition, matters of belief rest on clear antecedent evidence, to which we refer when express-
34) ing them (e.g., How do we know if this is a man?). Beliefs are also known as assumptions, and they may be true or false. They are true if verified or not

contradicted, but false if they are not verified or if they are contradicted. It was for this reason that the principle of "the problem awaiting verification" was introduced—for example, waiting to get close to the tower and find out how it looks close up.[30]

12. The feelings are two in number, according to the Epicureans, pleasure and pain. They are found in all animals, and the former is congenial, the latter naturally foreign. It is by means of these that acts of choice and aversion are decided upon.[31]

13. Some investigations have to do with actualities, others with mere verbiage.[32]

(At this point in his biography Diogenes inserted the *Letter to Herodotus* and *Letter to Pythocles*.)   (35–116

Let us review what Epicurus and those who came after him thought about the wise man.[33]   (117

1. Men inflict injuries from hatred, jealousy, or contempt, but the wise man masters all these passions by means of reason.

2. Once he has become wise, he no longer experiences the opposite state, nor does he voluntarily feign to. He will be more affected by feelings of pleasure and pain, but this will be no hindrance to wisdom.

3. A man cannot become wise in any and every bodily condition or in every nationality.

4. Even if the wise man is tortured he is happy.   (118 Nonetheless he will moan and groan under those conditions.

5. The wise man alone will show his gratitude and will continue to speak well of his friends, whether they are present or absent.

6. The wise man will not have intercourse with any woman with whom it is legally forbidden, as Diogenes tells us in his digest of Epicurus' ethical teachings.[34]

7. Nor will he punish his house slaves; he will show them mercy and grant pardon to any that are conscientious.

8. The Epicureans do not think that the wise man will fall in love, or worry about his burial.

9. Love is not divinely sent, Diogenes tells us.

10. The wise man will not make high-flown speeches in public.

11. Intercourse never helped any man, and it's a wonder that it hasn't hurt him.

119)   12. In addition, the wise man will marry and beget children, as Epicurus tells us in *Problems* and his work *On Nature*; but he will marry according to his station in life, whatever it may be.

13. He will avoid certain persons and certainly not make a fool of himself when drinking, as Epicurus remarks in the *Symposium*.

14. Nor will he meddle in politics (*Lives*, Bk. I), nor play the dictator, nor live like a Cynic[35] and beg alms (*Lives*, Bk. II).

15. Even if he goes blind he will still take part in life (*ibid.*).

16. He will likewise grieve,[36] as Diogenes tells us in Bk. V of his *Excerpts*.

120a)   17. He will plead his own case at law.

18. He will leave written works behind him, but not make set speeches in public.

19. He will be prudent about his property and provide for the future.

20. He will love country life.

21. He will confront adversity, because no one can count on the friendship of Lady Luck.

22. He will be careful about his good name to the extent of not losing public respect.

23. He will take greater pleasure than others in the festivals.[37]

24. He will set up likenesses of others but will be (121b
indifferent as to whether he has any of himself.

25. Only the wise man could talk properly about
music and poetry, but he would not actually compose poetry.

26. One sage is no wiser than another.[38]

27. He will make money if he stands in need of
it, but only by his profession.

28. He will, on occasion, wait upon a sovereign.

29. He will gloat over another's troubles—but
only as a means of setting him straight.

30. He will assemble a school but not for dema-
gogic purposes; he will lecture publicly but not of
his own free will; and he will speak dogmatically
without skeptical reservations.[39]

31. He will be the same asleep or awake.[40]

32. Sometimes he will die for a friend.

The Epicureans teach: (120b

That faults are not equal in importance;[41]

That health is a value for some persons but a
matter of indifference to others;

That courage does not arise naturally but from
utilitarian considerations;

That friendship arises because of its advantages;
that there must be a starting point, of course, Just as
we sow seed in the ground, but that friendship is
consolidated by the communal living of those who
have attained the full complement of pleasure;[42]

That happiness has two senses: supreme happi- (121a
ness, like that of the deity, which cannot be intensi-
fied, and the happiness that has to do with the
increase and decrease of pleasure.

(The *Letter to Menoeceus* was inserted at this (122–
point.)   135

In other works Epicurus rejected divination, e.g., (135
in *The Minor Epitome.* "Divination is nonexistent,"

he says, "and even if it did exist, events are to be
regarded as things not within our control."[43] So
much for the practical considerations that he has
treated in greater detail elsewhere.

136)   Epicurus differs from the Cyrenaics[44] regarding
pleasure, in that they sanction only dynamic pleasure and not static, whereas Epicurus sanctions both
types in the soul and in the body, as he tells us in *On
Choice and Aversion*, *The Purpose of Life*, Book I of
Lives, and in his letter to his friends in Mytilene.
Similarly Diogenes in Bk. 17 of his *Excerpts* and
Metrodorus in the *Timocrates* write that pleasure is
conceived as both dynamic and static. And Epicurus
says in *On Choice and Aversion* that "freedom from
mental and bodily pain is a static pleasure, whereas
joy and merriment are looked upon as dynamic, active pleasures."

137)   Epicurus also differed from the Cyrenaics in that
they taught that bodily pains are worse than mental
and pointed out that offenders undergo bodily punishment; whereas Epicurus held that pains of the
mind are worse, since the body is afflicted only
momentarily in the present, but the mind in the past,
present, and future. Similarly the pleasures of the
mind are greater. As proof that pleasure is the purpose of life he adduces the fact that all animals from
birth on are well content with pleasure but recoil
from pain naturally and non-rationally. Our own
experience, then, is the reason we avoid pain. . . .

138)   And the virtues are chosen not for themselves but
for their pleasurable consequences. . . . Virtue is the
only thing inseparable from pleasure; other things,
such as food, are separable. . . .

139–   (Diogenes concluded his biography with the
54)   *Leading Doctrines* of Epicurus.)

Letter to Herodotus

I. INTRODUCTION

I have already prepared a compendium[1] of my (35
entire philosophy, Herodotus, for the benefit of
those who are unable to study methodically all the
many volumes on nature that I have written or to
examine closely the major works I have composed,
in order that they may thereby get an adequate
grasp of the most important doctrines at least and
may be able to get help from time to time with the
leading ideas, to the extent that they concern themselves with physical theory. Also, those who are sufficiently advanced in their survey of the complete
works need to refresh their memories with a sketch
of the fundamentals of the entire philosophy, because one frequently needs a comprehensive grasp
of things and not so much a knowledge of particulars. One must return to the fundamentals and con- (36
stantly keep in mind just enough to provide an
authoritative grasp of the Epicurean system, and
then the scientific knowledge of particulars will all
be forthcoming, once the comprehensive outlines are
firmly grasped and remembered. With the accom-
plished Epicurean also, the hallmark of full scientific
knowledge is the ability to exercise rapid comprehension (both sensory and intellectual), and this can
come about only when everything is reduced to fun-

damental principles and formulas. For a condensation of the entire cycle of my works is impossible unless one can mentally compass in abbreviated formulas all that could be methodically expounded in the form of particulars. Since a procedure of this sort is serviceable to all who are at home in natural philosophy and since I recommend the constant pursuit of natural philosophy and find serenity myself primarily in a life of this sort, I have accordingly written for you a kind of primer and compendium of the whole body of my doctrines.

II. METHODOLOGY[2]

First of all, then, Herodotus, we must grasp the meanings associated with the word sounds in order that, by referring to these, we may be in a position to form judgments about matters of belief or about problems needing research or unresolved questions, and in order to avoid leaving matters in a state of confusion by expounding terms *ad infinitum* or by using meaningless verbiage. We must therefore look to the primary meaning in the case of each word and not require argument if we are to have a point of reference for our research problems, our unresolved questions, or matters of belief. Furthermore, we must keep all our judgments in line with our sensations (specifically our immediate perceptions, either of the mind or of any particular sense organ) and also in line with our actual feelings of pleasure and pain, in order to have the means with which to interpret a sense datum awaiting verification or a problem involving imperceptibles.

III. FIRST PRINCIPLES AND POSTULATES

1. Having made these distinctions, we must
now take a synoptic view of imperceptibles: to begin
with, the principle that nothing is generated from
the nonexistent. This is so because otherwise anything could be generated from anything and not require seminal particles.³ (L1) Second, if an object   (39
that passes from our view were completely annihilated, everything in the world would have perished,
since that into which things were dissipated would
be the nonexistent. Third, the totality of things was
always just as it is at present and will always remain
the same because there is nothing into which it can
change, inasmuch as there is nothing outside the
totality that could intrude and effect change.

2. Furthermore, the totality consists of bodies
and space. The fact of sensation itself universally
attests that there are bodies, and it is by reference to
sensation that we must rationally infer the existence
of imperceptible bodies, as I remarked previously. If
what we call "the void" or "space" or "impalpable   (40
being" were nonexistent, bodies would not have
anywhere to exist, nor would they have a medium
through which to move, as they manifestly do. In
addition to these two entities it is impossible to
think of anything else (by way of either concepts or
analogues of concepts) as being a complete and independent entity and not, rather, a property or accident of body and space. As regards bodies,
furthermore, some are compounds; others are the
components of which the compounds are made.   (41
These components are irreducible and immutable
atoms—assuming that things are not destined to be
completely annihilated but that something perdura-
ble is left over at the time of the decomposition of

the compounds—particles completely solid in nature and incapable of decomposition in any manner whatsoever. Thus the primal entities are necessarily indivisible corporeal atoms.

3. Furthermore, the totality of things is unlimited, because anything limited has an end point and this end point is seen against something else. But the totality, having no end point, has no limit and, having no limit, it must be infinite and without boundaries. In addition, the totality is infinite both in the quantity of atomic bodies and in spatial magnitude, because (1) if space were infinite but the atomic bodies finite in number, the atoms would not remain in any position but would be borne about and dispersed throughout infinite space, not having supporting bodies to stabilize them in their recoil from other atoms; and (2) if space were finite, the infinite number of atoms could not find positions anywhere. (L2)

4. In addition, the compact and irreducible atomic bodies out of which compounds are generated and into which they are resolved have an indeterminate number of different shapes, because it is impossible for so many different perceptible objects to be generated from the same shapes on the assumption that these are limited in number. Thus for each atomic configuration the number of similar atoms is plainly infinite; the various configurations, however, are plainly not infinite but simply indeterminate in number.

5. The atoms, furthermore, are in constant motion through endless time. [Some move perpendicularly; others deviate from the perpendicular (L3); still others move by internal vibration within compounds. Of the latter][4] some are separated by a considerable distance from each other, while others maintain an oscillating motion whenever they find

themselves turned aside by intertwining with others
or enveloped by an outer casing of atoms. The reason for this internal vibration is that the nature of   (44
the empty space that separates the individual atoms
produces this effect, since it is unable to provide any
support, and also the solidity characteristic of the
atoms causes them to rebound after collision to the
extent that intertwining permits reestablishment of
motion after collision. These vibrations have no   (45
starting point, the atoms themselves and empty space
being the causes. Now, if all these points are borne in
mind, this brief account suggests an outline adequate
for comprehending the physical nature of things.

6.   In addition, there are infinite worlds—worlds
like and unlike our own—because the atoms, being
infinite in number, as was just now shown, are in
motion extremely far out in space; and atoms of the
sort from which a single world could be generated,
or by which such a world could be constructed,
have not been used up on one world or on a finite
number of worlds, nor have they been used up on
all worlds such as ours or on all worlds different
from ours. So nothing stands in the way of there
being an infinity of worlds.

IV. SENSE PERCEPTION

1.   **Sight.** In addition, there are atomic images   (46a
similar in outline to solid external objects but differing greatly from these in their thinness or non-solidity.
It is not impossible that such atomic discharges
should be generated in the environment of objects,
nor that suitable circumstances for the production
of these hollow, thin films should exist, nor that
these emanations should maintain the successive

positions and structure that the particles had in the solid external bodies. We term these images *eidola*.

47) Also, nothing in our sensory experience witnesses against the fact that the *eidola* have an extraordinary thinness of composition, from which we may also infer that they have extraordinary speeds, since all their atoms have uniform velocities in addition to the fact that their outflow meets with little or no resistance, whereas structures composed of many or innumerable atoms do immediately encounter resistance. In addition to this, there is the fact that the

48) generating of *eidola* occurs as fast as a man can think, because the outflow from the surface of objects is continuous (but this does not become evident in loss of size because the atoms are replenished) and it maintains for a considerable period the position and structure of the atoms of the external object, even though at times it is thrown into disorder. Then, too, composite *eidola* are rapidly formed in the surrounding atmosphere because of the fact that it is unnecessary for the filling-up process to take place in depth; and there are various other ways in which composite images of this sort are generated. None of these points, indeed, is contradicted by our sensory experiences if one will only inspect the manner in which sensation conveys to us clear and distinct images of external objects and their qualities. (L4)

49) One must also assume that when *eidola* impinge on us from external objects we both see and think about their forms;[5] for such objects could not imprint their natural colors and shapes by means of an atmospheric impression formed midway between them and us, nor again by ocular rays or any conceivable emanation originating with us and moving out to the object.[6] These theories are less credible

than my own hypothesis that certain atomic films having the same colors and shapes as their objects impinge on us, entering either the eye or the mind, depending on the relative sizes of their atoms; that these films have a rapid course of movement and for (50 this reason present the phenomenon of a unitary and continuously existent object; and that they preserve the qualitative changes of the underlying physical object in their uniform impact on us from that source, which results from the atomic pulsations deep within the physical object.

Also, any perception of shape or qualities that we receive by atomic impingement on the mind or sense organs represents the true shape or quality of the physical object and is generated by the unbroken series of films or its residues, whereas falsity and error always consist of the element of belief superimposed on a percept which awaits verification or noncontradiction and which is then not verified or is contradicted. Thus the correspondence between (51 the perceptions that we take as representations (whether generated in our sleep or in our waking acts of attention, either mental or sensory) and what we call real existent objects could never arise unless certain entities of this sort were making their impact on us. On the other hand, error would not occur unless we were experiencing another kind of internal motion also, one connected with perceptualization but distinct from it. By virtue of this, an untrue judgment occurs whenever this process does not undergo verification or is disconfirmed and a true judgment whenever it is verified or not disconfirmed.[7] It is, therefore, absolutely necessary to (52 maintain this principle in order to prevent the standards of judgment that involve clear and distinct perceptions from being abridged and likewise to prevent error from becoming entrenched and confounding everything.

2. Hearing. Hearing also occurs when a flow of atoms moves off from anything that talks or makes a sound or noise or produces an acoustic reaction in any way whatsoever. This outflow is broken up into atomic masses having similar parts, and these masses simultaneously preserve a corresponding structure as well as a specific identity that extends back to the point of origin and in most cases causes perception in the person or else simply renders the external ob-

53) ject obvious. Indeed, aural perception would not occur unless a corresponding atomic structure were conveyed from the point of origin to the hearer. Accordingly one should not imagine that the atmosphere as such is given a shape[8] by the words we utter or by kindred sounds (for it would require a great deal for it to be affected in this way), but rather that the percussion that occurs internally whenever we utter sounds immediately causes the ejection of certain atomic masses (these effecting an outflow having the nature of breath), which produce in us an auditory reaction.

3. Smell. In the case of smell, furthermore, as in the case of hearing, we must again suppose that nothing would ever produce this reaction except certain atomic masses that move off from the object and are suited to activating the sense organ—some of them in an irregular manner foreign to its make-up, others in an orderly manner congenial to it.[9]

V. ATOMS AND THEIR CHARACTERISTICS

54)   **1. Properties of Atoms.** In addition, we should note that atoms do not present any of the character-

istics of phenomena except shape, weight, and size
and everything that is necessarily associated with
shape.[10] All phenomenal qualities change, but the
atoms do not change in any way because something
has to remain firm and irreducible when compounds
are broken up, something that will bring about
change—not change into nonbeing or from nonbeing
but changes produced by the transposition of certain
atoms or by the addition or subtraction of others.
Hence it is necessary that these transposed atoms be
indestructible and not have the nature of changing
phenomena, but have particles and structures peculiar
to themselves; for at least this much must remain   (55
immutable. Even in the case of objects all around us
that undergo change of form through attrition we
observe that shape persists, whereas qualities do not
persist in the changing body in the same way as
shape but disappear entirely. Thus it is the residual
atoms that are sufficient to bring about differences in
compounds, inasmuch as some bodies at any rate
must be residual and not subject to annihilation.

In order not to run the risk of being contradicted
by phenomena, we should not assume that all sizes
of atom are to be found but only that certain varia-
tions in size exist, because on this assumption our
affective and sensory experience will be better accounted for. In any case the existence of all sizes of   (56
atoms is of no use in accounting for qualitative differences, and furthermore certain sizes would have
to come within our sensory range and become visible; but this we never observe, nor is it possible to
conceive how an atom could become visible.

2. Parts of the Atom. Furthermore, it should not
be assumed that there are infinite particles or particles infinitely tiny inside a finite body. In order not
to undermine the structure of things in general and,

in the case of compound formations, to avoid being compelled to fritter away existing things by compressing them into nothingness, we must accordingly give up the idea of infinite divisibility into smaller and smaller particles.[11] Nor can we even pass in thought from the small to the smaller *ad infinitum*

57) in the case of finite bodies, because the moment one says there are infinite particles or particles infinitely tiny in a body, it becomes impossible to conceive how this could be so, and furthermore how could such a body still be finite in size? For it is obvious that the infinite particles are of certain sizes, and, however tiny they are, the body would also be infinite in size. (L5)

Also, since a finite body has an end point[12] that is distinguishable if not actually visible, it is impossible to conceive that the point next in order is not of the same sort, nor is it possible, by moving forward point by point in this manner, to proceed mentally to infinity. We should also observe that the perceptual minimum is not of the same nature as a partite body, nor is it in every respect dissimilar. It occupies

58) a certain common ground with partite bodies, but it has no discrete parts. If by virtue of this resemblance, or common ground, we suppose that we can make divisions in it—one on this side, another on that—the eye necessarily encounters only another minimal point of equal extension. We see these points one after another; beginning with the first, and we see them not as internally partite or as partite bodies touching other partite bodies but rather, in their own idiosyncratic way, as measurements of magnitude, more points constituting a larger body, fewer points a smaller body.

By the same token it must be assumed that the

59) minimal parts of the atom play an analogous role.[13]

It is obvious that they differ in size from the perceptual minimum, but they have the same relationship. We have, of course, indicated on the analogy of phenomena that the atom has size; only we scaled it far down. Also, in our logical theorizing about atoms that we do not see, we should regard their minimal, uncompounded parts as the ultimate limits of matter, which provide in themselves, as fundamental units, the measure of magnitude for atoms of all sizes, whether large or small. The common relationship that these minimal parts share with empirical minima suffices to bring the present discussion to a conclusion. In any case it is impossible that such particles were ever endowed with independent motion or that they coalesced into atoms.

3. **Motion of Atoms.** Furthermore, the atoms necessarily have equal velocities whenever they are (61 propelled through empty space, where they meet with no resistance. Thus heavy atoms will not move any faster than small, light ones—at least when nothing collides with them—nor will small atoms move faster than large ones but will maintain a uniform rate of motion so long as they encounter no resistance. Upward or diagonal motion that is brought about by collisions is no faster, nor is the downward motion that is caused by their respective weights. So long as any of these motions obtains, the atom will maintain a velocity as fast as a man can think, until it is deflected by something external or by its own mass recoiling from the force of an impact. Furthermore, in its transit through space under (46b conditions where it meets with no bodies likely to oppose it, it completes any determinate distance in an inconceivably brief period of time; for the appearance of relative slowness and speed is created by external resistance and nonresistance.[14]

62)

In addition, the claim will be made in the case of compounds that one atom moves more rapidly than another (when actually they all have the same velocity) because the atoms in such collections move in one direction even during the smallest continuous period of time that is perceptible. This claim will be made despite the fact that atoms do not move in one direction during time spans that are so brief as to be only mentally conceivable. On the contrary, they are in constant internal collision [and by these collisions they retard the motion of the whole collection] until such time as their path becomes perceptible as a continuum. The inference made regarding the subempirical level, viz., that time spans that are mentally conceivable will also show a continuous path, is not true in cases such as these, since "true" means either that which is empirically observed or that which is mentally apprehended.

47b)

Nor is it true in the case of these mentally conceivable time spans that the moving object also completes the same large number of trajectories as its component atoms; this is inconceivable. Furthermore such an object, on arriving as a unit at a perceived moment of time from any given quarter of infinite space, will not have started from the spot from which we see it coming. The moving object will thus be the sensory counterpart of its internal collisions, even though we grant that up to the moment of perception its velocity is not subject to retardation because of such collisions. It will prove useful to keep this principle in mind also.[15]

60)

In addition, we should not predicate "up" and "down" of infinite space, as though there were an absolute standard of highest and lowest. Assuming, however, that it is possible to prolong to infinity a line overhead from wherever we may be standing or a line to infinity beneath a hypothetical point, we know that this segment of space will never appear to us to be simultaneously "up" and "down" with reference to the same assumed point, because this is inconceivable.[16] Consequently it is possible to take the motion that we regard as infinite motion upward as a single entity, and the motion we regard as infinite motion downward as a single entity, even though in thousands of cases what travels from us into the spaces overhead arrives at the feet of beings above us and what travels downward from us reaches the heads of beings below us. Despite this fact, this is the case because we regard these motions, taken as wholes, as opposed each to the other *ad infinitum*.

VI. THE SOUL AND ITS NATURE (L6)

By referring to our sensations and feelings, which (63 will provide the most reliable basis for our beliefs, we must next take into account the fact that the soul is a body composed of fine particles that are dispersed throughout the entire organism, and that it bears the closest resemblance to breath with a certain admixture of heat, being similar in some ways to the one and in some ways to the other. There is also a third component that shows an even greater difference in fineness of structure than the other two and is for this reason more adapted to the rest of the organism. This is all clearly evidenced by the functions and affections of the soul, by the ease of its movements and thought processes, and by the privations that cause our death.

In addition you must bear in mind that the soul plays the most important role in causing sensation

64) but would never have achieved sensation unless it were somehow incorporated in the rest of the organism. The latter in turn, after providing the soul with this ground for sensation, has itself come to participate in the same function, thanks to the soul, but not in all the functions that the soul has. Hence when death releases the soul, the body does not have sensation, because it never possessed this capacity in and of itself but made it possible for another entity, generated at the same time as itself, to have sensation. This second entity, by actualizing its òwn potentiality through motion, at once achieved the function of sensation for itself and imparted it to the body also as a result of its proximity and congruence with the latter, as I said before. (L7)

65) Hence as long as the soul is present it will never cease to have sensation, even though some other part of the organism has been removed. On the contrary, if the soul persists at all it will have sensation, whatever particles of it are lost at the same time as its bodily casing is destroyed either in whole or in part.[17] The rest of the organism, on the other hand, may continue to exist in whole or in part but will no longer have sensation once it has lost the mass of atoms, whatever its size, that constitutes the nature of the soul. Furthermore, on the dissolution of the entire organism the soul is scattered abroad and no longer has its usual functions, nor does it undergo motion, with the result that it does not have sensa-

66) tion either. It is impossible to think of it as sentient if it is not present in a composite whole and if it does not enjoy its usual movements at such times as its housing and environment are not the same as the present environment in which it carries out these movements.

In addition, we should note that in the ordinary

usage of the term, "incorporeal" is used of some-   (67
thing that can be thought of as a thing in itself, and
that it is impossible to think of the incorporeal as a
thing in itself except in the case of empty space.
Now, empty space can neither act upon nor be acted
upon; it merely presents the opportunity for bodies
to move through it. Hence those who maintain that
the soul is incorporeal are talking nonsense, because
it would not be able to act upon or be acted upon if
it were of such a nature; but in actuality both these
functions are clearly distinguishable in the case of
the soul. (L8)

Now, if one refers all these observations about
the soul to empirical standards of feeling and sensa-   (68
tion, and recalls what was said at the beginning of
this letter, he will see that this outline is sufficiently
comprehensive for him to elaborate the details with
precision from what is said here.

VII. PROPERTIES AND ACCIDENTS (L9)

Next, as regards the characteristics of shape,
color, size, weight, and all the other qualities that
are predicated of body as so-called "concomitants"
or properties of all bodies in general or of bodies
that can be seen and are known to us as a result of
perceiving these qualities:[18] We should not think of
these as self-existent essences (for this is inconceivable) or as completely nonexistent or as immaterial   (69
entities having a different existence from body and
supervening upon it or as detachable parts of body.
On the contrary, we should think of a body in its
wholeness as having its own lasting existence from
all these—not as though it were an assemblage of
properties that had been brought together (as when

a larger aggregate is put together from the component parts themselves, such as the primary particles
or other quantities smaller than a given whole) but
simply, as I said, as having its own lasting existence
from all these. All these properties, furthermore, can
be observed in their own right and distinguished, as
long as the object as a whole accompanies such perception and is in no way detached but takes on the
predicate "body" from our thinking of its qualities
as a whole.[19]

70)   In addition, bodies frequently have accidental
characteristics which are not permanent concomitants and which we should not regard as coming
under the head of entities that are invisible, imperceptible, or nonmaterial. Consequently when we use
the term "accident" in its ordinary sense, we are
making it obvious that these contingencies have neither the nature of the whole object that we apprehend in its entirety and call "body" nor the nature
of those permanent properties in whose absence
body is inconceivable. Assuming that the object as a
whole is present, each of these contingencies might
71)   be called an accident as a result of various acts of
perception, but only when they are each observed to
occur, since accidents are not permanent concomitants. Also, we should not deny existence to these
clear and distinct phenomena on the ground that
they do not have the nature of the whole object of
which they are accidents or the nature of permanent
properties. Nor, on the other hand, should we regard them as things in themselves, because this is
unthinkable in the case of both accidents and permanent properties. On the contrary, we should think
of them all as accidents associated with bodies, as
our senses indicate—not as permanent properties,
not as entities having natural status as things in

themselves, but as what perception itself shows their peculiar nature to be.

We must take great pains to note in addition that   (72
we should not investigate the nature of time[20] as we do all the other properties and accidents of an object that we inquire into, i.e., by reference to concepts we have in our minds. On the contrary, we should consider those clear and distinct impressions in the light of which we speak of "a long time" or "a short time" and apply those impressions to time as we do in analogous cases. Nor should we substitute other expressions that are supposedly better, but use the already existing ones. Nor should we predicate some other entity of time, as some do, on the assumption that it has the same essence as this unique quality. Rather we should give our attention exclusively to what we associate this unique quality with and what we measure it by. Actually it requires no proof, simply reflection, to see, first, that we connect   (73
time with day and night or portions of these, and also with states of emotion or freedom from emotion, and with states of motion and rest; and, second, that we regard it as a unique type of accident associated with all these phenomena and accordingly give it the name "time."

VIII. OTHER WORLDS (L10)

In addition to the foregoing, we should consider that other worlds—i.e., every finite aggregate that bears a strong resemblance to the phenomena we see—have been generated from the infinite;[21] that all these systems, whether large or small, disengaged themselves from separate condensations of matter; and that they are all broken down again into their components—some more rapidly, others more slowly, some being acted upon by factors of one sort, others by factors of another sort. Also we should consider

74) that these worlds do not necessarily have a single form [or, on the other hand, every possible form; furthermore, that in all these worlds there are animals, plants, and other things such as we see in our own world].[22] For nobody can demonstrate that one such world might or might not have contained the kind of seminal particles of which animals, plants, and everything else we see are composed, but that in another such world this would have been an impossibility.

IX. GROWTH OF LANGUAGE AND CULTURE (L11)

Also, we must assume that at first actual condi-

75) tions taught and compelled mankind to do many things of various sorts, and that later on reasoning perfected nature's instructions and made additional discoveries, more rapidly in some cases than in others and with greater progress in some periods than in others. Thus the names of things were not originally created by convention. On the contrary, the various ethnic groups of mankind, on experiencing their own peculiar emotions and sensory impressions, uttered sounds conforming to these various emotions and impressions, each in its own way, corresponding to the geographical differences of the

76) groups. But later on, characteristic terms were assigned by common agreement in the various ethnic groups in order to make their intentions mutually more intelligible and to convey them more concisely.[23] Also, people who knew them brought in certain things never seen before and suggested certain

words for them. Sometimes these persons were
forced to invent natural sounds for the objects; at
other times they chose the sounds by a rational process in conformance with ordinary conventions,
thereby clarifying their meaning.

X. THE HEAVENLY BODIES

Furthermore, we should not regard the courses
and revolutions of the heavenly bodies—their eclipses, risings and settings, and the like—as the operations of some deity who dutifully performs these
functions, who decrees or did decree them, and who
simultaneously enjoys absolute blessedness as well
as immortality. (For management of business affairs, (77
worries, feelings of anger, and good will do not
harmonize with the state of blessedness but are
found where there is lack of strength and where we
fear and have need of those around us.) Nor, on the
other hand, should one imagine that these bodies,
which are actually aggregations of fiery matter, enjoy divine blessedness themselves and take on these
motions by an act of will. On the contrary, we must
preserve the full dignity of the divine in all expressions we use in connection with ideas such as these,
in order that notions contradictory to the divine
majesty may not arise from this source; otherwise
this very contradictoriness will produce the gravest
spiritual disturbances.[24] (L12) Hence we should
hold the opinion that this necessary cyclical movement of the heavenly bodies came about through the
original enclosure of these collections of matter at
the genesis of the world.

In addition, we must consider that it is the task (78
of natural science to determine with precision the

causes of the most important phenomena and that
our happiness is bound up with causal knowledge of
the heavenly bodies, i.e., with the understanding of
the nature of celestial phenomena, and everything
else that is germane to scientific knowledge relating
to human happiness. We should also realize that
phenomena that have a variety of causes and can
occur in more than one way do not belong here. On
the contrary, anything that suggests uncertainty or
confusion has absolutely no place in our conception
of the deathless and blessed nature of the divine.
This point can be rationally apprehended with com-
79) plete certainty. On the other hand, everything that
falls under the detailed investigation of the risings
and settings of these bodies—their revolutions,
eclipses, and kindred phenomena—makes no contribution to the happiness associated with causal
knowledge. On the contrary, those who have observed such phenomena, but are ignorant of their
nature and ultimate causes, stand in awe of them as
much as if they had no knowledge of them; and
their fear may well be greater if the wonderment
occasioned by observation of such phenomena fails
to find an explanation in a system of ultimate causes.
Hence even if we find more than one cause for these
80) revolutions, risings, settings, eclipses, and the like, as
we did in our detailed treatise, we must not suppose
that we have not acquired the scientific knowledge
needed to contribute to our serenity and happiness.
Hence we should investigate the causes of all celestial and nonperceptible phenomena by making a
comparison of these with the various ways in which
an analogous phenomenon takes place in our own
experience. And we should hold a low opinion of
those who fail to distinguish between phenomena
having a single cause and, in the case of objects

making a sensory impression on us from a distance, phenomena that have more than one cause; and a low opinion also of those who are ignorant of the conditions in which it is impossible to have an undisturbed mind. Accordingly if we suppose that it is possible for an event to take place in one particular way, under conditions where it is equally possible for us to feel unconcerned if we recognize that it may have more than one cause, we shall feel as undisturbed as if we knew that it occurs in one particular way.[25] (L13)

XI. CONCLUSION

In addition to all these general considerations we (81 must realize that the most important types of spiritual confusion consist (1) in men's believing that the heavenly bodies are themselves blessed and immortal and at the same time have wills, activities, and motives that are contrary to such properties (L14); (2) in their constantly anticipating or imagining some frightful everlasting fate, like those in the myths of hell, or dreading the loss of sensation at the time of death as though this were relevant to "themselves" (L15); and (3) in undergoing all this suffering not as a result of rational judgment but because of some irrational drive (and by not setting limits to mental suffering, they consequently experience turmoil equal to or even more intense than they would if they rationally entertained such beliefs). But mental serenity means achieving release from all such fears and keeping the most important (82 general principles constantly in mind. (L16)

Thus we should give our attention to our immediate feelings and sensations, in both their general

and their particular aspects, according to the circumstances, and to our existing clear and distinct
perceptions, in conformance with each of the criteria of judgment.[26] If we attend to these we shall cor-
rectly discern the causes that gave rise to confusion
and fear, and by investigating the causes of celestial
phenomena and all the other occurrences that are
constantly taking place we shall liberate ourselves
from everything that drives other men to the ex-
tremes of fear.

83)   These are the main topics of my system as a
whole, Herodotus, which I have epitomized for you
in such a way that the present account can be com-
prehended with precision. In my opinion, even if a
person did not go on to study all the scientific details, he would still enjoy an incomparable advantage over others, because he would make clear to
himself many of the points that are investigated in
detail in my general treatise, and these, once deposited in the memory, will be of constant assistance to
him. These principles are of such a nature that those
who are already studying the system in considerable
or complete detail can do most of their research into
the structure of the whole by analysis along these
lines. On the other hand, some of those who are not
fully matured Epicureans can promote their spiritual
tranquillity by making a rapid survey of the essentials through this voiceless method.[27]

Parallel Passages from Lucretius

L1 =
Herod.
38

Conspicuously absent from Epicurus' present letter is the notorious tirade against popular religion so
marked in Lucretius' poem. In a long passage
(1.146–214) Lucretius attempts to establish the prin-

ciple of regular and uniform natural causation as against popular belief in random and spontaneous creation of things from nothing by divine agency.

This darkling terror in the mind must needs be routed, not by the sun's rays, not by bright shafts of daylight, but by the observation and rational inspection of nature. Whence our first principle takes its rise: No thing is ever generated from nothingness by divine action. The minds of men are beset by awe because they see much taking place on earth and in the heavens, the causes of which they can in no wise comprehend and which they suppose comes about by divine will. Hence when we have understood that nothing can be created from nothing, we shall more rightly grasp the object of our search—the sources from which things severally originate and the manner in which things take place without the gods' assistance.

If things came into being from nothingness, then every species of thing could be born from everything, and nothing would need seed. Mankind might first arise from the sea, scaly fish from the land, and birds could emerge from sky. Plough animals and other kine, every species of wild beast, having no certain issue, would tenant lands both tilled and desert. Nor would trees have their wonted fruits; they would change about and any tree could bear any fruit. Indeed, if each species had not its own genetic bodies, how could things have definite parentage? In reality, since things are severally produced from determinate seed, each entity is born and issues into the realm of light from a source that contains its peculiar matter and primal bodies. And for this reason it is impossible for everything to be generated from everything, since discrete powers inhere in determinate bodies. [1.146–73]

L2 =
Herod.
42

Compare the more graphic *reductio ad absurdum* of Lucretius:

If the world's whole room were everywhere enclosed by fixed limits, if it were finite, then the whole mass of matter would already have coursed together to the bottom by reason of its solidity and weight. Not a thing would transpire beneath the roof of heaven; there would indeed be no heaven, no sunlight, if all matter lay in a heap after sinking to the bottom throughout endless time. Actually, to be sure, no rest from their motion has ever been vouchsafed to the primal bodies, since there is no "bottom" whatsoever in which they may congregate, so to speak, and find their repose. All is agog with ceaseless motion from this quarter and that, and the corpuscles of matter are roused and fetched from infinite depths below. [1.988–1001]

L3 =
Herod.
43

This refers to the notorious atomic "swerve," an absurd *ad hoc* hypothesis set up by Epicurus (but not by Democritus) to account for two things of major importance: (1) how atoms falling freely and at uniform velocities in infinite space can combine to form atomic aggregates (e.g., objects and whole worlds) and (2) why human beings have moral freedom of choice and action and are not merely mechanical in their ethical behavior. Since the swerve is nowhere discussed in this letter by Epicurus, we must turn to Lucretius' account:

I. In this context I also desire you to recognize that when the atomic bodies are borne straight down through the void of their own weight, they deviate a bit from the perpendicular at quite unpredictable times and places, but only enough for one to say that their course of motion has been altered. If they were not in the habit of swerving thus, they would all keep raining down through the vastness of the void like water drops, and no occasion would present itself for them to collide and strike together—with the result that nature would have wrought nothing. . . . [2.216–24]

II. If every motion of atoms is always continuous with another and if new motion always originates from old in determinate sequence, and if it is the case that the primal bodies do not swerve and at least begin to break the bonds of determinism, thus preventing cause from following cause in perpetuity, then why do living creatures throughout the world have freedom of the will, this freedom torn from necessity that allows each of us to go where his pleasure bids? Why are our motions unpredictable both in time and direction? Why do we move where the mind listeth? It is past doubting that our wills initiate motion in all such cases and that movement is channeled from this source throughout the frame. . . . You must see now that although a force from without drives many to move against their wills and often compels them to rush ahead pell-mell, there is nonetheless something in our hearts that can fight against such force and block its way. It is at the bidding of our wills that a quantity of matter is forced on occasion to deploy itself throughout limbs and frame and, when thus extended, is bridled in again and settles back once more. . . . Thus it is this slight deviation of the primal bodies, at indeterminate times and places, that keeps the mind as such from experiencing an inner compulsion in doing everything it does and from being forced to endure and suffer like a captive in chains. [2.251–62, 277–83, 289–93]

L4 = Herod. 48

According to the Epicureans, all sensing or thinking is imagistic. It is either a kind of vision produced directly in any of the sense organs or in the mind (without intervening sense organs) by the impact of fine-textured *eidola* from outside, or it is indirectly derived from the residues of such impacts in the past, as in the case of our general ideas, such as "man," "horse," etc. When we think about nonexistent animals such as centaurs, unicorns, etc., we are "seeing" composite or hybrid images that have accidentally taken shape in transit as the result of the collision of the images of real beings (e.g., man and horse). Quite apart from such unusual composite images, it is worth noting that any thought (or any dream, for that matter) we may have must have its external physical source, immediate or ultimate. Without such material stimulation the mind would be a *tabula rasa* and we should have no mental life at all. See Introduction IV.3 and V.2.b.

To begin with, let me say that many fine-textured *eidola* (such as spider's web and leaf of gold) range abroad in every conceivable direction and manner and that these readily join together when they encounter each other in the atmosphere, because they are much finer of texture than those images that fall upon the eye and stimulate vision, inasmuch as they enter through the pores of the body, wakening the subtle substance of the mind within and stirring its sensibilities. . . . To be sure, the centaur's likeness does not come from any living thing, because there never was such an existent creature, but when the *eidola* of horse and man meet by accident they readily coalesce forthwith (as I noted previously), because of their rarefied substance and fine textures. And everything else of this sort is created in the same manner. Since they move with speed and utmost ease, any single such likeness readily stirs the mind by a single impact, since the mind is itself rarefied and marvelously mobile.

The fact that this all takes place as I am telling it, you may ascertain from the following: What we see with the mind and what we see with the eyes must necessarily be produced by similar processes, inasmuch as the one phenomenon is similar to the other. Thus since I have shown that I perceive a lion (for example) by means of *eidola* that strike upon my eyes, it follows that my mind is activated in like manner and sees the lion and everything else it sees just as much by means of *eidola* as do my eyes, with the difference that my mind perceives images of finer texture. [4.724–56]

Lucretius points up the absurdity of the infinite divisibility of matter still further by showing that on this assumption there would be no difference between the universe and the smallest thing in the universe; both would be equal in containing infinite parts. This absurdity forces him to the conclusion that the atom is made up of minimal parts that are the ultimate and irreducible components of matter.

L5 = Herod. 57

If there are not irreducible parts in the atom, the smallest objects will contain infinite parts, because the half of every half will always have its half and nothing will prescribe any limit to this. What, then, will be the difference between the sum total of things and the smallest of things? No difference at all! Even though the sum total is absolutely infinite, the smallest objects will likewise consist of infinite parts! Since sound reasoning demurs at this and denies that the mind can believe it, you must be prevailed upon to admit that there are atomic parts that are possessed of no parts at all and are irreducible in nature. And since there are such entities, you must likewise admit that atoms are solid and eternal. [1.615–27]

L6 = Herod. 63

Since Lucretius used a fuller source than we have here in the present letter, his account of the nature of the soul differs in two important respects: (1) Although the soul is a single material entity composed of specialized atoms, it is bifurcated into *animus* (the mind, or reason, localized in the breast) and *anima* (the source of life and sensation, the atoms of which are not localized but distributed throughout the body). (2) The soul has a fourfold structure; it is composed of breath, heat, air, and a fourth unnamed element that plays a most important role in producing sensation.

I. Now, I hold that mind and soul are conjoined as one and between them compose one nature but that the head (so to speak) and master of the entire body is the counselor that we call the mind or reason. This has its place and seat in the mid space of the breast; for it is here that dread and terror riot, and hereabouts are the joys that caress. Here, then, are the mind and the reason. The remainder of the soul is seeded throughout the entire body and is obedient to the mind, moving at its behest and prompting. Only the mind is sentient and knows pleasures all its own at times when neither soul nor body is affected. Just as the whole body is not racked when head or eye aches with the onset of pain, so oftentimes the mind knows pain of its own or blooms with joy when the rest of the soul, throughout limb and frame, experiences no novel excitation. However, when the mind is excited by some more violent fear we observe that the entire soul shows fellow feeling in every member. Sweat and pallor appear in every part of the body, the tongue falters, the voice miscarries, the eyes mist over, the ears ring, the limbs give way. In fact, we often see men collapse from terror in the mind. From this, one may readily realize that soul and mind are conjoined, for when the soul is dealt a forceful blow by the mind it forthwith thrusts into the body and activates it. [3.136–60]

II. But we must not suppose that the soul is a simple entity, for a kind of attenuated breath mingled with warmth quits the dying, and warmth carries with it air also. There is no heat in which air is not mingled. Since its nature is rarefied, many prime bodies of air necessarily move within it. We have now found that the soul's nature is threefold, but these three taken all together are not enough to create sensation, since reason will not admit that any one of them is able to produce the sense-giving motions that cause what we think in our minds. To these,

then, some fourth entity must be assigned. It is
wholly without name, but there exists nothing
more mobile than this, nothing more rarefied or
with elements more small and smooth. [3.231–
44] . . . Thus the mingling of heat and air and
the unseen potency of wind constitute a single
entity, together with that mobile force which ap-
portions to these the original motion that gives
rise to sensory movements throughout the frame.
Deep within is this invisible power, nor is there
anything more deep lying in our bodies; it is, furthermore, the soul of the total soul. Just as in
our limbs and body the powers of mind and soul
are intermingled unseen, because formed of particles few and small, so this force without a
name is likewise invisible, made up as it is of
minute bodies; and it is, in a manner of speaking, the soul of the whole soul to boot, master of
the entire body. [3.269–81]

L7 =
Herod.
64
[The fourth component of the soul] is the
first to deploy sense-giving motion throughout
the limbs, since it is first excited, being composed of tiny forms. From it motion is imparted
to heat and to the invisible potency of breath
and then to air. After this everything is made active. The blood is stirred; the viscera tingle all
through with feeling; and, last of all, to bones
and marrow is allotted pleasure or the opposite
affection. [3.245–51] . . . This entity, then, the
soul, is wholly enclosed by the body and is itself
the body's warden and the ground of its well-
being. They are rooted each to each in unity and
clearly cannot be divorced without ruination.
Not easily can the scent be eradicated from
lumps of incense without destroying its exis-

tence. No more easy is it to extract from the whole body the being of mind and soul without the dissolution of the whole. They come into being from the very first with primal bodies thus intertwined and endowed with a conjugal life, nor without the potency of the other can either body or mind have sensation separately. On the contrary, it is by the shared movements of both that feeling is fired and kindled in our frame. Furthermore, the body neither comes into being nor grows by itself, nor do we see it endure after death. [3.323–38]

In attempting to show the material nature of the mind and soul, Lucretius does not use the abstract deductive logic of Epicurus but the concrete imagery of the poet. By giving empirical evidence of the direct action (via atomic contact) of the mind on the body and of the body on the mind, he not only touches on the body-mind problem but advances the materialistic argument to a point not reached by Epicurus in this connection, viz., that body and soul together form a single material unit.

L8 = Herod. 67

This same reasoning shows the nature of mind and soul to be corporeal. When we observe it animating the limbs, fetching the body out of sleep, altering the look of the face, in short, guiding and controlling the whole man (none of which could come about without touch, nor touch in turn without material body), must we not concede that mind and soul are of corporeal character? Furthermore, we observe that the mind acts in company with the body and has fellow feeling for it while in the body. If the ghastly force of steel plunges within, exposing bone and sinew, but fails

to pierce the life itself, it is nonetheless followed
by faintness, by a grateful lapse to earth, a tide of
feeling on the ground, and now and again a vacil-
lating will to rise. Thus the nature of the mind
must needs be physical, since it is anguished by
the stab of physical weapons. [3.161–76]

L9 =
Herod.
68–71

Thus besides empty space and material body
there remains no autonomous third entity in the
catalogue of nature, nothing that is ever subject
to our perception, nothing that the mind's reasoning can apprehend. Anything whatsoever that
has a name you will find to be either a property
of body and space or an accident of these. A
property is that which cannot be disjoined and
severed without the ruinous dissolution of a
thing; thus weight is a property of rocks, heat a
property of fire, liquidity of water, tangibility of
all bodies, intangibility of empty space. On the
other hand, slavery, poverty and riches, war,
peace and freedom, as well as all other conditions whose presence or absence leaves the being
of a thing unimpaired, these we are wont to call
accidents, as is proper. [1.445–58]

L10 =
Herod.
73–74

Lucretius argues here in effect that, given infinite
space, an infinite store of atoms, and the dynamics
of nature that have already constructed one world,
there must therefore exist an indefinite number of
other worlds similar to our own. This weighty conclusion is clearly a deductive inference from a set of
a priori premises and does not rest on empirical observations. Elsewhere (Book 5) he describes our local system as geocentric, with the earth, the heaviest
of the Greek elements, naturally forming the fixed
center. Surrounding the earth at varying distances
are moon, sun, stars, and a final ring of ether consti-

tuting "the fiery walls of the world." By analogy (a favorite Epicurean device frequently used as a substitute for knowledge) this same astronomical structure is then extended to each of the countless other worlds, all of which, like our own, support life in its various forms.

The second passage in this group deals with an important point not emphasized by Epicurus himself in the present letter—namely, that our world (and presumably all other worlds) is a "fortuitous concourse of atoms," i.e., the end product of blind mechanical processes, many of them previously eliminated as unstable or not "harmonious," and not the result of divine agency or intelligent design on the part of a cosmic mind or of the atoms themselves. By adopting this heterodox and unpopular principle of ateleology the Epicureans were able to give free play to the scientific concept of mechanism implicit in atomic materialism, and also to avoid the contradiction of maintaining that the gods were completely impassive and yet at the same time responsible for the creation and maintenance of the universe.

I. When space lies open, infinite on every side, and when atoms numberless in number spin to and fro eternally on their multifarious paths in the cosmic depths, it is in no wise plausible to believe that this earth and this heaven were created alone and that all the bodies of matter beyond have wrought nothing. Particularly is this true since this world was naturally formed after atomic bodies, colliding accidentally and spontaneously in their multitudinous paths, came together blindly, fruitlessly, and to no avail until the sudden coalescence of those masses that were to become ever the beginnings of great enterprises—

land and sea and sky and the host of living things. Thus you must needs concede a hundred times over that there exist elsewhere other concourses of matter like this of ours which ether holds in hot embrace. [2.1052–66] . . . Moreover, in the cosmos there is nothing single, nothing unique in its birth, nothing single and solitary in its growth. A thing is always of some class, and there are exceedingly many members of the same kind. . . . Hence by the same token you must allow that heaven and earth, sun, moon, sea, and all else that is, are not unique but on the contrary numberless, for the reason that a limit of life set deep within waits upon them, and their substance comes to the birth quite as much as that of every earthly species that abounds in its kind. [2.1077–89]

II. Not by design, certainly, not by conscious intelligence did the primal bodies array themselves severally in order, nor did they agree among themselves what motions each would carry out. . . . After packing together in a rabble during a long eternity and after essaying motions and couplings of every kind, it came to pass at length that certain bodies met together whose sudden conjunctions often became the beginnings of great enterprises—earth and sea and sky and the host of living things. At that time the wheel of the sun was not to be seen riding high in his amplitude of light, nor the stars of our mighty cosmos, nor sea nor sky, nor earth nor air, nor indeed anything like to our own world. Instead there was a kind of primeval tempest— an assembled mob of primal bodies of every kind, whose warrings and variance made a tumult of their interspaces, paths, and linkings, their masses and blows, their combinings and motions, because, owing to their unlike shapes and diverse figures, they could not remain thus conjoined or share, one with the other, motions that were congruent. Thereafter the parts of space began to separate from the mass, and like linked with like. A world began to disengage itself, to apportion its members and array its greater parts—that is, to sever high heaven from the lands and sequester the sea with its waters apart, and likewise ether with its fires unmixed and set apart. [5.419–48]

If you recognize and cling to these truths, you will see that Nature is freed forthwith and delivered from her haughty overlords and that she does all of her own will without divine action. By the holy godheads who pass the placid eternity of their serene lives in tranquil peace! *Who* is able to rule the boundless all? *Who* has the power to hold in his hand the stout checkreins of the abyss? *Who* can make all the skies to revolve together? *Who* can warm all fruitful lands with ether's fires? *Who* has the power to be omnipresent at all times, ready to darken the skies with clouds and shatter heaven's calm with a blast, to hurl bolts and oftentimes ruin one's own temples, or, withdrawing into the wastes, to wreak havoc with the lightning shaft that often passes by the guilty and kills the innocent and undeserving? [2.1090–1104]

In a long section on the development of early man and his civilization (5.925–1457) Lucretius fully illustrates Epicurus' naturalistic principle that

L11 =
Herod.
75–76

"at first actual conditions taught and compelled mankind to do many things of various sorts, and later on reasoning perfected nature's instructions." But he differs from Epicurus in assigning to nature the chief role in the early development of language, thereby implicitly denying that convention (reason) played any part.

I. Origin of fire and cooking.

It was the lightning bolt that first brought down fire to earth for mankind, and from it is disseminated every fire and flame. Many a thing do we see set aglow by the spur of heaven's fires after the shaft from the sky has bestowed its gift of heat. Or again, when a branching tree is smitten by winds, and swings and billows to and fro, tree leaning on the branches of tree, fire is sometimes pressed out by the force of the rubbing, and whilst branches and boles grind one upon the other, the fiery heat of flame bursts forth. Either of these happenings could have given men fire. Thereafter the sun taught them to cook their food and soften it by the fire's heat, for in the fields they saw many things grow ripe when overpowered by his heat and the scourging of his rays. [5.1092–1104]

II. Metalworking.

Copper and gold and iron were discovered, and at the same time massive silver and puissant lead, after a fire had cremated huge forests on great mountainsides. Either lightning had fallen from the sky, or men in waging their forest warfare had brought in fire to terrify the enemy or were led by the goodness of the ground to lay bare fertile fields and render the lands fit for pasture. . . . Whatever the reason may be, rivulets of silver and gold as well as copper and lead ran from the burning veins and converged in hollow places of the land. And when later they saw these hardened masses gleaming on the ground in their clear colors, they lifted them up, captivated by their smooth and elegant charm; and they observed that they had taken on shapes similar to the markings of their several concavities. It then occurred to them that these metals when molten would run into any shape or figure whatsoever, and could furthermore be forged by hammering into points and edges, however sharp and thin. In this way they could ready themselves weapons, cut down the forests, hew timber, scrape their logs smooth, even bore, punch, and drill holes. [5.1241–48 and 1255–68]

III. Language.

Nature compelled mankind to utter the tongue's divers sounds, and utility molded the names of things. . . . It is foolish to suppose that any one person at that time allotted names to things and that mankind learned its first words from him. For why should this person have been able to designate things by words and utter the tongue's divers sounds when it is assumed that others were unable to do the same? Moreover, if others had not also used words amongst themselves, how was the notion of their use instilled in him? How did he come by the original power of knowing and mentally discerning what he wanted to do? One man could not compel the many, could not tame and constrain them to learn by rote the names of things. Nor is it by any means easy to persuade and teach the deaf what they should do. They would not tolerate it, nor would they allow the sounds of the voice to pound upon their ears unheard and to no avail. In short, is it so very remarkable that the human race, vigorous as it is in tongue and voice, should variously designate things according to its various feelings, when dumb cattle and the species of wild beasts are wont to make diverse and various sounds whenever they are in fear and pain or when their pleasure swells? ... If, then, their various feelings compel the beasts, dumb though they are, to utter various sounds, is it not more reasonable to assume that mankind should at that time have been able to designate differing things by differing sounds? [5.1028–90]

L12 = Herod. 76–77

I. I shall also recount how Nature's forces control and govern the passage of sun and moon, lest it be supposed perchance that these bodies voluntarily and of their own accord traverse their yearly paths midway between sky and earth with a gracious intent to prosper crops and living things, or that they revolve in accordance with some reasonable divine scheme. For those who have rightly learned that the gods lead lives of unconcern may yet marvel at times how things take place, particularly those occurrences that we observe overhead in the spaces of heaven, and they may again lapse into the antique no-

tions of religion by acknowledging gods as the
fierce lords of nature, and in their piteous ignorance of what can and what cannot be they may
believe them omnipotent, not understanding the
manner in which each thing's natural power is
hedged by a limit set deep within. [5.76–90]

A person who has only superficially accepted
Epicurus' materialistic view of the world and his
idealizing theology may lapse into the cruder
forms of anthropomorphism, believing once more
that the gods are "fierce lords" who control the
various departments of nature by their capricious
wills. A lapse of this sort is accompanied by "the
gravest spiritual disturbances," which are here described by Lucretius. In modern terms, this immature intellectual view of the world has its own
psychological syndrome, the leading characteristics
of which are fear, anxiety, and the expectation of
divine retribution. A person caught in this vicious
circle is cut off from the chief spiritual benefits of
Epicureanism, viz., the mental composure that
stems from scientific knowledge, and those the-
ophanies, or manifestations of the divine nature,
that are transmitted by means of atomic images to
those able to receive them. Thus in Epicurus' view
science, spiritual health, and the higher contempla-
tive forms of religion are all intimately bound up
together; he is an enemy only of popular anthropomorphic religion.

II. Unless you cast such notions out of your
mind and cease altogether to think thoughts unbecoming to the gods and alien to their tranquillity, the holy godheads that you have yourself
impaired may ofttimes work you harm—not

that you could profane the gods' high estate or
that they would wrathfully thirst for hot vengeance but that you in your own mind would picture these serene beings, in their utter calm,
rolling up great tides of wrath against you, and
you would come to their shrines with unquiet
heart and have neither strength nor peace of
mind sufficient to receive those messengers of
deity, the images that flow from their holy bodies into the minds of men. [6.68–78]

L13 =
Herod.
79–80 "If we find more than one cause for these revolutions, risings, settings, eclipses, and the like" should
be interpreted to mean that, in the absence of adequate experimental techniques for determining natural causes with precision, the Epicureans had to be
content with setting up a number of alternative hypotheses, to all of which they were equally hospitable on principle, so long as the hypothesis in
question was empirical or at least not contradicted
by our terrestrial experience. This principle of plurality of causes (actually plurality of hypotheses) is
amply illustrated in Book 5 of Lucretius, where, for
example, he explains the phases of the moon (lines
705–50) in three different ways, without deciding
between the rival hypotheses. Thus the moon's
phases may be explained by assuming (1) that the
moon shines by reflected light, (2) that it shines by
its own light, and (3) that the moon is created anew
every day by a regular succession of forms. Each of
these explanations is on a par with the other two,
and since there was no way then of testing hypotheses involving remote phenomena, each was confi-
dently regarded as a coordinate "cause" of the
moon's phases. In other words, the term "cause"
was confused with what we today call a causal ex-

planation or hypothesis, and since none of these
three "causes" was contradicted by ordinary terrestrial experience they were all regarded as "true
causes." This points up the relative impotence of
empirical science at this stage of its history and gives
weight to the truism in science today that a hypothesis which cannot be tested by some crucial experiment is without value.

The confusion of cause and causal explanation is
equally apparent in Lucretius' account of solar and
lunar eclipses. In each case three hypotheses are presented as coordinate causes:

> We must likewise assume that the failure of
> the sun's light and the cloaking of the moon can
> occur from several causes. Why should the moon
> be able to screen earth from the sun's light by
> lifting her head high above the lands to oppose
> him and casting her invisible disk against his
> blazing rays, unless we assume at the same time
> that some other body, which glides by forever
> lightless and opaque, can do the same? Or again,
> why should an enfeebled sun not be able to dis-
> band his fires at certain times and again rekindle
> them, after he has passed through regions infested
> with atmospheres that cause his lights to be
> quenched and die?
>
> Again, why should the earth in her turn be
> able to despoil the moon of light by riding high
> above a sun humbled below her, whilst the men-
> strual moon glides through the numbing shad-
> ows of the cone, unless some other unseen body
> is likewise able to pass beneath the moon or
> move over the disk of the sun, to intercept his
> rays and flooding light? Be that as it may, if the
> moon shines with her own light, why should she

not become enfeebled in certain quarters of the world, when she traverses regions that are hostile to her light? [5.751–70]

L14 =
Herod.
81

See note L10, Part II, and L12.

L15 =
Herod.
81

I. Hell.

The hound of hell, the Furies, the eclipse of day, Tartarus vomiting dreadful tides of heat from the pit—these nowhere exist, nor can they in truth. Rather it is the fear of punishment for our evil deeds in this life—a fear as marked as they are marked; it is the reparation for our crimes—the prison or the fearful hurling from the precipice, the hangman's whips, the oaken block, the pitch, the heated plate, the brands. Absent though these may be, yet the guilty mind, fearful for its deeds betimes, applies the prick and flagellates itself. And in the meanwhile it sees no end to its ills, no limit to its punishments, and it fears lest they may be more grievous in death. In short, the life of simpletons is made into a hell here and now. [3.1011–23]

II. Loss of sensation in death.

Since the soul's substance is seen to be mortal, death is nothing to us, nor does it concern us in the least. In times long past we knew no ill when the Carthaginian assembled from every quarter for the fight; when the whole earth, shaken by the tumult and alarms of war, quailed in fright beneath heaven's high strand and it was

unknown which side was destined to bear the
rule over humankind on land and sea. Just so,
when we shall no longer be, after the divorcing
of body and soul, of which twain we are fitly
joined, nothing whatsoever will have the power
to affect us, since we shall not then be; nothing
be able to move our senses—no, not if earth
shall be confounded with sea and sea with sky.
[3.830–42] . . .

When a man while alive pictures to himself
that wild beasts and birds of prey may rend his
body in death, he commiserates with himself, because he does not distinguish himself from his
corpse or put himself at a sufficient distance
from his cast-off body; he imagines it to be himself, and as he stands by he imbues it with his
own sensation. Thus he feels resentful that he
was born mortal, nor does he see that in actual
death there will be no other "self" that will live
to mourn his own demise or will stand by and
grieve that "he" is lying there being torn apart or
burning on the pyre. [3.879–87]

III. Unreason and reason.

If we see that all this is laughable and a matter for mockery and if in actuality the fears and
anxieties that hound men do not dread the noise
of arms or the deadly shaft but move with bold-
ness amidst kings and potentates, reverencing
neither their golden glitter nor the bright splen-
dor of their purple raiment—can you then doubt
that all such power is reason's, particularly when
the whole of life labors in darkness? Just as children quail in the blinding dark and are fearful of

L16 =
Herod.
81–82

all, so we in the light of day are often terrified by things that are no more to be feared than what children tremble at in the dark and think are going to happen. This darkling terror in the mind must then be routed not by the sun's rays, not by the bright shafts of day, but by the observation and rational inspection of nature. [2.47–61]

Letter to Pythocles

Cleon brought me a letter from you in which you (84
continue to show affectionate regard for me com-
mensurate with my own feelings toward you and in
which you rather convincingly attempt to recall the
lines of reasoning that tend to promote the happy
life. You ask me to send you a sketch or concise account of celestial phenomena for easy review.[1] You
say that what I have written elsewhere on the subject is hard to remember, even though you claim that
my books are constantly in your hands. I greeted
your request with pleasure and feel obliged to com-
ply with it because of my fond hopes for you. Since
I have finished all my other writing I shall therefore (85
carry out your wishes, with the expectation that this
account will be serviceable to many others also, especially those who have recently come into contact
with genuine natural science as well as people who
are rather deeply involved in everyday business affairs. Consider it well, then, and go through it sys-
tematically, bearing the various points in mind
together with my other remarks in the shorter epitome that I sent to Herodotus.

I. PROCEDURE

First of all, then, we must assume that no other
end is served by the study of celestial phenomena,

whether considered by themselves or in some larger context, than mental composure and a sturdy self-reliance, just as in the case of the other disciplines.

86) We must not force an impossible explanation on these phenomena or make our treatment similar in all respects to an ethical discourse or to an explication of the problems of noncelestial physics—as seen, for example, in the statements "The universe consists of bodies and an intangible substance" or "Atoms are indivisible" and in all other such cases where there is but a single explanation that is consistent with phenomena.[2] This is not the case with the heavenly bodies. Their origins have more than one cause, and there is more than one set of predications relating to their nature that is compatible with our sensory experience. We should not carry on the study of nature by means of meaningless axioms and scientific decrees but should allow phenomena

87) to elicit their own explanations; for we have no use now for personal prejudice and meaningless guesswork if we are to live the unperturbed life. In the case of occurrences which have more than one explanation that is consistent with the phenomena, nothing need shake our composure if we are willing to concede, as we must, that theories about them are only probable. But if a person takes one explanation and throws out another that is equally compatible with the phenomenon, it is obvious that he is departing completely from scientific procedure and has slipped into religious superstition. From terrestrial phenomena it is possible to derive certain indications of what takes place in the heavenly bodies. It can be observed how the former occur but not how celestial phenomena occur, because it is possible for

88) the latter to happen from a variety of causes. However, we must give heed to the sensory impression in

each case, and in our judgments connected with it we must determine those cases where multiple causation is not contradicted by terrestrial phenomena.[3]

II. WORLDS

A world is a circumscribed section of the heavens and includes a sun, moon, stars, an earth, and all that occurs in the heavens; at its dissolution everything in it will be thrown into disorder. It is a segment of infinite space and terminates in a periphery that is either rarefied or dense, either in circular motion or in a state of rest, either spherical or triangular or of any other shape. All these possibilities exist, inasmuch as they are not contradicted by any phenomenon in our own world where it is impossible to lay hold of a terminal point.[4]

Furthermore, we can readily grasp the fact that (89 such worlds are infinite in number[5] and that any such world may be generated within a world or in the cosmic interspaces (i.e., the spaces between worlds) in a region containing a good deal of empty space but not in a pure vacuum of great size, as some persons claim. The birth of a world occurs after the necessary atoms have streamed in from one or more worlds or interspaces, gradually form organized aggregates, and effect the transfer of matter to various areas of the system as chance dictates, feeding in the appropriate materials until the world is completed. It then remains in equilibrium as long as the foundations that have been laid down are capable of receiving additional matter. (L17) Thus the (90 formation of a world requires more than merely a congregating of atoms and a vortex in a vacuum supposedly generated by Necessity.[6] Nor can a world keep on growing until it collides with another world, as one of the so-called cosmologists claims, because this runs counter to our experience. (L18)

III. THE HEAVENLY BODIES

1. Their Creation, Size, Movements, etc. The sun, moon, and other heavenly bodies were not generated separately and incorporated later into the world, but were formed at once and augmented by the conjunctions of swirling masses composed of tiny particles having the nature of air or fire or both; for this is what the senses suggest. The size of 91) the sun, moon, and other heavenly bodies is from our point of view just what it appears to be. From an absolute point of view it is either somewhat greater than what we see or somewhat smaller or exactly the same, because this is the way that fiery objects on earth appear to the senses when viewed from a distance. (L19) Any objection to this part of the argument will easily be resolved if we attend to our clear and distinct perceptions, as I point out in my work *On Nature*.

92)   The risings and settings of the sun, the moon, and the other heavenly bodies may come about from the lighting up and quenching of their fires, if the conditions at the place of their rising or setting are such as to bring about the aforementioned effects; for nothing in our sensory experience runs counter to this hypothesis. Or the said effects may be caused by the emergence of these bodies from a point above the earth and again by the earth's position in front of them; for nothing in our sensory experience is against this.[7]

It is not impossible that the movements of these

bodies may occur because of the rotation of the heavens as a whole, or the latter may be stationary and the heavenly bodies may rotate because of the necessary eastward motion that was generated originally at the birth of the world. * * * * * (L20)

It is possible that the tropics, or turning points of (93 the sun and moon,[8] are brought about by the slanting of the sky, which is forced into this position by the seasons; or, equally possible, by transverse air currents; or because the right sort of fuel is always ignited in due order as the previous supply leaves off burning; or because this kind of rotary motion was originally forced upon these bodies, with the result that they move in a kind of spiral.

Now, none of these theories or theories related to these are incompatible with our clear and distinct perceptions of things, provided we hold to the possible in these matters and are able to refer each theory to some phenomenal counterpart and not stand in awe of the slavish fabrications of the astronomers.[9]

2. The Moon. The waning and waxing of the (94 moon may take place because of this body's rotation, or, equally well, because of the structure of the atmosphere,[10] or again because some other body places itself in front of the moon. In fact, the phases of the moon may occur in any of the ways in which events in our own experience prompt us to give an account of this lunar phenomenon, provided we do not become overly fond of the "one cause" principle and irresponsibly reject other explanations without first considering what can and what cannot be observed, and consequently end up desiring to observe the impossible.[11]

Again, it is possible that the moon may have her own light and also possible that she has it from the

95) sun, because in our own experience we observe many objects that have their own light and many that get light from other sources. No celestial phenomenon stands in the way of these hypotheses, if we always keep in mind the principle of multiple causation and consider as a group the causal hypotheses that are relevant to the events, and do not concentrate on the irrelevant and rashly exaggerate it or lean in one way or another to the "one cause" method.

The apparent face in the moon may be caused by the variation of its physical features or by some ob-
96) ject in front of the moon or by any one of a number of observable factors that harmonize with phenomena on earth. Thus one should never neglect this method of investigation in the case of the heavenly bodies, because if a person fights the clear evidence of his senses he will never be able to share in genuine tranquillity.

3. Eclipses, Periods, etc. An eclipse of the sun or moon may occur because of the dying out of its fires, a thing we see occurring on earth also; or from other bodies passing in front of them, such as the earth or some invisible object or something else of this sort. We must thus consider as a group explanations that belong together and recognize that the simultaneous conjunction of certain causes is not an impossibility. (L21)

97) Again, the regularity of the celestial periods is comparable to the way in which certain occurrences take place in our own experience.[12] The divine nature, once more, should never be brought into these events. Let us exempt it from such responsibilities and keep it in the full state of blessedness. If we fail to do this, our whole causal theory regarding celestial phenomena will be meaningless, as it has al-

ready become for those who have not availed themselves of the method of possibility.[13] These persons have resorted to the meaningless practice of thinking that things happen only in one way and of rejecting all the other methods that accord with the principle of the possible. They turn to the irrational and are unable to examine the terrestrial phenomena that we must accept as the analogues of celestial occurrences.

The varying length of night and day may be (98 caused by the fact that the sun's movements over the earth are alternately fast and slow because it crosses areas of varying length or passes over certain areas more rapidly than others. There are analogous cases in our own experience, and in speaking of the heavenly bodies our theories must harmonize with such cases. Those who hold to one cause, however, resist such evidence and have failed to observe whether it is possible for human beings to use the empirical method. (L22)

IV. METEOROLOGY

Weather Signs, Clouds, Rain, Lightning, etc.

1. Weather signs may occur through a conjunction of events (as in the case of animals seen by all of us) and also from alterations and changes in the atmosphere.[14] Neither of these runs counter to experience, but it is impossible to determine which par- (99 ticular cause operates under given conditions.

2. Clouds may be brought together and generated by the thickening of the atmosphere under wind pressure, by the twining together of the interlocking atoms needed to bring about this effect, or

by the collecting of streams of moisture from the earth and its waters; in addition, there are several other ways in which such formations may quite possibly occur. Once clouds are formed, rain water may be produced from them if certain areas are com-
100)   pressed or if they undergo certain other changes.[15] Another cause of rain is the downflow of winds moving through the atmosphere out of the right quarter. Heavier precipitation is caused by the atomic aggregations needed for such downpours.

3. It is possible that thunder may be caused by the rolling around of the wind in the hollows of the clouds (analogously to our own storage jars);[16] by the booming of wind-inflated fire inside the clouds; by the rupturing and tearing apart of clouds; or by the rubbing together and fracturing of clouds after they have taken on an icelike solidity. Empirical considerations call upon us to apply the principle of multiple causation to this department of meteorology as we do in general.

101)   4. Lightning is likewise caused in several ways:[17] (1) Because of the rubbing together and colliding of clouds, the fire-producing configuration of atoms escapes and generates lightning, and the atomic bodies that produced this flash are hurled out of the clouds by winds; or the cause may be a squeezing-out process that takes place when the clouds are compressed either by each other or by winds. (2) The light that is disseminated by the heavenly bodies may be enclosed in the clouds, then become concentrated by the motion of clouds and winds, and fall out through the clouds; or light composed of extremely fine particles may filter through the clouds, and in this way the clouds may be ignited by the fire and thunder be produced by
102)   the fire's motion. (3) Wind may be ignited by its in-

tensity of motion and violent swirling about; or clouds may be shattered by winds, and the fire-producing atoms may fall out, causing the phenomenon of lightning. In addition, it will be easy to discover several other ways if we hold consistently to the evidence of the senses and are able to observe there what resembles the celestial events.

In cloud conditions such as these, lightning precedes thunder (1) because the atomic configuration that causes the lightning is thrust out at the same time as the wind rushes in, and subsequently the swirling wind produces the boom of thunder; or (2) because they are both ejected simultaneously, but lightning moves toward us at a greater velocity, with the thunder following after, analogously to certain objects that are seen at a distance and make differing sensory impacts.[18]   (103

5. Thunderbolts may possibly occur (1) because of dense accumulations of winds that swirl about and ignite in a powerful flame, a portion of which is ripped loose and descends violently to the ground below (the breaking loose of the bolt occurs because the masses of cloud become increasingly close packed, owing to compression); or (2) because of the actual ejection of the swirling fire (comparable to the way thunder is produced), when the flame becomes too massive and too violently inflated with wind; it then ruptures the cloud, since it is unable to go back to the adjoining areas because of the steady compression of the cloud masses one against the other. And it is possible that thunderbolts may be   (104
caused in still other ways. Only let there be an end to mythologizing![19] And there will be if we rightly follow the evidence of the senses in gleaning hints about things unseen.

6. Cyclones may be caused (1) by the descent of

a cloud in the form of a column to the earth below, the cloud being thrust downward by compacted wind and driven by massive gusts, while at the same time the wind outside it pushes it sideways; (2) by the formation of the wind into a spiral, air being forced down upon it from above; or (3) when a strong current of wind is generated and is unable to flow through the cloud mass sideways because of the compression of the atmosphere around it. When

105) the cyclonic winds reach down as far as the earth, whirlwinds of every sort are generated corresponding to the various wind motions, whereas over the sea waterspouts result.

7. Earthquakes may be caused (1) by the trapping of wind in the earth,[20] the displacing of the ground in small masses, and the adjacent motion, all of which produces a quaking of the earth. The latter either takes in this wind from the outside and encloses it, or else chunks of ground fall into cavernous depressions in the earth and churn up the air trapped there. In addition, (2) it is possible for earthquakes to be produced by the actual diffusion of the motion caused by the caving in of masses of earth and the countermotion that occurs when the former meets with thick concentrations of earth. There are also many other ways in which these

106) movements of the earth may occur.

*   *   *   *   * 21

8. Hail is caused (1) by a process of heavy freezing when certain wind particles are grouped together from all around and then broken up into pellets; or (2) by a more moderate freezing of water particles accompanied by a breaking-up process—in other words, the simultaneous compression and

splitting up of the hailstones, with the effect that both the parts and the wholes solidify as they freeze.[22] The roundness of the stones may quite (107 possibly be caused by the sharp points melting away all around or because at the time of their formation (so the claim goes) certain water particles or wind particles are evenly compounded in a circle, part by part.

9. Snow may be caused (1) by fine rain precipitating from the clouds through pores of suitable size due to strong wind pressure on the right sort of clouds; this rain then assumes a frozen state in transit due to certain conditions of intense cold in the clouds at lower levels. Due to freezing in clouds which have a uniform porosity, precipitation of this sort might be produced (2) by rain clouds that lie side by side and press against each other, just as they produce hail by causing compression, a very frequent atmospheric occurrence. Due to the friction of (108 clouds that have assumed a frozen state, this snow formation (3) may be whirled off. And there are still other ways in which it is possible for snow to be produced.

10. Dew is produced (1) by the coming together of those atmospheric particles that are productive of this kind of moisture[23] and (2) by the evaporation of particles from damp spots or places containing water, in which dew is generally produced. These water-bearing particles then come together, produce moisture, and again precipitate to the earth below, a phenomenon we see occurring in many cases in our own experience.[24] In addition, frost is produced (109 when drops of dew are altered in such a way as to assume a kind of frozen state due to the circumstance that the atmosphere is cold.

11. Ice is produced (1) by the extrusion of parti-

cles of round formation from water and the compression of the uneven and acute-angled particles existent in the water; (2) by the assimilation from outside of particles of the latter sort, which on being forced together cause freezing in the water by pressing out a certain number of round particles.

12. The rainbow is produced (1) by sunlight shining on an atmosphere full of water particles; or (2) by a special combination of light and air that often causes the special characteristics of these colors, either collectively or severally; because it reflects light, the adjacent areas of the atmosphere will often take on the coloring we see, due to the shining of 110) the light on its various parts. The well-known phenomenon of the rainbow's circularity is caused by the fact that the eye sees it at an equal distance from all its points or (2) because the atoms in the air or those in the clouds that are received from sunlight have become compressed in this way and the combination of the two stretches earthward in a kind of circle.[25]

13. A halo around the moon is produced (1) when air advances from every quarter toward the moon; or (2) when the atmosphere holds back effluvia discharged by the moon, uniformly and in such a way as to spread them around in a circle in this cloudlike formation, with no inequalities whatsoever; or (3) when it holds back the atmosphere around the moon symmetrically at every point, so as to spread it thickly in a circle. This occurs in various parts of the sky either because some external current 111) forces the air around or because heat stops up the atmospheric channels in a way necessary to produce this effect.

V. MISCELLANEOUS CELESTIAL PHENOMENA

Comets, Fixed Stars, Planets, etc.

1. Comets[26] occur (1) when fire accumulates in certain areas of the upper air during certain periods, after the occurrence of a certain atomic formation; (2) because the heavens overhead have a particular motion at certain times, with the result that stars of this sort become visible; (3) because they start to move independently at certain times because of special circumstances and come into areas of the heavens over us and thus become visible. The disappearance of these bodies is brought about by causes opposite to the above.

2. Certain stars "turn on the very spot."[27] This comes about (1) not merely because this part of the world is fixed and the rest of the sky revolves around it (as some maintain) but also because a vortex of air encircles it, which is an impediment to their ranging about as the other stars do; or (2) because they do not have the necessary supply of fuel except in this region of the sky where we see that they are fixed. There are also a number of other ways in which it is possible for this phenomenon to occur, provided we are able to make deductions that are consistent with the evidence of the senses.   (112

3. The fact that certain of the stars are planets, or "wanderers"[28] (if such is actually the case), whereas certain others do not have these erratic movements, may possibly be explained as follows: (1) Necessity from the very beginning compelled some of them, as they moved in their circular paths, to rotate in the same regular orbits and forced others at the same time to follow courses that have certain irregularities. (2) It is also possible that in some   (113

of the regions where they move there are level stretches of atmosphere that successively thrust them forward in the same direction by providing a uniform supply of fuel, as well as other stretches that are uneven, with the result that the deviations in orbit that we observe are brought about. Application of the "one cause" method to these events, when the phenomena call for multiple explanation, is a mad and improper practice of persons who have espoused the worthless science of astrology and who reduce causal theory to meaninglessness when they fail to release the deity from such duties.[29]

4. The fact that certain stars are observed to lag

114) behind others comes about (1) because they move in the same circular orbit but rotate more slowly than the others, (2) because they move in the opposite direction but are held back by the revolution of the other stars,[30] or (3) because all stars traverse the same circular path, but some rotate over a greater area, others over a lesser. To offer the simple "one cause" explanation of such phenomena is appropriate for people who want to parade their superstitions before the mob.

5. So-called falling stars may be caused in part (1) by a collision of stars and the subsequent falling out of debris, which occurs whenever there is a discharge of wind, as we remarked in connection with

115) lightning;[31] (2) by an aggregation of atoms that produce fire (assuming that there has been a meeting of cognate bodies to this end) and by their fall in the direction of the original impetus imparted to them by their coming together; (3) by a concourse of winds in dense, mistlike concentrations; this mass then ignites because of compression, bursts out of the surrounding matter, and falls toward whatever region its impetus carries it. And there are still other

ways in which this phenomenon may occur, ways that have nothing to do with myth.

6. The weather signs provided by certain animals come about through a conjunction of events, since animals do not bring any influence to bear on winter's coming to an end, nor does some divine being sit and watch them coming out of hibernation and then bring these portents to pass! Not even an insig- (116 nificant creature would be guilty of such stupidity (though trifles give more pleasure, they say), not to mention a being that has attained to perfect happiness.

VI. CONCLUSION

If you remember these various points, Pythocles, you will keep clear of religious superstition for the most part and be able to comprehend related matters. Devote yourself particularly to the study of metaphysical origins, infinity, and kindred topics, as well as the criteria of truth, the feelings, and the purpose for which we reflect on all these matters.[32] It is particularly the synoptic view of these topics as a group that will make it easy for you to study causation in detail. But those who have not fully committed themselves emotionally to these matters cannot properly view them as they are, nor have they grasped the purpose and the need for studying them.[33]

Parallel Passages from Lucretius

Through collisions the primal bodies are sev-   L17 = erally distributed from every side, each falling   Pyth. back to its own kind. Water goes to water, and   89 from the substance of earth the earth waxes. Fire fashions fire and ether ether, until Nature, the creator and perfecter of all, brings the whole to its final term of growth. This befalls when that which is added to the channels of life is no more than what flows out and falls away. [2.1112–19]

L18 =
Pyth.
90

That is, the unlimited growth of anything, including worlds, "runs counter to our experience," as Lucretius explains by the analogy of living organisms, which grow to the point of atomic equilibrium and then begin to decline, i.e., lose more particles than they take in.

When that which is added to the channels of life is no more than what flows out and falls away—at this point the youth of everything must come to a halt, and here Nature reins in the increase of her own powers. All that we see increasing in gladsome growth, ascending little by little the stair of ripening years, these things take to themselves more primal bodies than they give out, so long as food is readily infused into their veins and their expanse is not so great that they emit many particles or cause more to be expended than their youth feeds on. Assuredly it must be admitted that many corpuscles flow out and fall away from things, but more must enter in until things have reached the apex of their increase. Thereafter time crumbles their powers and robust maturity bit by bit, and life slips into its lesser half. . . . With reason do they perish, therefore, when they have become tenuous from the flux of atoms and succumb to attacks from without; for sustenance fails the aged life in the end, and the hostile bodies that beat upon it un-

ceasingly from without subdue and vanquish it
by assault. Thus even the circling walls of the
mighty cosmos will be assailed and sink in
squalid ruin. [2.1118–32 and 1139–45]

By the principle of "naïve realism" natural objects
and events are believed to be pretty much what the
senses represent them to be, and both Epicurus and
Lucretius accordingly held that the actual size of sun,
moon, and stars is approximately what we see. As
supporting evidence Lucretius adduces what purport
to be analogies from our own experience. He agrees
with Epicurus that "this is the way that fiery objects
on earth appear to the senses when viewed from a
distance," but he attaches two conditions (as Epicurus probably did also in his larger work *On Nature*):
Such objects do not appear to diminish in size (1) if
they continue to send out light and heat and (2) if
their outlines remain clear and unblurred.

L19 =
Pyth.
91

Nor can the sun's fiery wheel be very much
greater or smaller than it appears to our senses.
For, however great the interval, so long as fires
can cast their glow and waft their warmth and
heat upon our bodies, they subtract naught from
the bulk of their flames by reason of distance;
the blaze that falls upon the eye is in no way
lessened. Thus since the sun's heat and its
streaming light come through to our senses and
caress the earth, its shape and contours must be
truly seen from here, so much so that one can
neither add to it nor take away.

The moon likewise, whether she encompasses
the lands with a spurious light or casts her
beams from her own body, moves aloft in any
case with a bulk no greater than what we see

with the eye. For objects that we view at a far distance through long reaches of air seem indistinct in shape before their contours are reduced in size. Thus since the moon on high presents a distinct appearance and unblurred form whenever her outer rim is well defined, she must necessarily appear to us from here exactly as she is.

And finally, the fires we see here on earth appear now and again to change their magnitude only very slightly in either direction the further distant they are, so long as their quivering flames are clearly discerned. From this we may gather that the fires of heaven that we see from here on earth are a little smaller or a tiny bit larger than they appear. [5.564–91]

L20 = Pyth. 92

A loss of several lines in the Greek text at this point may possibly be filled in from the corresponding passage in Lucretius:

It may also be that the whole heaven remains stationary whilst the bright constellations revolve. And this comes about either because swirling tides of ether are there imprisoned, which seeking exit turn round and round and wheel the fires of night hither and yon across the quarters of the sky; or a flow of air issuing from somewhere beyond may turn and propel these fires; or they may proceed of their own motions; each moving whither its food beckons and invites, each pasturing its fiery body in various quarters of the sky. [5.517–25]

L21 = Pyth. 96

We must likewise assume that the failure of the sun's light and the cloaking of the moon can occur from several causes. Why should the moon be able to screen earth from the sun's light by lifting her head high above the lands to oppose him and casting her invisible disk against his blazing rays, unless we assume at the same time that some other body, which glides by forever lightless and opaque, can do the same? Or again, why should an enfeebled sun not be able to disband his fires at certain times and again rekindle them, after he has passed through regions infested with atmospheres that cause his lights to be quenched and die?

Again, why should the earth in her turn be able to despoil the moon of light by riding high above a sun humbled below her, whilst the menstrual moon glides through the numbing shadows of the cone, unless some other unseen body is likewise able to pass beneath the moon or move over the disk of the sun, to intercept his rays and flooding light? Be that as it may, if the moon shines with her own light, why should she not become enfeebled in certain quarters of the world, when she traverses regions that are hostile to her light? [5.751–70]

L22 =
Pyth.
98

It is possible that days grow longer and the nights languish, or contrariwise that the light of day lessens whilst nights increase, because the same sun as he runs his course beneath the earth and over it severs the round of heaven in revolutions unequal, dividing his daily circuit into unlike halves. And if he has taken away something from one portion he restores that much more to the one opposite as he revolves, until he comes to that constellation in the sky where the equinox makes the dark of night equal to the light of day. . . . Or it may be because the atmosphere in certain quarters is thicker and hence the tremulous beam of fire pauses beneath the earth and cannot readily pierce through and come forth to its rising. On this account the nights linger long in wintertime till the coming of the bright standard of day. Or again, it may be because the fires that cause the rising of the sun in a certain quarter are disposed to assemble more slowly or more quickly in alternate portions of the year. [5.680–88 and 696–703]

Letter to Menoeceus

No one should postpone the study of philosophy when he is young, nor should he weary of it when (122
he becomes mature, because the search for mental
health is never untimely or out of season.[1] To say
that the time to study philosophy has not yet arrived or that it is past is like saying that the time
for happiness is not yet at hand or is no longer present. Thus both the young and the mature should
pursue philosophy, the latter in order to be rejuve-
nated as they age by the blessings that accrue from
pleasurable past experience, and the youthful in
order to become mature immediately through having no fear of the future. Hence we should make a
practice of the things that make for happiness, for
assuredly when we have this we have everything,
and we do everything we can to get it when we
don't have it.

THE PRECONDITIONS OF HAPPINESS

I.   You should do and practice all the things I (123
constantly recommended to you, with the knowledge that they are the fundamentals of the good life.
(1) First of all, you should think of deity as imper-
ishable and blessed being (as delineated in the universal conception of it common to all men),[2] and

you should not attribute to it anything foreign to its immortality or inconsistent with its blessedness. On the contrary, you should hold every doctrine that is capable of safeguarding its blessedness in common with its imperishability. (L23) The gods do indeed exist, since our knowledge of them is a matter of clear and distinct perception; but they are not like what the masses suppose them to be, because most people do not maintain the pure conception of the gods. The irreligious man is not the person who destroys the gods of the masses but the person who imposes the ideas of the masses on the gods. (L24) The opinions held by most people about the gods

124) are not true conceptions of them but fallacious notions, according to which awful penalties are meted out to the evil and the greatest of blessings to the good. (L25) The masses, by assimilating the gods in every respect to their own moral qualities, accept deities similar to themselves and regard anything not of this sort as alien.[3]

(2) Second, you should accustom yourself to believing that death means nothing to us, since every good and every evil lies in sensation; but death is the privation of sensation. Hence a correct comprehension of the fact that death means nothing to us makes the mortal aspect of life pleasurable, not by conferring on us a boundless period of time but by removing the yearning for deathlessness.[4] There is

125) nothing fearful in living for the person who has really laid hold of the fact that there is nothing fearful in not living. So it is silly for a person to say that he dreads death—not because it will be painful when it arrives but because it pains him now as a future certainty; for that which makes no trouble for us when it arrives is a meaningless pain when we await it. This, the most horrifying of evils, means nothing to

us, then, because so long as we are existent death is not present and whenever it is present we are nonexistent. Thus it is of no concern either to the living or to those who have completed their lives. For the former it is nonexistent, and the latter are themselves nonexistent. (L26)

Most people, however, recoil from death as though it were the greatest of evils; at other times they welcome it as the end-all of life's ills. The sophisticated person,[5] on the other hand, neither begs off from living nor dreads not living. Life is not a stumbling block to him, nor does he regard not being alive as any sort of evil. As in the case of food he prefers the most savory dish to merely the larger portion, so in the case of time he garners to himself the most agreeable moments rather than the longest span. (126

Anyone who urges the youth to lead a good life but counsels the older man to end his life in good style is silly, not merely because of the welcome character of life but because of the fact that living well and dying well are one and the same discipline.[6] Much worse off, however, is the person who says it were well not to have been born "but once born to pass Hades' portals as swiftly as may be." Now if he says such a thing from inner persuasion (127 why does he not withdraw from life? Everything is in readiness for him once he has firmly resolved on this course. But if he speaks facetiously he is a trifler standing in the midst of men who do not welcome him.

It should be borne in mind, then, that the time to come is neither ours nor altogether not ours. In this way we shall neither expect the future outright as something destined to be nor despair of it as something absolutely not destined to be.[7]

THE GOOD LIFE

II. It should be recognized that within the category of desire certain desires are natural, certain others unnecessary and trivial; that in the case of the natural desires certain ones are necessary, certain others merely natural; and that in the case of necessary desires certain ones are necessary for happiness, others to promote freedom from bodily discomfort, others for the maintenance of life itself.[8] A steady
128) view of these matters shows us how to refer all moral choice and aversion to bodily health and imperturbability of mind, these being the twin goals of happy living. It is on this account that we do everything we do—to achieve freedom from pain and freedom from fear. When once we come by this, the tumult in the soul is calmed and the human being does not have to go about looking for something that is lacking or to search for something additional with which to supplement the welfare of soul and body. Accordingly we have need of pleasure only when we feel pain because of the absence of pleasure, but whenever we do not feel pain we no longer
129) stand in need of pleasure.[9] And so we speak of pleasure as the starting point and the goal of the happy life because we realize that it is our primary native good, because every act of choice and aversion originates with it, and because we come back to it when we judge every good by using the pleasure feeling as our criterion. (L27)

Because of the very fact that pleasure is our primary and congenital good we do not select every pleasure; there are times when we forgo certain pleasures, particularly when they are followed by too much unpleasantness.[10] Furthermore, we regard certain states of pain as preferable to pleasures, particularly when greater satisfaction results from our having submitted to discomforts for a long period of time.[11] Thus every pleasure is a good by reason of its having a nature akin to our own, but not every pleasure is desirable. In like manner every state of pain is an evil, but not all pains are uniformly to be rejected. At any rate, it is our duty to judge all such (130 cases by measuring pleasures against pains, with a view to their respective assets and liabilities, inasmuch as we do experience the good as being bad at times and, contrariwise, the bad as being good.

In addition, we consider limitation of the appetites a major good, and we recommend this practice not for the purpose of enjoying just a few things and no more but rather for the purpose of enjoying those few in case we do not have much.[12] We are firmly convinced that those who need expensive fare least are the ones who relish it most keenly and that a natural way of life is easily procured, while trivialities are hard to come by.[13] Plain foods afford pleasure equivalent to that of a sumptuous diet, provided that the pains of penury are wholly eliminated. Barley bread and water yield the peak of pleasure (131 whenever a person who needs them sets them in front of himself. Hence becoming habituated to a simple rather than a lavish way of life provides us with the full complement of health; it makes a person ready for the necessary business of life; it puts us in a position of advantage when we happen upon sumptuous fare at intervals and prepares us to be fearless in facing fortune.[14]

Thus when I say that pleasure is the goal of living I do not mean the pleasures of libertines or the pleasures inherent in positive enjoyment, as is supposed by certain persons who are ignorant of our doctrine or who are not in agreement with it or who

132) interpret it perversely.[15] I mean, on the contrary, the pleasure that consists in freedom from bodily pain and mental agitation. The pleasant life is not the product of one drinking party after another or of sexual intercourse with women and boys or of the sea food and other delicacies afforded by a luxurious table. (L28) On the contrary, it is the result of sober thinking—namely, investigation of the reasons for every act of choice and aversion and elimination of those false ideas about the gods and death which are the chief source of mental disturbances.[16]

The starting point of this whole scheme and the most important of its values is good judgment, which consequently is more highly esteemed even than philosophy.[17] All the other virtues stem from sound judgment, which shows us that it is impossible to live the pleasant Epicurean life without also living sensibly, nobly, and justly and, vice versa, that it is impossible to live sensibly, nobly, and justly without living pleasantly. The traditional virtues grow up together with the pleasant life; they are

133) indivisible.[18] Can you think of anyone more moral than the person who has devout beliefs about the gods, who is consistently without fears about death, and who has pondered man's natural end? Or who realizes that the goal of the good life is easily gained and achieved and that the term of evil is brief, both in extent of time and duration of pain?[19] Or the man who laughs at the "decrees of Fate," a deity whom some people have set up as sovereign of all? * * * * *[20]

The good Epicurean believes that certain events occur deterministically, that others are chance events, and that still others are in our own hands. He sees also that necessity cannot be held morally responsible and that chance is an unpredictable thing, but that what is in our own hands, since it has no master, is naturally associated with blameworthiness and the opposite.[21] (Actually it would be better to subscribe (134 to the popular mythology than to become a slave by accepting the determinism of the natural philosophers, because popular religion underwrites the hope of supplicating the gods by offerings but determinism contains an element of necessity, which is inexorable.) As for chance, the Epicurean does not assume that it is a deity (as in popular belief)[22] because a god does nothing irregular; nor does he regard it as an unpredictable cause of all events. It is his belief that good and evil are not the chance contributions of a deity, donated to mankind for the happy life, but rather that the initial circumstances for great good and evil are sometimes provided by chance. He (135 thinks it preferable to have bad luck rationally than good luck irrationally. In other words, in human action it is better for a rational choice to be unsuccessful than for an irrational choice to succeed through the agency of chance.

Think about these and related matters day and night, by yourself and in company with someone like yourself. If you do, you will never experience anxiety, waking or sleeping, but you will live like a god among men. For a human being who lives in the midst of immortal blessings is in no way like mortal man!

Parallel Passages from Lucretius

I. It is not possible for you to believe that   L23 = the gods have their sacred seats in any quarter of   Men. the world; for the tenuous substance of deity is   123 far removed from human sense and is scarce visible to the mind's eye. Since it escapes the touch and thrust of the hand, it must then touch nothing that we can touch; for that which cannot be touched itself is unable to touch. Hence their abodes must also be unlike our abodes and as tenuous as their bodies—all of which I shall later expound in ample style. [5.146–55]

II. As soon as the voice of reason rises from your [Epicurus'] godlike mind to enunciate the nature of things, the terror in the soul dissolves, the walls of the world fall back, and I see what comes to pass throughout the void. The holy godheads are manifested, and their tranquil thrones; the winds do not buffet them or clouds bestrew them with storms, nor snow, clotted by piercing frost, profane them with falling hoar. An ever cloudless ether arches them over, smiling with its amplitude of light. Nature supplies all their wants, nor does anything vex their peace of mind at any season. [3.14–24]

L24 = Men. 123

Epicurus (and Lucretius after him) made a sharp distinction between his own idealizing theology and the vulgar forms of popular religion, all of which he regarded as erroneous and debasing to both gods and men. Chief among these misconceptions is the notion that the gods intervene constantly in the deterministic processes of nature and arbitrarily cause natural phenomena to occur. This kind of thinking is extremely bad in its effects on human happiness. It degrades the impassive majesty of the gods; it promotes a vulgar religion of fear, and fear is destructive of serenity and mental poise. It was, therefore, one of the chief social aims of Epicureanism to combat popular religion in all its forms and to substitute for it a theology that was ethically emancipating and elevating.

Those who have rightly learned that the gods
lead lives of unconcern may yet marvel at times
how things take place, particularly those occurrences that we observe overhead in the spaces of
heaven; and they may again lapse into the antique notions of religion by acknowledging gods
as the fierce lords of nature; and in their piteous
ignorance of what can and what cannot be they
may believe them omnipotent, not understanding the manner in which each thing's natural
power is hedged by a limit set deep within. . . .
Unless you cast such notions out of your mind
and cease altogether to think thoughts unbecoming to the gods and alien to their tranquillity, the
holy godheads which you have yourself impaired
may ofttimes work you harm—not that you
could profane the gods' high estate or that they
would wrathfully thirst for hot vengeance, but
that you in your own mind would picture these
serene beings, in their utter calm, rolling up
great tides of wrath against you and would come
to their shrines with unquiet heart and have neither strength nor peace of mind sufficient to receive those messengers of deity, the images that
flow from their holy bodies into the minds of
men. [6.58–78]

Another item in the Epicurean humanitarian program was to combat the fear of death and the afterlife, which in the troubled Hellenistic period
amounted to a mass phobia. Since "death means
nothing to us" because of the permanent breakup of
the atomic patterns of the soul at death, there can be
no possibility of future sensation or an afterlife of
any sort. The bizarre torments of the classical hell
(which are almost equal in ingenuity to the Christian)

L25 =
Men.
124

are physically nonexistent; they are explained by both Epicurus and Lucretius as mythological projections of the "hell on earth" that people create for themselves by their naïve religious fears, by their cravings for power, pleasure, excitement, etc. By demonstrating the meaninglessness of death and by exposing the psychological origins of the hell myths, the Epicureans attempted to cut at the roots of many types of human unhappiness and to apply mental therapy on a social scale to their own "age of anxiety."

I. If a man is perhaps to be wretched and in pain in the future, he must of course be existent at that time, if evil is to befall him. Now, since death does away with life and cancels the existence of everyone to whom such afflictions might accrue, we may infer that there is nothing in death for us to fear and that we cannot be wretched if we are nonexistent. In fact, when once the death that knows no death has done away with our mortal existence, it is no different than if we had never been born at all! [3.861–69]

No one desires himself or life at a time when mind and body are both at rest in slumber. As far as we are concerned, sleep could then be everlasting, since we have no feeling of wanting ourselves. And yet at the time a person starts out of his sleep and gathers himself together, the primal bodies scattered throughout his frame are by no means far distant from those movements that produce sensation. We should, therefore, consider that death means far less to us even than sleep, if there can be a quantity less than what we observe is nothing. For there ensues at death a greater turbulence and disbanding of matter than in sleep, and no one awakens or rises from his bed once the chill stoppage of life occurs. [3.919–30]

II. Assuredly all those torments that are reported to occur in the pit of hell are in our own lives. There is no unhappy Tantalus (as the story has it), benumbed with useless panic, who dreads the impending boulder from mid-air. Instead an inane fear of the gods besets mortal men in this life, and they dread the misfortune that chance may bring to each of them. No vultures bite into Tityos as he lies stretched out in Acheron, nor assuredly in an eternity of time can they find the food they are looking for in his cavernous chest. . . . Instead Tityos is here among us—the lovesick man whom the harpies tear to bits, the person fretted by carking care or rent by some other lust. Sisyphus also moves before our very eyes in life—the person who thirsts for the emblems of office, the fasces and dire axes, at the hands of the people and always retires from the contest disconsolate and beaten. To seek abortive power that is never granted and to endure unceasing hardship is so doing, this is like Sisyphus sweating to shove the stone uphill. At the very top it again rolls back and speedily descends to the level floor of the fields below. Then again, to be always feeding the good things of life to a jade and never be able to satisfy the ingrate, . . . this is like the story they tell about the Danaides, those virgins in the prime of their youth who keep pouring water into a perforated vessel which they are never able to fill. [3.978–1010]

The judgment that "death means nothing to us" is one of the most basic teachings in Epicureanism. The new convert who has accepted this teaching

L26 = Men. 125

with all its implications has undergone mental therapy that may revolutionize his whole attitude toward life and what is really valuable in living. He is now ready for the positive or constructive doctrines of Epicureanism, viz., that the moral good is pleasure (properly interpreted) and moral evil is pain. With an almost neurotic zeal to prove this point, Lucretius adduces more than twenty-five arguments, covering some four hundred lines (3.425–829), to show that the soul is just as mortal as the body. These arguments are not all of equal worth or weight. One of the better ones starts with the naturalistic assumption that body and soul are not two mutually exclusive entities but together form an organic unit, and then proceeds to give psychosomatic evidence that changes in the body are accompanied by changes in the soul and vice versa. The conclusion to be drawn from this evidence is that neither body nor soul can survive the atomic disruption of organic functions that we call death.

We observe furthermore that the mind comes into being at the same time as the body, grows along with the body, and becomes senile at the same time as the body. Thus the wavering steps that young children take with their weak bodies are accompanied by slender powers of judgment. And when they mature to their full physical strength, their discretion is likewise greater and their powers of mind increased. Finally, after the body has been assailed by the heavy onslaught of time and the frame has given way and its powers have been blunted, then the intelligence begins to lag, the tongue babbles, the mind slips. Everything fails and is found wanting at one and the same time. Thus it is natural that the soul's being should be wholly annulled, like smoke, in the winds of high heaven, since we see that it comes into being and grows along with the body and, as I have shown, grows faint and flaccid at the same time as the aging body.

We observe, in addition, that just as the body undergoes frightful diseases and brutal pain, the mind suffers its own fierce anxieties, its grief and dread; and hence it is natural that it too should share in extinction. Furthermore, when the body is diseased, the mind oftentimes wanders far afield. It becomes deranged and speaks deliriously, and sometimes in deep coma it plunges into an everlasting sleep, head and eyelids drooping, in which it can neither hear the voices nor recognize the faces of those who stand round about, their lips and cheeks bedewed with tears—those who would summon it back to life. Since the taints of disease penetrate the mind, you must concede that it too is subject to annihilation. For mental suffering and bodily sickness are each of them architects of death, as we have learned from the demise of many heretofore. [3.445–73]

The doctrine that pleasure is the highest ethical good lends itself to immediate misunderstanding because of the unfortunate ambiguity of the key term "pleasure." The Epicureans were purposely misrepresented as sensualists and "high livers" by their philosophical rivals and later by the Christian Fathers. Actually they were rather ascetic and even puritanical both in teaching and in practice, and this fact is borne in on anyone who reads the surviving Epicurean texts sympathetically. Epicurus regarded pleasure and pain as the two fundamental facts of human psychology that can serve as the basis for a

L27 = Men. 129

naturalistic theory of the good life. He interpreted *pleasure* as the logical opposite of *pain*; in other words, for him *pleasure* meant *non-pain* or the (relative) absence of pain in mind and body. The good life, therefore, is not at all one of sensual enjoyments, excitement, competition, social prestige, and monetary success (the ingredients of the American way of life, as popularly understood and practiced). The good life for the Epicurean involved disciplining of the appetites, curtailment of desires and needs to the absolute minimum necessary for healthy living, detachment from most of the goals and values that are most highly regarded, and withdrawal from active participation in the life of the community, in the company of a few select friends—in a word, plain living and high thinking. The good Epicurean, like Epicurus himself, lived on a high plateau of serenity with no emotional peaks of sensuality or excitement and no valleys of depression. From this vantage point he could look out with understanding on the universe at large. He could also look down on ordinary mortals with disdain and pity, and congratulate himself that he was not as other men.

When the winds are roiling the plains of the great sea, it is pleasant to view the massive exertions of others from the land, not because you take delight or joy in another's troubles but because it is good to see the evils you yourself are free from. It is likewise pleasant to watch mighty hosts in full panoply warring on the field of battle when your own life is not in jeopardy. But nothing is more gratifying than to occupy a calm and lofty eminence that is fully fortified by the teachings of the sages. From here you may look down on other men as they rove about and search hither and yon for a way of life; from here you may watch them fighting it out with their wits, disputing over prestige, and working day and night with consummate effort to get to the top of the heap and become lords and masters.

How unhappy are the lives of men! How purblind their hearts! In what black ignorance and dark peril their small lives are spent! They do not see how little Nature cries out for. She demands only the secession of pain from the body; she requires only that the mind be secluded from anxiety and dread and enjoy feelings of pleasure. We see, then, that few things, all told, are necessary for the body's well-being—in fact, only those that shut out pain. It may be gratifying at times to have luxuries strewn at our feet, but Nature does not demand them. Nor does she take it amiss if there are no golden statues of young men in your house supporting flambeaux in their hands to provide illumination for the feastings of the night, nor is she concerned if your house does not gleam with silver and flash with gold and if there are no paneled and gilded ceilings re-echoing to the lute. Nature is not concerned about these things when people may together recline on the soft grass beneath the branches of a tall tree near a stream of water and joyously care for their bodily wants at no great expense. . . . Thus since riches, noble lineage, and the prestige of power in no way profit the body of a man, we may surmise that they profit his mind no more. [2.1–39]

After a highly circumstantial and sensual account of sexual passion and copulation Lucretius renders the expected Epicurean verdict: Sex is a kind of

L28 = Men. 132

madness or chronic illness, especially where there is
a consuming attachment to one object, whether boy,
man, or woman. It may culminate in an ecstasy of
pleasure, but such pleasure is an extreme of irra-
tionality and a far cry indeed from the spiritual
composure demanded by Epicurus. The moral of all
this is clear: Avoid sex altogether or, if this is impossible, diversify your interests, avoiding all entangling
alliances, whether homosexual or heterosexual.

A man who has felt the stab of Venus' shafts,
whether he be smitten by a boy with woman's
limbs or by a woman whose whole body exudes
lust, makes for the source of his wounding,
yearning to have union, to draw his sperm and
cast it from body into body. The muteness of his
passion foretells the joy to come.

This is what we mean by Venus; this is the
source of the word "love," the source whence
drops of Venus' sweets are first distilled in the
human heart; succeeded soon by woes that chill.
The object of your love may be distant; yet its
image is ready to hand, and the lovely name
hovers at your ear. It is well to eschew such images and to be rid of the pabulum of love. Turn
your thoughts elsewhere; inject the sperm gar-
nered for one into all and sundry without re-
straint. By setting your heart once and for all on
a single passion you lay up woes for yourself
and certain grief. Love's ulcer grows with feeding and becomes inveterate. The madness swells
from day to day. The distress worsens unless you
rout the first assault by new sallies, unless you
cure the fresh wound by riding some whore or
divert elsewhere the motions of the mind.

He who shuns a single love is not without the

fruits of venery; rather he gathers bounties that are without pain and penalty, for assuredly the sane have a more exquisite pleasure from this than the demented. Even at the moment of coition the heat of lovers fluctuates in an uncertain tide, nor are they sure what eye and hand shall first enjoy. Whatever they crave they closely press and put the body in pain; and oftentimes their teeth lash the lips with kisses that come like blows—this because their pleasure is impure. There are latent spurs that bid them harm the very thing, whatever it may be, that begets the germs of frenzy. [4.1052–83] . . .

A thirsty man in a dream may crave to drink, and when no liquid is forthcoming to quench the pangs in his flesh, he seeks instead an imaged water and vainly struggles with his thirst though drinking in the midst of a rushing stream. So it is in love. Venus tricks her lovers with fantasies, and they are unable to sate themselves even by gazing full face on each other, nor can they rub aught from the young flesh as their hands wander deviously over their bodies. Finally, when they taste the vintage of youth with limbs conjoined and their bodies foretell the bliss to come, and it is the moment when Venus seeds the fields of woman, flesh fastens avidly on flesh, tongue lubricates tongue, and they breathe kisses with teeth pressed hard upon the lips—but all to no avail, for they are unable to rub aught away, unable to enter in and wholly fuse, body with body. This, it seems, is often their aim and will, so hotly do they cling together in the jointure of love, whilst bodies quiver and melt from pleasure's power. At length, after the mass of lust has erupted in the sinews, there comes a brief pause in passion's furious heat. But only for a little while, for then the same frenzy returns and madness possesses them once more. In their search to find what it is they really want to achieve they are unable to discover any agent to subdue their sickness; they languish from the wound within, forever confused. [4.1097–1120]

Leading Doctrines[1]

1–5: Five Fundamental Teachings Bearing on the Good Life.

1. The blessed and indestructible being of the divine has no concerns of its own, nor does it make trouble for others. It is not affected by feelings of anger or benevolence, because these are found where there is lack of strength.[2]

2. Death means nothing to us, because that which has been broken down into atoms has no sensation and that which has no sensation is no concern of ours.[3]

3. The quantitative limit of pleasure is the elimination of all feelings of pain. Wherever the pleasurable state exists, there is neither bodily pain nor mental pain nor both together, so long as the state continues.[4]

4. Bodily pain does not last continuously. The peak is present for a very brief period, and pains that barely exceed the state of bodily pleasure do not continue for many days. On the other hand, protracted illnesses show a balance of bodily pleasure over pain.

5. It is impossible to live the pleasant life without also living sensibly, nobly, and justly, and conversely it is impossible to live sensibly, nobly, and justly without living pleasantly. A person who does not have a pleasant life is not living sensibly, nobly, and justly, and conversely the person who does not have these virtues cannot live pleasantly.[5]

6–7: Personal Security and the Good Life.[6]

6. Any means by which it is possible to procure freedom from fearing other men is a natural good.

7. Some men have desired to gain reputation and to be well regarded, thinking in this way to gain protection from other people. If the lives of such men are secure, they have acquired a natural blessing; but if they are not, they do not possess what they originally reached for by natural instinct.

8–9: How to Choose Pleasures.

8. No pleasure is bad in itself. But the things that make for pleasure in certain cases entail disturbances many times greater than the pleasures themselves.[7]

9. If all pleasures could be compressed in time and intensity, and were characteristic of the whole man or his more important aspects, the various pleasures would not differ from each other.[8]

10–13: The Good Life Is Dependent on Science.[9]

10. If the things that produce the debauchee's pleasures dissolved the mind's fears regarding the heavenly bodies, death, and pain and also told us how to limit our desires, we would never have any reason to find fault with such people, because they would be glutting themselves with every sort of pleasure and never suffer physical or mental pain, which is the real evil.

11. We would have no need for natural science unless we were worried by apprehensiveness regarding the heavenly bodies, by anxiety about the meaning of death, and also by our failure to understand the limitations of pain and desire.[10]

12. It is impossible to get rid of our anxieties about essentials if we do not understand the nature of the universe

and are apprehensive about some of the theological accounts. Hence it is impossible to enjoy our pleasures
unadulterated without natural science.[11]

13. There is no advantage in gaining security with regard
to other people if phenomena occurring above and beneath the earth—in a word, everything in the infinite
universe—are objects of anxiety.

14: Withdrawal into Obscurity Is the Best Form of Security.[12]

14. The simplest means of procuring protection from other
men (which is gained to a certain extent by deterrent
force) is the security of quiet solitude and withdrawal
from the mass of people.

15: Wealth, Natural and Unnatural.

15. Nature's wealth is restricted and easily won, while that
of empty convention runs on to infinity.[13]

16: Luck vs. Reason in the Good Life.

16. Bad luck strikes the sophisticated man in a few cases,
but reason has directed the big, essential things, and for
the duration of life it is and will be the guide.[14]

17: Justice and Mental Health.

17. The just man is the least disturbed by passion, the unjust man the most highly disturbed.[15]

18–21: The Limits of True Pleasure.

18. Bodily pleasure is not enlarged once the pains brought
on by need have been done away with; it is only diver-

sified. And the limit of mental pleasure is established by rational reflection on pleasures themselves and those kindred emotions that once instilled extreme fear in human minds.[16]

19. Infinite time contains no greater pleasure than does finite time, if one determines the limits of pleasure rationally.[17]

20. The body takes the limits of pleasure to be infinite, and infinite time would provide such pleasure. But the mind has provided us with the complete life by a rational examination of the body's goal and limitations and by dispelling our fears about a life after death; and so we no longer need unlimited time. On the other hand, it does not avoid pleasure, nor, when conditions occasion our departure from life, does it come to the end in a manner that would suggest that it had fallen short in any way of the best possible existence.[18]

21. One who understands the limits of the good life knows that what eliminates the pains brought on by need and what makes the whole of life perfect is easily obtained, so that there is no need for enterprises that entail the struggle for success.[19]

22–25: Empirical Considerations.

22. It is necessary to take into account both the actual goal of life and the whole body of clear and distinct percepts to which we refer our judgments. If we fail to do this, everything will be in disorder and confusion.[20]

23. If you reject all sensations, you will not have any point of reference by which to judge even the ones you claim are false.[21]

24. If you summarily rule out any single sensation and do not make a distinction between the element of belief that is superimposed on a percept that awaits verification and what is actually present in sensation or in the

feelings or some percept of the mind itself, you will cast
doubt on all other sensations by your unfounded interpretation and consequently abandon all the criteria of
truth. On the other hand, in cases of interpreted data, if
you accept as true those that need verification as well
as those that do not, you will still be in error, since the
whole question at issue in every judgment of what is
true or not true will be left intact.[22]

25. If at any time you fail to refer each of your acts to nature's standard, and turn off instead in some other direction when making a choice to avoid or pursue, your
actions will not be consistent with your creed.[23]

26, 29, 30: Classification of Human Desires.

29. Some desires are (1) natural and necessary, others (2)
natural but not necessary, still others (3) neither natural
nor necessary but generated by senseless whims.[24]

26. All desires that do not lead to physical pain if not satisfied are unnecessary, and involve cravings that are easily
resolved when they appear to entail harm or when the
object of desire is hard to get.[25]

30. If interest is intense in the case of those natural desires
that do not lead to physical pain when they are not satisfied, then such desires are generated by idle fancy, and
it is not because of their own nature that they are not
dissipated but because of the person's own senseless
whims.[26]

27–28: Friendship.[27]

27. Of all the things that wisdom provides for the happiness of the whole man, by far the most important is the
acquisition of friendship.

28. It is the same judgment that has made us feel confident
that nothing fearful is of long duration or everlasting,

and that has seen personal security during our limited span of life most nearly perfected by friendship.

31–38: Justice and Injustice.[28]

31. The justice that seeks nature's goal is a utilitarian pledge of men not to harm each other or be harmed.[29]

32. Nothing is either just or unjust in the eyes of those animals that have been unable to make agreements not to harm each other or be harmed. The same is true of those peoples who are unable or unwilling to make covenants not to harm or be harmed.[30]

33. Justice was never an entity in itself. It is a kind of agreement not to harm or be harmed, made when men associate with each other at any time and in communities of any size whatsoever.[31]

34. Injustice is not an evil in itself. Its evil lies in the anxious fear that you will not elude those who have authority to punish such misdeeds.[32]

35. It is impossible for a person who underhandedly breaks the agreement not to harm or be harmed to feel sure that he will escape punishment, even though he manages to do so time after time; for up to the very end of his life he cannot be sure that he will actually escape.

36. In its general meaning, justice is the same for all because of its utility in the relations of men to each other, but in its specific application to countries and various other circumstances it does not follow that the same thing is just for all.[33]

37. In the case of actions that are legally regarded as just, those that are of tested utility in meeting the needs of human society have the hallmark of justice, whether they turn out to be equally just in all cases or not. On the other hand, if somebody lays down a law and it does not prove to be of advantage in human relations, then such a law no longer has the true character of jus-

tice. And even if the element of utility should undergo a change after harmonizing for a time with the conception of justice, the law was still just during that period, in the judgment of those who are not confused by meaningless words but who look at the actualities.[34]

38. In cases where the surrounding conditions are not new and where laws regarded as just have been shown to be inconsistent with the conception of justice in their actual workings, such laws are unjust. Again, in cases where the circumstances are new and where the same laws, once deemed to be just, are no longer serviceable, the laws in this case were just as long as they were useful to the community of citizens, but later when they were no longer useful they became unjust.

39–40: The Sectarian Spirit and Life.

39. The person who is the most successful in controlling the disturbing elements that come from the outside world has assimilated to himself what he could, and what he could not assimilate he has at least not alienated. Where he could not do even this, he has dissociated himself or eliminated all that it was expedient to treat in this way.[35]

40. All who have the capacity to gain security, especially from those who live around them, live a most agreeable life together, since they have the firm assurance of friendship; and after enjoying their comradeship to the full they do not bewail the early demise of a departed friend as if it were a pitiable thing.[36]

The Vatican Collection of Aphorisms[1]

4. All pain is readily discounted. Intense pain has a short life, and longer lasting bodily pain is weak.[2]
9. Necessity is bad, but there is no necessity to live under necessity.[3]
11. For most people leisure is stupor, and activity frenzy.
14. We are born once. We cannot be born a second time, and throughout eternity we shall of necessity no longer exist. You have no power over the morrow, and yet you put off your pleasure. Life is ruined by procrastination, and every one of us dies deep in his affairs.[4]
18. If you subtract seeing, social contact, and sexual intercourse, the erotic passion dissolves.[5]
23. Every friendship is desirable for itself, but it has its origin in personal advantage.
24. Dreams have neither divine character nor prophetic power but are generated by the influx of atomic images.[6]
25. Poverty, when measured by the goals that nature has set, is great wealth, whereas unlimited wealth is great poverty.[7]
29. When discoursing on nature I personally should prefer to speak oracularly, even though no one were likely to listen, and candidly utter truths that are beneficial to all men, rather than acquiesce in conventional opinion and reap a fat harvest of popular plaudits.
31. It is possible to get protection against other things, but when it comes to death, all of us human beings live in a city without walls.
34. It is not so much friends' services that we find serviceable as the assurance of their services.

37. As regards evil, human nature is feeble—not as regards good; for we are protected by pleasure but destroyed by pain.[8]

38. The person who has a number of good reasons for making his exit from life is puny indeed.

40. The person who says that everything happens necessarily cannot criticize the person who says that things do not happen necessarily; for he has to admit that this too is a necessary happening![9]

41. We must laugh and philosophize and manage our households and look after our other affairs all at the same time, and never stop proclaiming the words of the true philosophy.

44. The wise man, after adjusting himself to the bare necessities of life, understands better how to share than to take—so large is the fund of self-sufficiency that he has discovered.

45. The study of nature does not cause men to give out big words and boasts or to show off those accomplishments that the public fights over; it makes them disdainful and independent, puffed up over their own good qualities rather than the worth of their possessions.[10]

48. We must try to make the latter part of the journey better than the first, so long as we are en route; and when we reach the end, we must keep an even keel and remain cheerful.

51. I learn from your letter that carnal disturbances make you excessively inclined to sexual intercourse. Well, so long as you do not break any laws or disturb well-established conventions or annoy any of your neighbors or wear down your body or use up your funds, you may carry out your own plans as you like. However, it is impossible not to be affected by at least one of these things. Sex never benefited any man, and it's a marvel if it hasn't injured him!

52. Friendship dances round the world, summoning every one of us to awaken to the gospel of the happy life.[11]

53. We should envy no man. The good are undeserving of envy; as for the bad, the more successful they are, the more they mutilate themselves.

58. We must get out of the prison house of routine duties and politics.

59. It is not the belly that cannot be satisfied, as people believe, but the false belief about the belly's having unlimited capacity.

60. Every man departs this life as though he had just been born.[12]

64. Approval on the part of others must come voluntarily; it is our business to get on with our own self-therapy.[13]

65. It is senseless to ask the gods for what a man is able to provide for himself.

66. Let us show our sympathy for our departed friends not by mourning them but by taking thought.

67. A free man cannot acquire many possessions, because this is no easy feat without becoming a hireling of mobs or dynasts. And yet he has a constant abundance of everything, and if he should chance to gain many possessions, he could easily portion them out so as to win his neighbors' good will.

68. Nothing is sufficient for the person who finds sufficiency too little.

71. We must put the following question to each of our desires: What will happen to me if the object of my desire is achieved? What will happen if it is not?[14]

77. The most important consequence of self-sufficiency is freedom.

79. The impassive soul disturbs neither itself nor others.

81. Spiritual disorder cannot be resolved—or joy worthy of the name produced—by wealth however great, by popular acclaim and respect, or by anything that causes unrestrained desire.

Abbreviations

Herod. = *Letter to Herodotus*

L.D. = *Leading Doctrines*

Lucr. = *Lucretius, De Rerum Natura (On Nature)*

Men. = *Letter to Menoeceus*

Pyth. = *Letter to Pythocles*

V.C. = *The Vatican Collection of Aphorisms*

L1, L2, etc., refer to parallel passages of Lucretius.

NOTES

Introduction

1. In this short historical sketch I am indebted to two excellent secondary sources both for data relative to the history of ideas and for quotations from the pre-Socratics: B. A. G. Fuller, *A History of Philosophy*, 3rd ed., revised by Sterling M. McMurrin (New York, Henry Holt & Co., 1955), and W. T. Jones, *A History of Western Philosophy* (New York, Harcourt, Brace & Co., 1952).

2. A later follower of Parmenides got him out of this logical predicament by postulating the real as nonspherical and infinite in extent.

3. For all his insistence on logic Parmenides seems to be guilty of a breach of logic in his first and all-important premise that nothingness is nonexistent. It is certainly true that when we think of nothingness we think something, i.e., a concept called "nothing." In other words, according to Parmenides, to think "nothing" is to think a contradiction, and since a contradiction represents an unreal situation, "nothing" must be unreal, or nonexistent. The semanticist today would point out that Parmenides is here confusing the *meaning* of "nothing" with its *referent* in nature. To think "nothing" is to think of a meaning with a definite positive content and does not involve a contradiction, because the meaning of the term is quite different from the natural state to which it refers. As we shall see, the assertion of the real existence of nothingness in the form of empty space was one of the revolutionary departures from Parmenidean logic made by the atomists.

4. The word "atom" itself in Greek means "indivisible," "irreducible."

5. There are a number of good laymen's accounts to be had—for

example, Fritz Kahn, *Design of the Universe* (New York, Crown Publishers, Inc., 1954), especially pp. 51–127. Also Lancelot Whyte, *Essay on Atomism: From Democritus to 1960* (London, Thomas Nelson & Sons, 1961).

6. *Herod.* 38; cf. Lucr. 1.146–73 (=L1).

7. *Herod.* 39; cf. Lucr. 1.232–37: "Infinite time and a day long past must necessarily have consumed all that is of mortal frame; but if in that span of time long past there have existed bodies out of which this universe of things is made new and now consists, such things of a certainty are gifted with a deathless substance. Hence no thing can revert to nothingness."

8. *Herod.* 39.

9. *Herod.* 41. All that remains of the ancient atomic theory today are the terms "atoms" and "particles"; in all other respects Epicurus' description is completely wrong. The atom is not solid, it is not irreducible or immutable, and it is decomposable. Even the conception of "corporeality," or matter, is radically different today; see note 5 above. However, it is worth noting from a purely historical point of view that the indivisibility of the atom was firmly accepted in nineteenth- and early twentieth-century physics. By the 1930s the atom was pictured as a relatively simple structure, something like a miniature solar system, in which electrons moved in orbits around a central nucleus composed of protons and neutrons. But this simplicity of structure has been radically changed by the advanced techniques and refined instruments that have been developed more recently. Today the atom could more accurately be pictured as a jungle of elementary particles, some forty of which have so far been discovered, and the expectation is that still more remain to be discovered.

10. *Herod.* 39; cf. Lucr. 1.265–328.

11. *Herod.* 39–40. The student should note that the existence of empty space is proved indirectly by an argument called the *reductio ad absurdum* (which is also a great favorite of Lucretius). This consists in assuming the truth of *the opposite* of the proposition you wish to prove and then showing that this leads to an absurdity. Given a pair of contradictories (e.g., here, "space either exists or does not exist"), if one is shown

to be absurd or false, the other is necessarily true. By assuming hypothetically that space is nonexistent, two absurdities follow: "Bodies would not have anywhere to exist, nor would they have a medium through which to move." Since bodies obviously do have a place to exist and do move, Epicurus has indirectly proved the desired proposition: "Space exists."

In this connection it is noteworthy that Epicurus makes no mention of time, which conceivably might be a third basic entity in the system of the universe. See *Herod.* 72–73 for his (rather unsatisfactory) treatment of time, and note 20 to that letter.

12. See 1.503 ff.

13. *Herod.* 41.

14. *Herod.* 42. Note the use of the *reductio ad absurdum* (note 11, above).

15. *Herod.* 45. As we see from *Pyth.* 88–90 the general assumption made by the Epicureans was that each of these infinite worlds is geocentric, with a sun, moon, and stars. This, even in the absence of adequate observational techniques, would seem to indicate an excessive and uncritical reliance on analogy. A wide variety of shapes is allowed. Some worlds are spherical, others oval, others triangular, etc. "All these possibilities exist, inasmuch as they are not contradicted by any phenomenon in our own world." The atomic generation of any such world is described in some detail in *Pyth.* 89.

16. See *Herod.* 43.

17. See *Herod.* 62.

18. See *Herod.* 47b.

19. *Herod.* 62.

20. Epicurus, if pressed, might have evaded this difficulty by a technical rejoinder: The sensed motion of any compound is an *accident* (i.e., nonessential characteristic) of a particular collection of atoms, just as color, shape, and size are *properties* (i.e., essential characteristics) of all atomic aggregates (*Herod.* 68–71). "We should not deny existence to these clear and distinct phenomena on the ground that they do not have the nature of the whole object of which they are accidents or the nature of permanent properties. Nor, on the other hand,

should we regard them as things in themselves, because this is unthinkable in the case of both accidents and permanent properties. On the contrary, we should think of them . . . as what perception itself shows their peculiar nature to be." (*Herod.* 71) This quotation grants a kind of existence to accidents such as sensed motion, but it does not tell us explicitly whether this existence is as real as that of atoms and void. "Things in themselves" does not refer to atoms and void but to supposed metaphysical entities such as motion *per se*, color *per se*, etc. Democritus, on the other hand, took the strict view: "In reality there are atoms and void. That is, the objects of sense are supposed to be real, and it is customary to regard them as such, but in truth they are not. Only the atoms and the void are real." (Frag. o; from Charles M. Bakewell, *Source Book in Ancient Philosophy*; New York, Scribner's, 1907).

21. See *Herod.* 61.
22. For the complete context, see Lucr. 2.251–93 (=L3, part II).
23. The good name of Democritus should be protected from these criticisms. He was a complete determinist in both physics and ethics, which is much to his credit today, although not in ancient times. Most ancient philosophers upheld moral freedom in one sense or another and attempted to make man a partial exception to the natural order of "necessity." Today the doctrine of metaphysical free will appears to us as one of those archaic relics of traditional religion that Epicurus and Lucretius should have done their utmost to combat. Moral freedom and determinism are by no means incompatible. Man is himself a causal agent in nature and is morally responsible when he acts "freely," i.e., from his own settled character and in his own capacity as an individual, *provided he is exempt from external force or pressure*. His settled character may be partially determined by inherited psychological traits and by environmental influences, but as a causal agent in his own right he has some capacity to alter himself in one direction or another. In general the modern tendency is to regard moral freedom not as freedom from determinism but as freedom from coercion (such as physical force and the various pressures exerted by governments, corporations, and society itself).

24. *Herod.* 63–64.
25. See note 20, above.
26. *Herod.* 65–66.
27. On the nullity of death and hell, see Lucr. 3.445–73, 3.861–69, 919–30, 978–1010 (=*Men.* L25 and L26).
28. *Herod.* 49–50. Note that certain images may bypass the senses and enter the mind directly. This occurs when we dream or when we contemplate the divine beings whom we can never perceive with any of the senses. We may dream, for example, of a dead friend, and see and talk to him. In such a case the images are not fallacious; they are free-floating films that have persisted from times when the friend was still living. Cf. Lucr. 4.757–76.
29. "The fact of sensation itself universally attests that there are bodies, and it is by reference to sensation that we must rationally infer the existence of imperceptible bodies," or atoms (*Herod.* 39).
30. *Herod.* 51.
31. *Herod.* 50.
32. Cf. Lucr. 4.482–85: "What should we consider as having greater validity than sensation? Will reasoning that takes its rise from 'false' sensation have power to contradict the senses when it originates wholly from them? If they are not true, all reasoning likewise becomes false." Lucretius devotes a long passage (4.379–521) to the infallibility of the senses and the false inferences we draw from sensory data. The example of the round tower was suggested by Lucr. 4.353 ff.
33. *L.D.* 24.
34. This whole development, both religious and philosophical, is beautifully sketched out by Gilbert Murray in his *Five Stages of Greek Religion* (New York, Columbia University Press, 1925); see especially Chap. III and IV, "The Great Schools" and "The Failure of Nerve." Many centuries later Kant was equally alarmed by contemporary eighteenth-century developments, especially the devastating skepticism of Hume, and took the appropriate dogmatic steps to rehabilitate the validity of scientific knowledge.
35. *Pyth.* 85.

36. *Herod.* 78.
37. Especially by Professor DeWitt in his recent important study of Epicurus; see Norman W. DeWitt, *Epicurus and His Philosophy* (Minneapolis, University of Minnesota Press, 1954), pp. 7, 26, and elsewhere. See notes 27 and 29 to Diogenes Laertius' *Life of Epicurus* for a fuller treatment of his objections.
38. *Herod.* 38; cf. also *Herod.* 82, where "our immediate feelings and sensations" and "our existing clear and distinct perceptions" are listed as definitive criteria.
39. See the important quotation on this point from *L.D.* 24, given in full in IV. 4, above.
40. Cf. also Lucr. 1.423–25: "Unless there is a fundamental and persistent faith in the sensations we have in common, there will be nothing to which we can resort when we attempt a rational demonstration of difficult questions."
41. *Pyth.* 96.
42. *Men.* 123.
43. Diogenes Laertius, *Life of Epicurus* 32 and 33. Cf. also Lucr. 4.478–79, "You will find that the concept of truth arose first from the senses and that the senses cannot be refuted." For Professor DeWitt's antiempirical views see notes 27 and 29 to the *Life of Epicurus*.
44. *Herod.* 46a.
45. *Pyth.* 92.
46. See *Pyth.* 90 and Lucr. 2.1118–45 (=L18).
47. *Herod.* 80. Cf. also *Pyth.* 87: "From terrestrial phenomena it is possible to derive certain indications of what takes place in the heavenly bodies. It can be observed how the former occur but not how celestial phenomena occur, because it is possible for the latter to happen from a variety of causes." Analogy was also used to draw inferences about the subempirical. Epicurus' atoms "fall" through infinite space by analogy to falling bodies on earth, and in *Herod.* 59 inferences are drawn concerning the minimal parts of the atom by analogy to "perceptual minima," i.e., the smallest points that can be seen by the naked eye.

Lucretius abounds in analogies, some prosaic and commonplace, others poetic or merely decorative. For example in

2.317 ff. we have the beautiful picture of sheep grazing on a distant hillside. They appear as a stationary blur but are actually in motion. In the same way the atomic configurations we call things may be at rest as gross objects while their component atoms are all in motion.

48. See, e.g., *Pyth.* 99–115 on the multiple causes of clouds, rain, thunder, lightning, cyclones, earthquakes, falling stars, the rainbow, etc.

49. It should be noted that causation always remained an unanalyzed metaphysical postulate with the ancient materialists and never underwent the stringent examination that it later received at the hands of thoroughgoing empiricists such as Hume. It must have seemed completely obvious to Democritus, Epicurus, and Lucretius that any causal sequence (e.g., lightning striking a dead tree and immediately setting it on fire) could successfully be explained in terms of atomic movements and impacts and that no closer inspection of so "natural" a process was needed. But this common-sense assumption was far from obvious to Hume, who insisted on viewing causation not in terms of unperceived (and therefore nonempirical) atoms but strictly in terms of observed experiences. According to Hume any causal sequence (such as a burning candle giving out light and warmth) is to be analyzed into two separate events, A and B, which are always observed "in constant conjunction." What we always *fail* to observe, however, is the transfer of causal energy or force from A to B, with the result that, *empirically* speaking, we never find ourselves in the position where we can say that there is a "necessary connection" between A and B, such that A is the "cause" of B. If these two events are actually separate and disconnected, and if we are not justified in saying that one is the cause and the other the effect, how do we happen to have the firm belief that they are causally (i.e., necessarily) connected? Hume explains our belief in psychological terms: A and B are vividly associated as mental impressions on every occurrence, and the "habit" or "custom" of always experiencing them together unconsciously gives rise to the belief that they are necessarily connected. Thus Hume demolishes causality as a "natural"

and necessary connection between events, and allows it only a kind of shadow existence as an illegitimate inference from "habit." His analysis would probably have been rejected as fantastic or oversubtle by a thinker such as Epicurus, but this only serves to point up the vast difference between an open, analytical empiricism and a doctrinaire empiricism that had hardened into dogmatism in the struggle with the competing epistemologies of Platonism and Skepticism.

Far from undermining the possibility of science, as Kant and others feared, Hume's analysis lends itself today quite readily to the current phenomenological conception of causation as statistical probability. Events A and B, now shorn of the psychological interpretation given them by Hume, are viewed as causally connected or "correlated" according to the statistical regularity with which they are observed to occur together, and to that extent they provide a basis for scientific predictions having either high or low probability.

50. The Epicureans stoutly defended the feelings of pleasure and pain as the sole criteria of good and evil in the moral sphere, against all other competing standards such as reason, duty, convention, and so on. This criterion is quite consistent with the "one cause" atomic principle they used in their physics and metaphysics, since the feelings are themselves atomic aggregates.

51. *Pyth.* 86 and 94.

52. See *Herod.* 46a–53 (perception), 54–55 (natural change), 63–68 (the soul and sensation), 73–74 (other worlds). On the atomic genesis of worlds, see also *Pyth.* 89–90, where other theories are discarded as inadequate.

53. Cf. *Herod.* 76: "We should not regard the courses and revolutions of the heavenly bodies—their eclipses, risings and settings, and the like—as the operations of some deity who dutifully performs these functions, who decrees or did decree them, and who simultaneously enjoys absolute blessedness as well as immortality."

54. See *Pyth.* 93, 94, 97, 98, and 113.

55. It should be noted that on occasion they defended multiple causation on the ground that the phenomena were remote and

their causes "imperceptible," and that it was better to have a number of theories regarding a given event (say a solar eclipse), provided these were all "probable," than to use the stereotyped theological explanation. See, e.g., *Pyth.* 87. As regards scientific knowledge of the heavens, the Epicureans were in much the same primitive stage of development as we are today in understanding UFO's, the Unidentified Flying Objects whose real existence now seems undeniable despite consistent attempts by the U.S. Air Force to suppress all information relating to them. In his latest crusading ("tell the American people all") book on UFO's, Major Keyhoe relates the following:

> It had swung around, was drawing abreast, pacing them at about one hundred yards. For a moment he had a clear glimpse of the monster.
> Its sheer bulk was amazing; its diameter was three to four times the Constellation's wing span. At least thirty feet thick at the center, it was like a gigantic dish inverted on top of another. Seen at this distance, the glow along the rim was blurred and uneven. *Whether it was an electrical effect, a series of jet exhausts, or light from openings in the rim,* Benton could not tell. But the glow was bright enough to show the disc's curving surface, giving a hint of dully reflecting metal. (Italics mine. See Major Donald E. Keyhoe, *Flying Saucers: Top Secret*; New York, G. P. Putnam's Sons, 1960, p. 18).

The italicized words in this passage show that our present stage of ignorance is just as likely to breed multiple theories as it was in the case of the Epicureans.

56. See *Pyth.* 100 (thunder), 101 (lightning), 105 (earthquakes), 107 (snow), 109 (rainbow), and 111 (comets).
57. *Pyth.* 93 and 97.
58. *Men.* 123.
59. See V.2.b, above, on direct perceptions of the mind.
60. See Lucr. 5.156–234 for reasons why the gods did not create the world.
61. *Herod.* 76–77; Lucr. 6.58–78.

62. In 5.195–234 he cites various imperfections of the world as evidence that it could not have been created by perfect beings.

63. See, e.g., *Herod.* 77 and 80; *Men.* 123–24; *Pyth.* 93, 94, 97, 104, 113, 114, 115–16.

64. Iphigenia was brought to Aulis, a seaport of Boeotia, on the pretext that she was to be married to Achilles. Instead she was forced to become a human sacrifice in order to procure favorable winds for the Greek fleet, which was setting out from Aulis against Troy. Her own father, Agamemnon, was the hatchet man at the altar. This legendary event is of course intended to be typical of the thousands of barbarous acts committed throughout history in the name of religion—killings, poisonings, burnings at the stake, holy wars, exterminations of whole populations, and so on—a shocking list of sanctified crimes. *Tantum religio potuit suadere malorum!*

65. For Lucretius' account of the torments of hell interpreted as mythological projections of present woes and frustrations, see 3.978–1010 (=*Men.* L25: "Assuredly all those torments that are reported to occur in the pit of hell are in our own lives," etc.).

66. A difficult term to define precisely, but roughly equivalent to the traditional institutional religion or religions of a given country such as India (which has seven major religions), Britain (which has an established Church and various nonconformist sects), or the United States (which has a plurality of more than two hundred sects). Popular religion is emphatically *not* the religion of the philosophers (Aristotle, Leibniz, Spinoza, etc.) or the humanists (Comte, Dewey, etc.) or the astronomers and physicists (Eddington, Jeans, Einstein, etc.) or the existentialists (Kierkegaard, Tillich, etc.), all of whom have to be dealt with on their merits. It should also be noted that popular religion means the actual practices and beliefs of the people, not the ideal statements of theologians or scriptures.

67. Epicureanism had a long history of some five centuries. For its later dissemination in the Roman Empire after Lucretius' time, see DeWitt, *Epicurus and His Philosophy*, Chap. XV, "Extension, Submergence, and Revival."

68. Similar refocusings of feeling have often occurred where pre-

vious world views have been destroyed or altered. For example, the atheistic Communism which in part displaced the Orthodox Church in Russia has encouraged the cult values that cluster around the persons of Marx, Lenin and (until 1961) Stalin, and their various writings have the status of "orthodox" truth. And in this country the person of Mary Baker Eddy became an object of cult veneration even in her own lifetime, and her writings are publicly read in Christian Science churches along with the Christian Scriptures. Both Auguste Comte in France and John Dewey in America tried to displace traditional Christian values with a new religion of humanity, with dubious results, since humanity is a symbol of ambiguous value when regarded as an object of veneration or ideal aspiration.

69. The language of therapy and mental health is not being read into this context by anachronism; it is present in both Epicurus and Lucretius. Cf. *Men.* 122: "No one should postpone the study of philosophy when he is young, nor should he weary of it when he becomes mature, because the search for mental health is never untimely or out of season." The term for moral catharsis in Lucretius is *purgare*.

70. *Men.* 123–27.

71. 3.425–829.

72. *Men.* 128.

73. *Men.* 129.

74. *Men.* 131–32.

75. For Lucretius' circumstantial account of sexual passion and copulation, and his condemnation of the whole business of love, see 4.1052–1120 (=L28).

76. *Men.* 129–30.

77. The simple life of withdrawal from competition and politics is purely a matter of self-interest. It is the best protection against the demands and hostile acts of other people. Cf. *L.D.* 7: "Some men have desired to gain reputation and to be well regarded, thinking in this way to gain protection from other people. If the lives of such men are secure, they have acquired a natural blessing; but if they are not, they do not possess what they originally reached for by natural instinct"; and

L.D. 14: "The simplest means of procuring protection from other men (which is also gained to a certain extent by deterrent force) is the security of quiet solitude and withdrawal from the mass of people."

78. *Men.* 128 and 130–31; Lucr. 2.14–21.

79. Professor DeWitt makes the claim that "Epicureanism was the first and only real missionary philosophy produced by the Greeks. . . . It was Epicurus who first extended brotherly love to embrace mankind and exalted it as the impelling motive for revealing to men the way to happiness." See DeWitt, *op. cit.*, pp. 26–29.

80. *Men.* 133–34. This view of causation as a compulsive force operating inexorably in nature is now generally considered erroneous and untenable for semantic reasons. Only human beings can compel or force other human beings to do their will; only human beings are inexorable, in the sense that they cannot be appeased or bent by superior force of will. The fact that events in nature occur in (statistically) uniform and regular sequences and are often predictable with great accuracy does not mean that some metaphysical power is "compelling" them to behave as they do. Things behave as they do because that is the kind of world we live in. The older view of causation, which lingered on for centuries and finally evolved into the *logical* necessity of an unfolding Absolute Mind in the hands of Hegel in the early nineteenth century, was an unconscious anthropomorphic misreading of nonhuman nature. The newer view of the late nineteenth and present twentieth century has finally succeeded in dehumanizing nature. However, the same anthropomorphic connotations still attach themselves unconsciously and in subtle ways to the words "natural law," "force," "energy," and so on.

81. With the extension of the concept of determinism into *all* areas of scientific investigation, including psychology, during the last hundred years, it has become a forlorn hope that man's psychological or moral life can any longer be treated as an exception. For the reconciliation of moral freedom with determinism in present-day theory, see note 23, above.

Actually, a full determinism is much more compatible with

Epicurus' egoistic hedonism than indeterminism would be. If it is true that each of us always seeks his own pleasure or happiness, then the ethical imperative based on this fact of human nature—"Always seek your own pleasure and happiness"—makes sense only if it is sanctioned by some natural mechanism or drive. If our choices were free from causation (indeterminism) and were not rooted in some natural drive, the ethical imperative could not be stated in a consistently egoistic manner, as above.

82. For a concise and excellent discussion of the Heisenberg Principle and its irrelevance to ethics, see Lewis White Beck, *Philosophic Inquiry* (New York, Prentice-Hall, Inc., 1952), pp. 143–47.

83. See *Protagoras* 354–57.

84. *Men.* 130.

85. The distinction between *is* and *ought* is a modern one, but seems to be present in a vague way in the following statement of Epicurus (*Men.* 129): "And so we speak of pleasure as the starting point and the goal of the happy life because we realize that it is our primary native good, because every act of choice and aversion originates with it, and because we come back to it when we judge every good by using the pleasure feeling as our criterion." Here "our primary native good" may be the stage of psychological hedonism, and "the goal of the happy life" is obviously the ethical ideal.

86. There is also a well-known "refutation" of psychological hedonism by the eighteenth-century bishop, Joseph Butler (Sermon XI, sect. 3), to the effect that it is not pleasure primarily that we seek but some specific object or value such as steak X, girl Y, or movie Z. Pleasure ordinarily *accompanies* the attainment of a particular goal but is not the fundamental motive. Butler seems to have been at least half right. Is it not the-particular-steak-plus-the-particular-pleasure-of-eating-that-steak that is our real motive? If anticipated pleasure were not part of the motive, our desires would be feeble and lack substance in many instances, as in the case of the bored person who "has everything."

87. *Men.* 132.

88. Cf. DeWitt, *op. cit.*, pp. 128–32. Treatments of hedonism, specifically the egoistic hedonism with which we are here concerned, abound in the various college texts on ethics. For unusually good accounts, see Stephen C. Pepper, *Ethics* (New York, Appleton-Century-Crofts, Inc., 1960), Chap. 5; and Philip Wheelwright, *A Critical Introduction to Ethics* (New York, Odyssey Press, rev. ed., 1949), pp. 64–91.

A Note on the Translation

1. Edited by Achilles Vogliano in 1928 (Berlin, Weidmann) and provided with Latin interpretations of the fragments.
2. See Cyril Bailey, *Epicurus: The Extant Remains* (Oxford, Clarendon Press, 1926). I have relied chiefly on Bailey's conservative text in preference to that of Hermann Usener's *Epicurea* (Leipzig, Teubner, 1887), with its often brilliant, unnecessary, and exhibitionistic rewritings of the original manuscripts. Usener was the great nineteenth-century German pioneer who reopened the field of Epicurean studies, but many solid textual contributions had already been made in the seventeenth century by Pierre Gassendi, a contemporary of Descartes and the first modern to revive atomism after its long submergence.
3. For the poetic merits of Lucretius see the admirable account by the literary critic and historian J. Wight Duff, *A Literary History of Rome from the Origins to the Close of the Golden Age* (New York, Charles Scribner's Sons, 2nd ed., 1928), pp. 275–302.
4. See his *Lucretius: On the Nature of Things* (Oxford, Clarendon Press, 1924). I have used Bailey's latest revision of the Latin text (Oxford, 1947) as the basis for my own translations.
5. See Selected Bibliography.

Excerpts from the Life of Epicurus
by Diogenes Laertius

1. These selections are drawn from the tenth book of Dioge-
    nes Laertius' *Lives of the Philosophers*, a compilation of
    the second century A.D. The work is of uneven merit and
    reliability, although the biography of Epicurus happens to
    be the best single life of a philosopher that we have from
    antiquity.

    Epicurus was a very affectionate man and a great letter
    writer. The effusive language of some of his personal letters
    could easily be interpreted erotically by those who wished to
    do so, and apparently there were many malicious and cynical
    persons who did. Furthermore, the walled Garden in Athens
    was the habitat of a number of Epicurean "friends" of both
    sexes—male disciples such as Metrodorus and Hermarchus
    and female followers such as the free woman Themista and
    the three slave hetaerae, Leontion, Nicidion, and Mammarion
    ("Baby Lion," "Little Conquest," and "Sweet Mamma," re-
    spectively). The hetaerae were not only high-grade "call girls"
    but also semieducated professional entertainers, roughly com-
    parable to the Japanese geishas. The price of this (apparently)
    innocent and high-minded experiment in communal living
    was the inevitable charge of promiscuous sexual relations lev-
    eled by foes and rivals in the outside world. The opening selec-
    tions give us a sordid picture of the backbiting and vilification
    that were undoubtedly current in all the philosophical schools
    of the time, including the Epicurean. In true journalistic fash-
    ion Diogenes first gives us "the dirt" about his subject, then
    quickly takes pains to correct this impression by showing us
    the real Epicurus. The biography ends with a disjointed and
    choppy account of what Epicurus taught, some parts of which
    are nonetheless quite valuable and throw additional light on
    the meager remains of this prolific writer.

2. The recipient of the (second) letter bearing his name.

3. None other than the famous Stoic philosopher, who happened
    to live more than three centuries after Epicurus! The brickbats
    exchanged by the Greek schools remind us of the snide com-

ments made by the various Christian sects about each other over the years.

4. Almost twenty dollars.

5. Hedeia and Erotion were both common names in the trade, meaning "Sweetie" and "Lovey," respectively.

6. The language is fanciful, but the claim is not. The loyalty of successive generations of Epicureans to the person and teachings of the master was remarkable and a well-known fact in ancient times. Lucretius, who lived two centuries after Epicurus and was a non-Greek, is a prime example. "Deviationists" were almost unknown. This probably testifies to the strong religious feeling of the Epicurean communities, which made for solidarity among the "friends" as well as for philosophical purity.

7. The school had a continuous life of some five centuries, but by the time Diogenes wrote his biography it had already begun to assimilate itself, both in doctrine and membership, to the surrounding communities of Stoics and Christians, who were far better organized for survival. See DeWitt, *op. cit.*, Chap. XV, "Extension, Submergence, and Revival."

8. This name means "The Mouse."

9. Cf. *Men.* 123–24. The gods in question were the deities of the state religion, purified and redefined. See Introduction VI. 2.a, and DeWitt, *op. cit.*, pp. 278–83.

10. A famous disciple who had the nickname of "Despot of the Garden." He is mentioned later in the biography (sect. 25) as having more than four hundred rolls, or books, to his credit, one of which was *Annals*, a history of the school.

11. I.e., at the end of 342 B.C. or the beginning of 341 B.C. His death occurred in 270 B.C. An Olympiad was the four-year period between the celebration of the Olympic games.

12. Two cities of northwestern Asia Minor. Geography is of some importance here because it was in the coastal cities of Ionia further to the south that Greek materialism had its beginnings, rather than in Greece proper. Democritus, the founder of atomism, had lived and taught for many years at Abdera in Thrace, the district northwest of the Hellespont and not far distant from Mitylene and Lampsacus.

13. A favorite disciple who died seven years before Epicurus.

14. Epicurus always insisted that he was self-taught and owed no philosophical debts, even to Democritus. He denied that Leucippus, Democritus' predecessor, had ever lived (sect. 13). This dishonest or, at the least, disingenuous attitude was no doubt intended to magnify his own originality and authority, but it only succeeded in calling forth numerous charges of plagiarism. Professor DeWitt excuses Epicurus on the ground that he was a moral reformer and hence felt himself "absolved from debts of gratitude"; see his discussion, DeWitt, *op. cit.*, pp. 14 ff.

15. Diogenes interspersed his biography with the *Letter to Herodotus*, *Letter to Pythocles*, and *Letter to Menoeceus* as well as the important collection of ethical aphorisms entitled *Leading Doctrines*. We would have little or no knowledge of these works otherwise.

16. This is what we today would call his epistemology, which emphasizes the empirical basis of knowledge and the various tests for truth (sensation, direct mental perception, universal concepts; and the feelings of pleasure and pain) as against the dialectical or purely logical methods favored by Plato and other rationalists. See *Herod.* 37–38, *Pyth.* 85–88, Introduction V.2.

17. E.g., the *Letter to Herodotus*.

18. I.e., his personal letters, of which we have fragments, and also the *Letter to Menoeceus*.

19. Two important points:

    1. Epicurus rejected the dialectic of Plato, i.e., the method of logical argument that aimed at universal definitions (What is piety? What is justice? etc.) and at the discovery of eternal archetypes or Ideas (Piety, Justice, etc.). The Epicureans of course used deductive logic in building their system as much as anybody else, but they anchored it firmly to empirical data and never allowed it to become a free-floating, speculative method. Epicurus believed that if logic were divorced from fact it became mere verbalizing and led to "inconceivable" entities such as the Platonic Ideas, which to him were "empty words." The root cause of his break with Plato lay in the fact that in a "salvation"

philosophy the purpose of knowledge is necessarily practical and therapeutic and not theoretical or speculative. See
Introduction V.1, and DeWitt, *op. cit.*, pp. 22–24,128–32.

    2. "The names of things" (e.g. "horse," "ox," "man")
immediately evoke their corresponding concepts, which
have been generated in the mind by repeated sensory experience (of horses, oxen, and men). The point of this obscure
remark is that it is unnecessary and misleading to engage
in a long search for definitions, in Platonic fashion, since
our experience of natural objects already provides us with
clear and distinct mental images. Cf. *Herod.* 37–38: "We
must grasp the meanings associated with the word sounds
in order . . . to avoid leaving matters in a state of confusion by expounding terms *ad infinitum* or by using meaningless verbiage. We must therefore look to the primary
concept in the case of each word and not require exposi-
tion. . . ." See also sect. 33 of this biography.

20. See Introduction V.2. The numbered items following in the
translation are snippets from *The Canon*, or theory of
knowledge, a treatise now lost. Note the order that they follow: sensations, concepts, feelings. This is one of the more important sections of the biography.

21. Cf. *Herod.* 38.

22. I.e., sensation is self-evident in its truth value and does not
need proof. Every sensation is autonomous and self-contained,
and neither gains nor loses by comparison with another, except when the mind misinterprets what is given in sensation—
as in the case of a mirage, where something is added.

23. E.g., taste cannot refute taste. A says, "This martini is very
dry"; B says, "It isn't dry at all." This apparent contradiction
doesn't destroy the reliability of the senses, as the Skeptics
claimed, but shows their relativity to the perceiver and makes
each sensation authoritative. In the second case, one sense
cannot contradict another; e.g., A says, "This martini *tastes* of
juniper berries," and B, "It *looks* like water." Obviously. What
is not mentioned here is the important fact that sensations are
often misinterpreted by the mind, in which case we need to
"refute" them by closer inspection. See the example of the ru-

ined pier of the aqueduct which was mistaken for a tower, Introduction IV.4.

24. Reason was an ancillary tool and was never listed as a primary test for truth. Cf. Lucr. 4.482–85, "What should we consider as having greater validity than sensation? Will reasoning that takes its rise from 'false' sensation have power to contradict the senses when it originates wholly from them? If they are not true, all reasoning likewise becomes false." Professor DeWitt (*op. cit.*, p. 136) strongly denies that this means that "the whole content of consciousness is derived from the sensations," and for this and other reasons refuses to regard Epicurus as an empiricist.

25. I.e., the fact that our sensations are not merely passively registered but actively cognized and fitted into the existing content of consciousness, witnesses to their truth.

26. There are two classes of material events that are not open to direct perception: (1) atoms and their behavior and (2) remote celestial phenomena such as comets and solar eclipses. In both cases our knowledge is inferential and derived from the "signs" that observed phenomena provide. Reason enables us to draw such inferences, but it is not the primary source of truth. Much the same attitude is seen today in statements such as "Science is a mental construct resting on the evidence of the senses."

27. This passage is discussed and illustrations provided in Introduction V.2.d. Professor DeWitt (*op. cit.*, p. 136) unconvincingly writes off this testimony of Diogenes as unreliable, although it is obviously part of a context extracted from Epicurus' lost treatise on the theory of knowledge. He would translate the Greek noun for "ideas" as "secondary or inferential ideas," i.e., ideas that are logically derived rather than built up from sense experience. In other words, DeWitt has strong prejudices against calling Epicurus an empiricist. On the other hand, it is certainly obvious that Diogenes was in error, or at least inexcusably vague, in saying that *all* our ideas "take their rise from sensation." For example, the proposition that "worlds are infinite in number" (*Herod.* 45) is clearly not given in sensation, but logically derived from the first princi-

ple that "the totality is infinite both in the quantity of atomic bodies and in spatial magnitude" (*Herod.* 42). Perhaps we should give Diogenes the benefit of the doubt by saying that by the term "ideas" he meant "universals" such as "man," "horse," "ox"; but DeWitt is not willing to concede even this (*op. cit.*, 112–13).

28. See Introduction V.2.b.
29. Cf. Lucr. 4.478–79: "You will find that the concept of truth arose first from the senses and that the senses cannot be refuted." This important passage from Diogenes is discussed in context in Introduction V.2.d. Professor DeWitt again writes off Diogenes' account of the empirical origin of concepts as the testimony of a two-bit hack. He attempts to reverse the generally accepted opinion on this point and by using a battery of arguments both good and bad (*op. cit.*, pp. 142–8), tries to prove that, far from being empirical in origin, Epicurus' "concepts" were *a priori* or innate ideas provided by nature as effective guides for thinking—just as it has provided the feelings of pleasure and pain as effective guides for the moral life. One of the pieces of evidence seemingly in favor of this view is the fact that the Greek noun for "concept" (*prolepsis*) means "anticipation"; hence "if an idea precedes or anticipates something, this can hardly be anything but experience" (p. 145). Thus, for example, nature has provided us with an innate idea of justice, so that when we mature we may be able to distinguish just acts from unjust. But if so, nature is a purposeful agent, and we have seen (Introduction VI.2.b) that ideas of purpose are utterly foreign to a materialism such as Epicureanism. It would seem, rather, that Diogenes has provided us with the correct interpretation of "anticipation": "We could not look into what we want to investigate *if we did not have prior knowledge of it.*" A concept is anticipatory in the sense of being a precondition to our identifying new occurrences of individuals of given classes (e.g., Is that a horse or an ox?) or as a preexisting means of delimiting some field of investigation (e.g., how could one write a book on baroque art without first having some conception of the meaning of "baroque," gained through hearing

baroque music and seeing baroque painting and architecture?). Both these meanings of "anticipatory" are compatible with the empirical origin of concepts.

In all fairness it must be admitted that other arguments adduced by DeWitt are very persuasive, among them the testimony of Cicero that the true conceptions of the gods were inborn. The question of the status of concepts in Epicurus is closely connected with the larger question of whether he was an empiricist, and DeWitt wages a concerted campaign on several fronts against the widely accepted opinion that he was. If he is right, then Epicurus was an intuitionalist and not an empiricist at all as far as the nature of concepts is concerned. But even so, the other two important criteria of truth—sensations and feelings—are unaffected and constitute major evidence for the empiricist side of the argument. In any case DeWitt's arguments must remain inconclusive, since the word for "concept" appears only four times in the extant writings of Epicurus, which is too slender a basis for decision, and because we lack an all-important document, Epicurus' *Canon*, or theory of knowledge.

30. For this principle of empirical verification, cf. *Herod.* 50–52 and *L.D.* 24, and see Introduction IV.4. Some beliefs are open to direct verification (e.g., Is that tower round or square?). Others are not, especially when they involve the causes of remote celestial phenomena (e.g., What is the cause of the rising and setting of the sun?). In the latter case, plural hypotheses are set up, and the principle of noncontradiction comes into play: Any hypothesis that is not contradicted by our terrestrial experience may be regarded as probable. See Introduction V.3.

31. I.e., decisions for or against various courses of action. See *Men.* 129.

32. Epicurus is contrasting his own empirical methods with the dialectical methods of the Platonists. See note 19, above.

33. What follows is a scrapbook of Epicurus' views on "the wise man," or ideal Epicurean. The recurring "will" is usually equivalent to "ought to." Everything is disjointed and run together, and the reader gets the impression that Epicurus was no better than a cracker-barrel moralist. Numbering has been

introduced into this melange to give a semblance of order. This section is capped by the *Letter to Menoeceus*.

34. Not the biographer, but Diogenes of Tarsus.

35. The "beat" philosophers of antiquity, who flouted all civilized conventions and lived like street dogs (whence their name).

36. Unlike the rival Stoic sage, who disciplined himself not to feel emotion, including grief at the loss of a child or friend.

37. Oddly enough, Epicurus was very punctilious in his own observance of the rites of the state religion and urged his followers "to sacrifice piously and properly." Whether his motives were defensive, hypocritical, or pious cannot be properly ascertained, but Professor DeWitt (*op. cit.*, 280–81) holds that they were completely sincere and gives good reasons for so believing.

38. It is suggested by Ettore Bignone, an Italian editor, that since Epicureanism was a closed, dogmatic system any idea of progress or of one Epicurean thinker advancing beyond another was automatically ruled out.

39. The Epicureans considered it a virtue and not a vice to have arrived at a complete system of positive dogmas about nature and human nature. This closed body of teachings they regarded as the only "true philosophy," in contradistinction to the speculative uncertainties of Platonism and the crippling excesses of Skepticism. Their dogmatism can be justified only in the light of their over-all aim—the cure of souls in an age of anxiety. See Introduction V.1, on the purpose of knowledge, and DeWitt, *op. cit.*, pp. 113–15.

40. I.e., equally unperturbed.

41. The Stoics, contrariwise, held that they are equal, since conduct is either moral or immoral, with no possible middle ground of partly moral, partly immoral.

42. I.e., by professional Epicureans who live the simple life of *ataraxia* in a group; cf. *L.D.* 40. "Those who have attained the full complement of pleasure" is a technical phrase for "perfect Epicureans." It may anticipate a similar technical phrase in St. Paul's Epistles (cf. Ephesians 3.19: "To know the love of Christ which passeth knowledge, that ye may be filled unto all the fullness of God," i.e., become perfect Christians).

43. I.e., it is impossible to read the future by supernatural means. Even if it were possible, things happen deterministically, and we can do nothing about them.

44. A fifth-century school founded by Aristippus of Cyrene, a student of Socrates'. Since it antedated the Epicurean school by more than a century and also taught that pleasure is the moral good, Epicurus was accused of plagiarizing from Aristippus (sect. 4 of Diogenes' biography). But the two conceptions of pleasure differed radically. Epicurus taught that pleasure was neutral and largely static, consisting in freedom from pain in body and mind, whereas Aristippus held that pleasure is positive and dynamic, consisting in the immediate, intense enjoyments of the moment, whatever they may be; also that there is no difference between "lower" and "higher" pleasures (e.g., sex and Brahms), because all pleasures are bodily states. The moral life consisted in rational regulation of our actions, with a view to maximizing the positive balance of pleasure over pain. In other words, Cyrenaicism was what Epicureanism has always tended to become in the hands of its lay practitioners (see the examples of "degenerate" Epicureans given in Introduction VII.1). Nevertheless it was fundamentally different from the sectarian practice of the Garden.

Letter to Herodotus

1. This was the so-called *Major Epitome*, a condensation of Epicurus' masterpiece *On Nature* (in thirty-seven rolls, or "books"), which is now lost except for certain fragments recovered at Herculaneum. *The Major Epitome*, also lost, was intended for beginning students and was probably the chief source book on which Lucretius based his poem *De Rerum Natura* (*On Nature*). The present *Letter to Herodotus*, also known as *The Minor Epitome*, was intended for advanced students of Epicureanism—which may account for the allusive and overly condensed style of certain sections.

2. This short section deals with the empirical methodology of Epicurus and is extracted in condensed form from his *Canon*,

the important treatise on the theory of knowledge that is now unfortunately lost. The student is first told to let the "word sounds" (e.g., "man," "horse," "ox") evoke their corresponding concepts and to avoid wasting time in wordy Platonic dialectic, which aimed at the discovery of universal definitions and their corresponding eternal archetypes, or Forms (e.g., "man-ness," "horse-ness," etc.). According to Epicurus, concepts such as "man" are neither transcendental nor innate in the Platonic sense, but empirically built up from repeated sensory experience of the various classes of natural objects, such as human beings, horses, and oxen. Hence the "primary meaning" of each word is closest to its empirical origin and is an important criterion of truth, which we must use "to form judgments about matters of belief or about problems needing research" (e.g., Is X a man or an ape?). This point is further developed by Diogenes Laertius in his *Life of Epicurus* sects. 32–33.

Other important criteria of truth mentioned here are our sensations and the feelings of pleasure and pain. The latter are appealed to primarily in deciding ethical questions of "right" and "wrong." The former are used "to interpret a sense datum awaiting verification." (E.g., Is that object in the distance a tower or the pier of a ruined aqueduct? Only direct inspection will provide the true answer.) However, there are two classes of physical events known as "imperceptibles," which are not open to direct sensory experience: (1) atoms and their motion through space and (2) remote events in the heavens and their causes, such as lunar and solar eclipses. In the latter case the Epicurean first determined by observation the various ways in which light may be obscured here on earth and then proceeded to infer that the eclipse may have occurred in some analogous way or ways. Note that reason is not listed as a primary test for truth but is used only secondarily as a means of inference, i.e., a way of passing from the observed to the unobservable. In general, a proposition involving "imperceptibles" is true if it is confirmed, or at least not contradicted, by empirical evidence. In the following section on first principles "imperceptibles" refers to atoms and their motion, infinite space, and the infinity of worlds in the cosmos. Since these all lie beyond the range of the senses, all propositions about them must be inferential, i.e., rationally deduced from objective conditions of our world, the world we know and experience through the senses. The various criteria of truth used by Epicurus are discussed in detail in Introduction V.2 and 3.

3. This is one of a number of technical terms for "atoms."

4. Conjectural passage.

5. Epicurus consistently held that thought consists of direct sensory images or of concepts derived from repeated sensory experience of objects. He also held that on rare occasions atomic films from remote objects—e.g., the gods—bypass the senses and impinge directly on the mind. In the latter case he might have argued, "Since we think about the gods, they must exist." His desire in part was to prevent his materialistic system from being stigmatized as atheistic.

6. Epicurus is here rejecting two current theories of perception in favor of his own: (1) the theory of Democritus, his predecessor, that we do not see and hear atomic images as such but atmospheric impressions of such films made in the air while the image is in transit; and (2) the more widely held theory attributed to Empedocles, Parmenides, and Plato that perception is an active process, involving the ejection of "rays" from the sense organ, and not simply a passive reception of the facsimiles of external objects.

7. The important question of truth and falsity in perception is discussed and illustrated in the Introduction IV.4.

8. Epicurus again rejects a rival theory of Democritus; cf. note 6, above.

9. He means that "olfactory" atoms that do not harmonize with the atoms of the sense organ produce disagreeable odors, while those that do harmonize produce pleasant odors.

10. Associated with shape are the inseparable "minimal parts" of the atoms discussed later in this section.

11. Epicurus is here arguing against a rival view (of the Eleatic school) which held that matter is infinitely divisible. If the components of matter could be pared down to infinitesimal size, the point of annihilation would ultimately be reached

and the whole structure of matter would collapse from lack of inner solidity and strength. Since this is not the case, he infers rather that there is a lower limit to the divisibility of matter—namely, the irreducible atoms themselves.

12. The "end point," or "perceptual minimum," is the smallest perceivable unit of a physical object (e.g., a line) that has parts or segments of equal or unequal size. Epicurus holds that (1) when the eye reaches such a point or minimum, we may think we can make further subdivisions but this is an illusion, because the eye has simply passed on to the next point which is of equal size (and there cannot be an infinity of equal points in a finite body without contradiction); (2) these points, or minima, are both like and unlike partite bodies, i.e., they have extension in space but have no parts; and (3) they are the units of measurement whereby we judge the various degrees of smallness or largeness in objects. By analogy to perceived objects he then goes on to argue (59) that atoms likewise have a finite number of minimal parts, or points, which are extended, indivisible, and inseparable and which determine the relative sizes of atoms.

13. In the absence of experimental techniques for verifying scientific hypotheses, the method of logical analogy became the characteristic and favorite Epicurean method of passing from the empirical level of sensory experience and observation to the sub-empirical level of the atom. By setting up a scheme of *assumed* similarities between phenomenal objects and unseen atoms, analogy permitted the Epicureans to arrive quickly and painlessly at a set of scientific and metaphysical "truths" by pure reason, unassisted by the laborious experimental and mathematical techniques of the present day. A scientific or metaphysical proposition is true, according to Epicurus, (1) if it is confirmed by ordinary sensory observation or (2) if it is not contradicted by the senses. (For example, in the case of the atomic images that are postulated by Epicurus to explain perception, the first criterion is not directly applicable, but the second criterion is applicable and is sufficient to make his hypothesis "true.")

The reader should note the heavy use throughout this letter

of such expressions as "we must (not) suppose," "it should (not) be assumed," etc., which indicate that "pure reason" or logic is coming into play. The Greek faith in logic as the chief instrument for arriving at truth is not borne out by modern logical theory, which holds that logic is "analytic" (i.e., merely reveals the implications of premises, whether these be factually true or false) and not "synthetic" (i.e., does not of itself provide us with truths about the world).

14. "Slow" and "fast" are, strictly speaking, predicates belonging to compound objects that we can perceive, and not to free atoms in space which we never perceive. Epicurus is here applying these terms by analogy to the compound bodies which he is about to discuss in the next section. A collection of atoms, or "body," becomes perceptible to us, he says, because of its internal atomic collisions, which have the effect of reducing normal atomic speeds to the range of human perceptions. A slow-moving body is therefore one in which internal atomic collisions are occurring at a relatively high rate, and by analogy "slowness" may be predicated of free single atoms in space whenever they meet with a relatively high degree of resistance from other atoms.

15. This obscure passage may be clarified by extracting the following points: (1) Atoms in a compound body are analogous to free atoms in space. Within the limited internal space of the body they too move at a uniform rate of speed unless temporarily checked by collisions with other atoms in their aggregate. A "slow" body is different from a "fast" body because of the higher rate of internal collisions (see note 14, above). (2) There are two kinds of motion in the world, both real— atomic motion and the observed motion of bodies. A moving object that we observe is the "sensory counterpart" or "appearance" of all the internal atomic motions that we do not observe. Its motion is its own. It is real and not illusory because the object is a sensed entity in its own right and not merely the sum total of its component motions. (3) What is true of the observed motion of bodies is not true of the subempirical motion of atoms, because the truth of the senses is different from truth that is logically deduced or "mentally

apprehended," even though the latter must be verified or at least not contradicted by empirical evidence. Thus our senses tell us that one object (e.g., a car or a ball) is moving faster than another, but we cannot infer that the atoms of the faster object are therefore moving faster than the atoms of the slower object. Atomic speed is one thing, a mental construct; the speed of atomic aggregates is another, a datum of sensation. Nor, conversely, can we infer that because the atoms of a compound follow a multitude of separate paths the compound itself follows the same paths.

16. Although there is no absolute top or bottom in infinite space, there may be an "up" and "down" relative to a hypothetical point in space such as the earth. To draw a line to infinity upward or downward from such a point and then to regard this segment of space as both up and down with reference to the hypothetical standpoint would be a contradiction. In other words, "up" and "down" may be meaningless in terms of cosmic space, but they are still logical contradictories relative to us. However, it is not a contradiction for us to speak of up and down and at the same time hold that space is infinite, because we are using two different frames of reference—one terrestrial, the other cosmic.

17. "Bodily casing" could here refer to some organ or limb, e.g., an arm or leg or eye.

18. Every empirical object is the sum total of certain perceived qualities such as shape, size, weight, color, etc.; these qualities are all physical and inseparable from the body. The body could not exist without them, nor do they exist as separate physical components in their own right (the view of the Stoics) or as nonmaterial Platonic Forms or essences (which is inconceivable to an empiricist such as Epicurus). Such essential and nondetachable qualities are what Epicurus here calls "properties." An empirical object is the sum total of such properties, and conversely a configuration of such properties is what we mean by "body." (For Epicurus, these properties are not only physical but objective, i.e., in the external body itself. Although an empiricist, he never arrived at the same conclusion as did the eighteenth-century empiricists Berkeley

and Hume—that these properties are all subjective, or "mental," since all we know about them is our own perceptions or experience of them.)

A second set of characteristics is known as "accidents." These are contingent or nonessential qualities of bodies whose presence or absence does not alter the essential nature of the object. Thus Socrates is essentially human whether he is a slave or a freeman, whether he speaks Greek or Persian. Modern examples of accidents would be the race, color, and creed of a given person.

It should be noted that the terms "property" and "accident" are relative and not absolute. Thus "having a head" is an accident of the class "body in general" but a property of the subclass "living human body."

19. Although we can mentally distinguish between these properties and isolate any one of them for study or esthetic contemplation, this must always take place in a context where the object is present as a whole unit. Epicurus emphasizes that the term "body" refers to a perceived complex of qualities, none of which is mechanically compounded with others to form an object in the sense that component parts are brought together to form artifacts, e.g., cars and houses. He is pressing home this common-sense point against his rivals, the Platonists and Stoics.

20. In a materialistic system one might expect time to be defined perhaps as "the durative aspect of matter in motion." But Epicurus held that time is unique and cannot be defined or discussed by reference to general concepts such as we use in discussing other properties and accidents. He is therefore driven to appeal to our common experience of time and to the ordinary linguistic expressions we use in talking about it. We intuit or experience time as "long" or "short" always in connection with other accidents of material reality such as day and night, emotional states, states of rest and motion, etc. In other words, time is an indefinable relation that might be described as "an accident of other accidents." Instead of giving time metaphysical status in nature along with atomic matter and empty space, Epicurus is content to speak of it simply as a

sensed quality of our experience. But if empty space is a metaphysical postulate necessitated by the motion of atoms, why
should time not also require such a postulate, since motion is
inseparable from duration of motion?

Lucretius takes the same view:

> Time is naught in itself; rather from actual events there
> flows the sense of what was concluded in the past, what is
> hard upon us now, and what will next ensue. One must
> needs allow that no man senses time by itself, divorced
> from the movement and placid calm of things. . . . You
> may thus discern that things past neither are nor exist in
> themselves as does body, nor do we speak of them in the
> same manner as we do the void; rather, you may with jus-
> tice call them accidents of body and space, wherein all
> takes place. [1.459 ff.]

21. In III.6 Epicurus has already postulated an infinite number of
other worlds existing in infinite space. His general conception
seems to have been that each of these was a *kosmos*, or order
system, like our own, consisting of an earth, sky, and heavenly
bodies. But not all *kosmoi* have the same shape; some are
spherical, others oval, etc.

22. Conjectural passage.

23. The moot question in antiquity whether language originated
naturally or by convention (i.e., deliberate rational invention
and standardization) is settled by Epicurus by a compromise.
The various racial groups at first evolved their own languages
naturally and spontaneously. These primitive tongues were the
physiological expressions of different emotional reactions to
their various environments. Later on, reason came into play in
the form of linguistic conventions, which served to standard-
ize both the structure of languages and the meanings of
words. This was presumably not accidental but done deliber-
ately, he says, to facilitate contact between the various racial
groups. The odd detail that the various primitive peoples had
quite different sensory and emotional reactions to their environments is not as naïve as it may seem. Epicurus apparently

reasoned that early languages are physical externalizations of internal psychological reactions to the environment (a straightforward materialist assumption), and since both languages and environments differ widely he inferred that primitive man's inner responses must likewise have differed widely. (This argument cannot meet the objection that primitive peoples occupying the *same* environment as settled residents, not migrants, often have entirely different languages.)

24. We cannot without contradiction (nor without "the gravest spiritual disturbances") believe (1) that a deity created the heavenly bodies and prescribed the laws of their regular motions and (2) that this deity is at the same time absolutely "blessed" and impassive, i.e., devoid of all activity, passion, concern, etc. Since Epicurus held that the deities are completely "blessed" and impassive, he logically rejected the idea of special creation and also the idea of divine governance of the world, since both of these involve activity on the part of the deity or deities. This left him with the alternative of maintaining that both the genesis and the regular motions of the heavenly bodies are mechanically determined by the motion of atomic aggregates. By adopting this alternative he kept both his theology and his materialism "pure," i.e., free from contradiction. For similar reasons he also rejected another religious conception that was widespread in the Hellenistic period, viz., that the heavenly bodies are themselves gods. This idea detracts from the "dignity" of the divine because it involves the principle of voluntary self-activation, which is contradictory to absolute impassivity. See Introduction VI.2.a.

25. It was important for the Epicurean to imitate the impassivity of the gods in his own human pursuit of serenity and a life lived without fear. An essential ingredient in this ideal of happiness was the general theory of natural causation, especially as this applied to the phenomena of the heavens, which were a chief source of religious awe and superstitious fear among the ignorant and the half-educated of the Hellenistic period. The realization that "the revolutions, risings, settings, and eclipses" of the heavenly bodies occur solely through impersonal mechanical processes and not by the arbitrary will of gods was

an indispensable piece of wisdom for the happy life. But a detailed empirical observation of these phenomena that is not accompanied by a theory of natural causation may simply deepen the fears of the observer and strengthen his conviction that it is the gods who manipulate the heavenly bodies.

Also, our failure to attain complete certainty about the specific causes of remote celestial phenomena need not disturb our peace of mind so long as we are in possession of the general theory of causation. Thus Epicurus allowed for more than one explanation of solar and lunar eclipses (see Pyth. 96 and Lucr. 5.751–70). In all such cases, he says, we cannot hope for a single correct explanation because of the remoteness of sun and moon from the earth and human observation. We must, therefore, be content to set up several alternative hypotheses, just as we do in the case of analogous occurrences on earth. For example, in explaining eclipses we must consider in how many different ways light may be obscured under earthly conditions, and having done this we may extend these explanations by analogy to the corresponding solar and lunar events. In this way Epicurus (1) maintained his empirical principle that a scientific explanation must be consistent with, or not contradicted by, experience and (2), more important, tried to allay any superstitious fears or uneasiness by adhering to a general principle of determinism, without claiming to have knowledge of specific causes in all cases. See Introduction V.4 and 5.

26. In Epicureanism knowledge about the world was always a means to the end of promoting the ethical ideal of serenity and spiritual composure. If our beliefs about the world (e.g., celestial phenomena) are such that this ideal is defeated, we shall lead lives of fear and anxiety. We are morally obligated, therefore, to submit our beliefs and inferences to the empirical testing which for Epicurus is the final court of appeal: "We must keep all our judgments in line with our sensations (specifically our immediate perceptions, either of the mind or of any particular sense organ) and also in line with our actual feelings of pleasure and pain, in order to have the means with which to interpret a sense datum awaiting verification or a

problem involving imperceptibles" (38). For the three criteria of truth (sensations, feelings, and concepts), see note 2, above.

In the eighteenth century another empiricist, David Hume, was also interested in checking our beliefs against bedrock sensory experience. Hume's motive, however, unlike Epicurus', was purely epistemological rather than therapeutic. He aimed to clear away the dead wood of erroneous and meaningless beliefs and arrive at a body of clear and distinct ideas for the sake of such ideas themselves. "All our ideas or more feeble perceptions are copies of our impressions or more lively ones. . . . All ideas, especially abstract ones, are naturally faint and obscure. . . . They are apt to be confounded with other resembling ideas, and when we have often employed any term, though without a distinct meaning, we are apt to imagine it has a determinate idea annexed to it. On the contrary, all impressions, that is, all sensations . . . are strong and vivid; the limits between them are more exactly determined, nor is it easy to fall into any error or mistake with regard to them. When we entertain, therefore, any suspicion that a philosophical term is employed without any meaning or idea (as is but too frequent), we need but enquire, from what impression is that supposed idea derived? And if it be impossible to assign any, this will serve to confirm our suspicion. By bringing ideas into so clear a light we may reasonably hope to remove all dispute which may arise concerning their nature and reality." (*An Enquiry concerning Human Understanding*, sect. II).

27. "This voiceless method," i.e., by reading this *Letter to Herodotus*. The ordinary method of instruction was oral, face to face with a teacher such as Epicurus himself.

Letter to Pythocles

1. The letter to Pythocles on celestial phenomena is addressed to a favorite student of Epicurus, but the letter itself has generally (even in antiquity) been regarded as the work of a later compiler and not of Epicurus himself. Stylistic and other considerations show that it is probably not from the hand of the

philosopher. But for all that, it is an authoritative Epicurean document, and when taken with the fifth and sixth books of Lucretius it helps to fill in many of the details from the larger work of Epicurus, *On Nature,* which is now lost.

With Epicurus the study of the heavenly bodies and related phenomena was not an end in itself but, like all his scientific investigations, was intended primarily to disabuse the reader's mind of superstitious ignorance and to contribute to his spiritual composure and peace of mind. This department of nature, however, was regarded as a particularly "sensitive area" in the Epicurean campaign against the beliefs of popular religion because of the remoteness of the events and the impossibility of assigning specific natural causes with precision. Consequently, in the absence of reliable scientific information, it was all too easy for even the intelligent layman of the Hellenistic period to fall back on the simple dogmatic answers of religion, viz., that divine powers have created the heavenly bodies and manipulate them at will or that the heavenly bodies are themselves divine beings. Rather than make such an easy surrender to dogmatic ignorance, it is better, says Epicurus, to accept approximate or probable knowledge about the heavenly bodies, as long as it is empirically based. It may be impossible to determine the one precise cause of a given event (e.g., a solar eclipse), but at least we can preserve our spiritual poise by assigning several alternative causes. Each of these causes (actually hypotheses) will be drawn from our terrestrial experience and extended by analogy to the distant celestial event, and each may be regarded as "probable" in so far as it is not contradicted by empirical observations of similar events here on earth. (In this connection the student should read the relevant passages in *Herod.* 77–80, and notes 25 and L12 to that letter.)

The student should note that this practice of assigning probability to any causal explanation that is not contradicted by empirical data has a striking similarity to the *ad ignorantiam* fallacy in logic, in which a proposition is supposedly true if it cannot be proved false. Thus it does not follow logically that "God exists" is true simply because we cannot conclusively prove the proposition false. Nor by the same token can we draw the inference that the setting of the sun is probably caused by the temporary extinguishing of the solar fires (see *Pyth*. 92), on the ground that this explanation is not contradicted by anything analogous in our experience on earth. In neither case is lack of conclusive evidence against something the same as evidence in favor of it. The Epicurean rule of thumb for determining the causes of celestial phenomena is therefore relatively worthless in the absence of more refined observation and experimental techniques of verification. The principle of multiple causation, by being hospitable to all sorts of "empirical" explanations, produced more fantasy than fact.

2. In contrast to celestial mechanics, in which it is impossible to ascertain single causes for single events, Epicurus held dogmatically that the problems of ethics, terrestrial physics, and metaphysics (dealing with the ultimate composition of the universe) admit of only one correct solution.

3. For example, we have the "sensory impression" of a solar eclipse. The "judgments connected with it" are the hypotheses we set up to explain this event: Has a third body intervened between earth and sun? If so, is this third body the moon or some opaque, invisible object in the sky? Or have the sun's fires temporarily died out? According to Epicurean procedure, any one of these explanations is "probable" as long as we can find a terrestrial occurrence analogous to it. If no negative evidence is forthcoming, a solar eclipse might thus have as many as three different "causes."

4. I.e., we cannot go out to the periphery of our own local world and determine whether it is rarefied, in motion, spherical in shape, etc. In other words, there is no negative evidence in our experience to prevent our making any of these assumptions about our own world or, by analogy, any other world.

5. Cf. *Herod*. 45 and 74.

6. Epicurus (or the compiler) is here criticizing his two predecessors, Leucippus and Democritus—the former because he oversimplified a complex situation, the latter because he postulated a metaphysical entity (Necessity) for which there is no empirical evidence. Democritus was a thoroughgoing determinist both in physics and ethics. Epicurus, by his counter postulate

of the atomic swerve, purposely introduced an element of indeterminism in order to escape the tyranny of blind Necessity,
especially in the area of the moral life (see *Men.* 134).

7. An excellent example of the Epicurean principle of multiple
causation, where the two "causes" were regarded as equally
possible since neither was contradicted by terrestrial phenomena. The first hypothesis was put forward by Heraclitus, the
second by Anaximenes, two preatomic cosmologists.

8. This section offers four separate explanations (all equally
"possible") of the apparent paths of the sun and moon, which
seem not only to circle the earth but to move up and down in
the sky, standing higher in the heavens at certain parts of their
orbits than at others. The ecliptic, or apparent path of the sun,
is oblique, i.e., set at an angle to the plane of the earth's equator. The sun reaches its northern turning point, or "tropic," in
the sign of Cancer about June 21 and its southern turning
point in the sign of Capricorn about December 21. The ancient theories of the ecliptic that are enumerated here are as
follows: (1) Assuming that the heavenly bodies do not move
independently but turn with the sky as a whole, their oblique
orbits, which slant with respect to the plane of the equator,
must be caused by the obliqueness of the sky itself (apparently
a theory of Empedocles). (2) Sun and moon would normally
revolve on the same plane as the earth, but they are pushed
out of orbit and toward the tropics by transverse air currents
(a theory of Anaxagoras). (3) The fuel that feeds the fires of
the celestial bodies lies along the ecliptic (possibly a Stoic theory). (4) The orbits of the heavenly bodies were imposed on
them from the very beginning by Necessity, and the combination of the daily revolution of sun and moon with their grad-
ual ascent or descent along the ecliptic to the two tropics
produces a spiral motion (the theory of Democritus).

9. "Slavish" because they bound themselves to one set theory
and did not favor the flexible methods of the Epicureans.

10. "The structure of the atmosphere" probably refers to the varying amounts of fuel available to the moon as it moves in orbit
through various atmospheric densities, a theory previously
met with in (3), note 8, above.

11. The "one cause" principle seems often to be a standard euphemism for divine causation. People who resort to this easy *ad hoc* explanation and "irresponsibly" reject the evidence of their senses "end up desiring to observe the impossible"; i.e., they will never be able to observe the gods controlling the heavenly bodies simply because the gods are impassive and never engage in such activity. The student will note at various points in this letter the insistent propaganda in favor of the empirical principle of multiple causation and the decrying of the "one cause" theological explanation. This was an important aspect of the Epicurean program of educating the public and was certainly a big step in the right direction, even though the empirical method as then employed left much to be desired (see note 1, above).

12. Lucretius, for example, draws a parallel between the regular succession of the seasons and the regularity of the moon's phases (5.737–50)

13. As usual, the possible is contrasted with the impossible, i.e., natural causation with divine causation. The latter is impossible logically because it is a contradiction of the gods' "blessed" or impassive nature.

14. A mackerel sky followed by rain may be (1) "a conjunction of events," i.e., mere coincidence without causal significance, or (2) due to "alterations and changes in the atmosphere." In any case, according to the writer, it is impossible to determine which "cause" applies. Similarly an early robin in late February may be a sign of spring, but again the two events are coincidental; the appearance of the robin has no causal effect on spring. This latter point is reinforced in sect. 115 of this letter.

15. These changes are explained by Lucretius (6.514–16): "The clouds, when smitten from above by the sun's heat, send forth their moisture and distill their rain, even as a mass of wax over a hot fire melts and becomes liquid."

16. An empirical analogy to explain the first cause of thunder. A tall, narrow-mouthed Greek jar, when blown into, gave out a kind of rumble.

17. An elaborate theory of lightning is broken down into three sets of equally possible causes, each set having two items: (1)

Atoms already contained in clouds are ejected as lightning by the collision or compression of the clouds. (2) Fire-atoms emanating from the heavenly bodies become concentrated in cloud masses and are ejected as lightning, or light filtering into the clouds from the surrounding atmosphere may ignite the clouds themselves. (3) Wind already present in the clouds may be ignited by its own motion, or winds may break the clouds open and eject atoms already present (similar to 1.)

18. Lucretius gives an example from "our own experience" (6.167–71): "If you see someone at a distance felling a huge tree with the twin-bladed ax, it happens that you may see the blow before its impact reaches the ear as sound; in the same way do we see the lightning flash before we hear thunder."

19. As his contribution to the Epicurean propaganda war against mythological religion, Lucretius devotes more than two hundred lines (6.219–422) to debunking the bolt as a terror weapon of the vengeful sky god Jupiter and to a very full account of its natural causes. The length of this passage alone is symbolic of the importance the Epicureans assigned to meteorology and astronomy in their campaign against superstition. The passage here in Epicurus ends with the usual exhortation to supplant myth with empirical observation, from which we are to glean "hints about things unseen," i.e., derive parallels or analogies that may serve as explanations of celestial events whose causes cannot be directly observed.

20. Earthquakes are treated under meteorology because of this theory that subterranean wind trapped in the earth is a probable cause. The wind theory persisted in various forms well into the eighteenth century when the terrible earthquake at Lisbon (1755) was accounted for in this and other unscientific ways.

21. At this point there is a considerable gap in the Greek text that cannot be filled in even conjecturally. The four remaining lines of this section make little sense in the absence of the larger context, and I have therefore omitted them from the translation.

22. This confused language simply means that there is a twofold process going on whenever hail is produced, regardless of

whether it is composed of wind particles or water particles:
(1) the freezing and solidifying of the parts of each hailstone
and (2) the splitting up of larger masses into individual stones.

23. The compiler of this treatise is sometimes guilty of presenting
us with tautologies rather than information. What he is saying
here amounts to "Dew is produced by particles that produce
dew," which may be true, like any tautology, but tells us nothing scientifically.

24. E.g., the condensation of steam into water droplets.

25. The two theories of the circularity of the rainbow correspond
to the two original explanations above: (1) If the rainbow is
caused "by sunlight shining on an atmosphere full of water
particles," then it is circular because all points of the reflected
sunlight are equidistant from the eye (which is a tautology).
(2) If it is caused "by a special combination of light and air," it
is circular because either the light atoms or the air atoms are
arranged in a circle and impart this form to the whole configuration (which seems like a question-begging, *ad hoc* explanation).

26. Comets are (1) chance aggregations of fiery atoms that come
and go; (2) actual stars that are usually concealed but make
their appearance when the heavens as a whole are in certain
positions; (3) stars that are normally concealed and stationary
but have independent motion under special conditions.

27. Referring to the "fixed stars" at the poles, which do not revolve with the heavens as a whole like the other stars. The
quotation is from Homer's *Iliad* (18.487).

28. "Wanderers" was the regular Greek term for planets, which
were so named because of their apparently erratic or irregular
courses as compared with the "regular" stars. Of the nine
planets five were known to the ancient astronomers (Mercury,
Venus, Mars, Jupiter, and Saturn). The earth was not known
to be a planet of the sun until the ancient geocentric theory
was displaced by the modern heliocentric theory of Coperni-
cus in the sixteenth century. Uranus, Neptune, and Pluto were
discovered in 1781, 1846, and 1930, respectively.

29. The "one cause" method is, as usual, the discredited theological method of assigning causal activity to the gods (see note

11, above, and sect. 97 of this letter). Releasing the deities from all such duties was the only course consistent with their serene and impassive nature, a fundamental assumption of Epicurus' theology. Note the contemptuous language used in reference to the theological reactionaries. The Epicureans were dogmatic and intolerant of the views of their rivals, whether Skeptics, Platonists, or "mythologizers."

30. I.e., they actually move in a direction opposite to that of the other stars but are retarded by the vortex created by the main orbit. This produces the illusion that they are traveling with the other stars but more slowly. The idea in item (3) is that certain orbits are located at a greater distance from the center of the local universe and hence have greater distances to cover than those located nearer the center.

31. See sect. 101 of this letter.

32. A survey of Epicurean fundamentals: the metaphysics of atoms and space; the infinity of atoms, space, and worlds; the criteria of scientific truth; the feelings of pleasure and pain as criteria of moral good and evil; the ethical goal of all knowledge—freedom from religious fears, and spiritual tranquillity.

33. In other words, there is more to Epicureanism than mastering an intellectual system. One must first have the desire to get rid of theological phobias and moral excesses before the philosophical abstractions become meaningful. We might almost say that this is the faith element that is present in any "salvation" philosophy such as Epicureanism or Stoicism. This prior existential commitment is well summed up in the later Christian formula "*Credo ut intelligam*" ("I believe in order to understand").

Letter to Menoeceus

1. This letter, together with the important collection of individual sayings and teachings known as *Leading Doctrines*, is the chief source of our knowledge about Epicurus' ethics and his theory of the good life. In it he sets forth, in a flowing and un-

technical style, the following salient points: the right attitude toward the gods (123–24) and toward death (124–27), the limitation of desires to those that are necessary and natural (127–29), the doctrine of pleasure and pain (hedonism, 129–32) and of *ataraxia* (freedom from pain in body and mind, 131), the role of reason or "good judgment" (132–33), and the role of determinism, chance, and freedom in the moral life (133–35).

2. The Greek verb here translated as "delineated" also means "traced in outline." On that basis Professor DeWitt holds that Epicurus believed "the universal conception" of the gods to be innate and *a priori*, rather than empirically derived (see DeWitt, *op. cit.*, pp. 145–47), especially since this view is confirmed by the testimony of Cicero. Plausible as this may seem at first sight, it is plainly contradicted by the words of Epicurus himself in this paragraph: "The gods do indeed exist, since our knowledge of them is a matter of clear and distinct perception." Here the adjective translated as "clear and distinct" is a standard term frequently used by Epicurus in connection with sense perception, especially at close range. In addition, we have the testimony of Lucretius (6.76–77 = L24) concerning the atomic images of the gods "that flow from their holy bodies into the minds of men" and are there perceived directly by the mind. This question is of more than pedantic interest since it bears on the larger question of whether Epicurus was a straightforward empiricist or not. See Diogenes Laertius, *Life of Epicurus*, sect. 33 and note, and Introduction V.2.b.

3. I.e., the Greek gods were made in the image of man. They were popularly represented as having human passions, vices, and virtues and as engaging in activities such as quarreling, lovemaking, creating, rewarding, and punishing—all of which Epicurus regarded as contradictory to their perfection, serenity, and self-contemplation. The "true conception" of the gods was no doubt set forth in detail by Epicurus in his treatise *On the Gods*, which is now lost, but there are plenty of hints to be found in the *Letter to Herodotus*, the *Letter to Pythocles*, and in Lucretius and Cicero. The gods were wholly concerned with their own perfection and bliss and had no interest whatever in

human beings or in the physical universe that they had no part in creating. See Introduction VI.2.

4. Cf. *L.D.* 19: "Infinite time contains no greater pleasure than does finite time, if one determines the limits of pleasure rationally." In other words, why long for immortality?

5. I.e., the Epicurean "wise man" or "sage," whose other merits are recited by Diogenes Laertius, sects. 117–21b.

6. I.e., a good life in the Epicurean sense is a preparation for dying well, without fear or repining. One who has lived the pleasant life of *ataraxia* can die with the serenity and composure that have become habitual.

7. The relaxed and self-sufficient Epicurean did not eagerly reach out for the future, nor did he write it off altogether. His habitual composure made him ready to extend a calm present into an equally calm future. By contrast, the Cyrenaic, who lived much more intensely, never banked on the future at all but lived by the motto "Only the present is ours." See Diogenes Laertius, *Life of Epicurus*, note 44.

8. In addition to the right attitude toward death and the gods, the curtailing of desires to the bare minimum was essential for the good life as Epicurus understood it. In *L.D.* 29 the classification of human desires is presented more simply and clearly than it is in the present passage: "Some desires are (1) natural and necessary, others (2) natural but not necessary, still others (3) neither natural nor necessary but generated by senseless whims." For the strict Epicurean the only legitimate desires are those whose fulfillment will produce freedom from pain in body and mind, which is what Epicurus meant by "pleasure" (simple diet and clothing, shelter, and companionship together with the right attitude toward death and the gods). All other desires that aim at positive satisfactions or intense pleasure (such as a rich diet, sex, esthetic pursuits) may add diversity to life but are in reality unnecessary and superfluous, or they may actually be harmful in their consequences (such as the pursuit of wealth, fame, power, excitement, etc.). These are characteristic of the worldly sophisticate or the crass Cyrenaic but must be forgone by the strict sectarian in his own self-interest. Cf. *L.D.* 26: "All desires that do not lead to physical

pain if not satisfied are unnecessary, and involve cravings that are easily resolved when they appear to entail harm or when the object of desire is hard to get."

9. Cf. *L.D.* 3: "The quantitative limit of pleasure is the elimination of all feelings of pain. Wherever the pleasurable state exists there is neither bodily pain nor mental pain nor both together, so long as the state continues." Pleasure is the "starting point," i.e., the natural psychological basis, of the happy life. Thus because of the ambiguity of "pleasure" Epicurus is able to say that "we speak of pleasure as the starting point and the goal of the happy life" and to make the claim that the good life is one lived in accordance with nature. But the ethical goal of *ataraxia* is a philosophical refinement of "our primary native good" and a far cry from the active pleasure that untutored nature craves. For this reason some have classified Epicurus as a neutral hedonist (or simply a "neutralist") rather than as a genuine hedonist.

10. E.g., the sexual act, which Epicurus regarded as natural but unnecessary except for reproductive purposes. Cf. *V.C.* 51, "Sex never benefited any man, and it's a marvel if it hasn't injured him!"

11. E.g., necessary surgery, if it is followed by physical comfort after convalescence.

12. Like the Stoics, the Epicureans made much of self-sufficiency (independence of what life gives or takes away) and maintained that the basic material requirements for the happy life are easily met. Cf. *V.C.* 25, "Poverty, when measured by the goals that nature has set, is great wealth, whereas unlimited wealth is great poverty," and *L.D.* 15, "Nature's wealth is restricted and easily won, while that of empty convention runs on to infinity."

13. Epicurus would have considered a good American steak dinner as falling under the rubric of "trivialities," not to mention the disgustingly opulent fare that Trimalchio set before his Roman guests in Petronius' *Satyricon*. Epicurus practiced what he preached. Cf. Diogenes Laertius, *Life of Epicurus*, sect. 11: "Epicurus himself remarked in his letters that he was satisfied with just water and plain bread. 'Send me a small pot

of cheese,' he wrote, 'so that I can have a costly meal whenever I like.' "

14. I.e., it makes for self-sufficiency. See note 12, above.

15. Any way of life based on pleasure is liable to be caricatured by malicious rivals (here Cyrenaics and Stoics) as sensual and "libertine," just as Carlyle in the nineteenth century caricatured Mill's social hedonism as "a swinish philosophy." The "high liver" is the least sophisticated of men; he is the creature of uncontrolled drives and ignorant fears. Cf. *L.D.* 10: "If the things that produce the debauchee's pleasures dissolved the mind's fears regarding the heavenly bodies, death, and pain and also told us how to limit our desires, we would never have any reason to find fault with such people, because they would be glutting themselves with every sort of pleasure and never suffer physical or mental pain, which is the real evil."

16. Far from being sensual, the pleasant life of the garden is synonymous with the philosophical life. Cf. *L.D.* 20: "The body takes the limits of pleasure to be infinite, and infinite time would provide such pleasure. But the mind has provided us with the complete life by a rational examination of the body's goal and limitations and by dispelling our fears about a life after death; and so we no longer need unlimited time."

17. "Good judgment" (often translated as "prudence") is here contrasted with, and given higher rank than, "philosophy," or the theoretical grasp of first principles. The same contrast between "intellectual virtue" and "practical wisdom" is found in Plato and Aristotle, but these two philosophers, being rationalists, rank theoretical knowledge higher. The theory of the good life takes precedence over the practical wisdom that is derived from experience. The empirically minded Epicurus shows his independence of the rationalist tradition by reversing the order of importance. The practical good sense that stems directly from nature is more to be esteemed than the body of theory which is the product of philosophical reason. It is this sound common sense that shows us how to discriminate among pleasures in concrete situations and limit our pleasures so as to avoid pain and prompts us to pursue the conventional virtues such as justice (discussed in detail in *L.D.*

31–38). Despite this new emphasis, Epicurus could hardly deny that a theoretical grasp of the atomic theory and its implications must precede the practice of the good life of *ataraxia.*

18. Because of the stigma attached to pleasure in the minds of the ignorant or the perverse, Epicurus emphasizes that the pleasant life of *ataraxia,* though unconventional and divorced from the everyday life of the community, actually supports and fosters all the conventional virtues—in fact that justice and nobility of character are impossible unless one adopts the Epicurean way of life. This whole section is a final answer to his critics. Far from being immoral or a radical departure from the past, Epicureanism continues to maintain the best elements of the Greek moral and religious tradition.

19. The therapeutic power of his philosophy to reduce or neutralize all forms of pain, both physical and mental, is often stressed by Epicurus as one of its most attractive features. Cf. *V.C.* 4: "All pain is readily discounted. Intense pain has a short life, and longer lasting bodily pain is weak." Also cf. *L.D.* 12: "It is impossible to get rid of our anxieties about essentials if we do not understand the nature of the universe and are apprehensive about some of the theological accounts. Hence it is impossible to enjoy our pleasures unadulterated without natural science."

20. Bailey, following the Italian editor Bignone, fills in this serious lacuna in the MSS with the words, "He thinks that with us lies the chief power in determining events, some of which happen by necessity, . . ."

21. Epicurus held that: (1) Physical events, such as the movements of the heavenly bodies, are governed by necessity or, as we should say, by natural determinism but that necessity is essentially amoral, and to regard human life as determined, as Democritus did, would be equivalent to reducing man to moral slavery (*V.C.* 9: "Necessity is bad, but there is no necessity to live under Necessity"). (2) Chance is not the cause of good and evil, but human intelligence can often use chance events for both good and evil purposes (*Men.* 134). (3) The greater part of our lives is "in our own hands," thanks to the rational control made possible by the freedom of the will; *we* are

therefore responsible for what we do and cannot blame either necessity or chance. For a general discussion of determinism and freedom, see Introduction VII.2 and DeWitt, *op. cit.*, pp. 171–78.

22. After the decay of the religion of the Olympian gods and of belief in their moral government of the world, control of human affairs (e.g., war and peace, famine, pestilence, etc.) was popularly assigned to a single new power, variously called Chance or Fortune. The worship of this deity was extremely widespread in the Hellenistic period among both Greeks and Romans and is often regarded as an evolutionary stage in the development of monotheism. (See Gilbert Murray, *Five Stages of Greek Religion*, Chap. IV, "The Failure of Nerve.")

Epicurus takes a naturalistic view of chance. It is not a deity, "as in popular belief," but apparently a type of causation, metaphysical in nature but not orderly and predictable like the mechanical necessity that governs the regular processes of nature. It is chance that causes certain atoms to swerve and collide with other atoms, thereby producing entire systems called worlds, and it is the chance swerving of soul atoms that makes possible free will. Paradoxically our moral freedom depends on chance, but the impact of chance events on our lives is minimized by Epicurus: "Bad luck strikes the sophisticated man in a few cases; but reason has directed the big, essential things, and for the duration of life it is and will be the guide" (*L.D.* 16).

Leading Doctrines

1. A miscellany of assorted and doubtless genuine sayings of Epicurus on questions of ethics, politics, and epistemology. This collection was a kind of manual for practicing (or prospective?) Epicureans, not a full presentation of all the leading ideas of the system. Some of the sayings are criticisms, open or implied, of rival points of view put forward by Cyrenaics, Platonists, or Skeptics. There is no systematic or logical development of ideas, but the sayings may be classified into groups

according to their content or purpose. The title is sometimes translated as "authoritative" or "authorized" doctrines.

2. The gods are impassive themselves and have no concern for human affairs. See Introduction VI.2, and cf. *Herod.* 77 and *Men.* 123–24.

3. Cf. *Men.* 124–27.

4. I.e., pleasure means the neutralization of pain in body or mind, and nothing more; it does not mean the enjoyment of *positive* pleasures, as the layman or Cyrenaic ordinarily thinks it does. For this negative limitation of pleasure, which was central to Epicurean ethics, see *Men.* 128–32 and the discussion in Introduction VII.1.a.

5. I.e., the pleasant Epicurean life is synonymous with practicing the conventional virtues and vice versa; cf. *Men.* 132.

6. The egocentric Epicurean life is defensive. In order to have freedom from pain one must protect one's personal security from the inroads of others. Some men attempt to do this by force, by reputation, or by political power, but the most effective way is to withdraw from competition and the life of the community: "Live obscurely." See *L.D.* 14, and the discussion in Introduction VII.1.b.

7. "Pleasure" is here used in the ordinary sense of positive enjoyment. Every such pleasure is a good because it is "akin to our nature," but the consequences of overindulgence often result in a balance of pain over pleasure. Hence the "sensible" Epicurean will seek only the pleasures that neutralize pain. See *L.D.* 3 and *Men.* 129.

8. Epicurus insisted that there is both a quantitative and a qualitative difference in pleasures, in opposition to the Cyrenaics, who held that "no pleasure differs from any other, nor is it more pleasant" (Diogenes Laertius 2.87). For them the good life was a hedonistic binge that included any and every intense pleasure, without discrimination. Epicurus of course held that we must be "sensible" and select long-term mental pleasures that do not entail pain, such as conversation, reading, study, music, etc. He did not regard sex as a painkiller and would have frowned on the following "compression" of pleasure related by Alciphron, a writer on erotica: "Zenocrates the Epi-

curean took the girl harpist in his arms, looked at her with half-shut eyes, and said, 'This is my flesh's balm, the quintessence of pleasure.'"

9. The good life is impossible if we fear gods, death, hell, and the heavenly phenomena supposedly caused by the gods, but atomism cancels all these fears. See Introduction II.2, IV.2, and VI.3.2.

10. For Epicurus' optimistic view of the limits of pain see *L.D.* 4. The ethical limit of desire or pleasure is stated in *L.D.* 3.

11. The "essentials" referred to are of course death, the gods, and the heavenly bodies. Cf. also *Herod.* 78.

12. Cf. also *L.D.* 6, 7, and 40; Introduction VII.1.c.

13. Cf. *Men.* 130–31.

14. Cf. *Men.* 134–35, where Epicurus argues that chance sometimes provides "the initial circumstances for great good and evil."

15. For this egocentric view of an important social value see Introduction VII.1.c.

16. See note 4, above. A banquet does not increase the quantity of real bodily pleasure. It merely presents more opportunities for satisfying appetite than, say, a diet of barley bread and water but at the same time involves far greater risks of subsequent discomfort. And as for the mind, its highest limit of pleasure is to understand the limitations of pleasure and the nature of mankind's perennial fears and cravings—gods, death, and immortality (cf. *Men.* 132). Note again the purely negative and defensive attitude of the strict Epicurean. The positive pleasures of the civilized mind—conversation, reading, study, the arts—do not increase the amount of mental pleasure; they merely diversify it. But unlike the physical pleasures they are innocuous, since they do not threaten *ataraxia*. See also Introduction VII.1.a.

17. Cf. *Men.* 124–25. This aphorism seems to mean, "If perfect pleasure is attainable here and now, why long for immortality?" See *L.D.* 20.

18. Cf. *Men.* 126–27. "The best possible existence" is, of course, freedom from pain in body and mind, and nothing more. Epicurus' claim that his ideal is not ascetic would hardly pass

muster with cultivated persons today, who would find this kind of life (by the strict interpretation) barren, sterile, and stultifying.

19. This refers especially to engaging in politics, the *bête noire* of the Epicureans.

20. This cryptic saying establishes a vital connection between ethics and empirical knowledge. If our choices are to be morally good, we must not only measure them against the goal of *ataraxia* but test them against the empirical evidence that favors or does not favor them. For example, I might form the "judgment" that politics is a good way of life by observing how Senator X wins friends and influences people and also how well he lives (he drives a Cadillac and lives in a fifty-thousand-dollar house). Would this judgment be a sound basis for a choice of politics as my career? I must test it (1) against the standard of *ataraxia* and (2) against the available evidence that supports or fails to support it. In the first instance I can see that the rough-and-tumble of politics is about as far removed from *ataraxia* as any way of life can be. In the second instance, I see that the senator's physical surroundings, though superficially attractive, are a denial of the simplicity demanded by the Epicurean life. I also learn that he suffers from insomnia, ulcers, and bad nerves as a result of his hectic life. On all counts, then, I can only conclude that it would be immoral for me to choose politics as my way of life.

21. Rejection of sensation in general as untrustworthy was the extreme Skeptic position that Epicurus combated. He is showing here that this position is self-refuting. If all sensations are untrustworthy, then sensation cannot judge sensation to be false (nor can reason, since it is based on sensation, as he shows elsewhere). If the sensations are to be doubted, then all possibility of knowledge disappears. It is not the senses that deceive us, Epicurus teaches, but the false interpretations we often place on sensory data. See the discussion in Introduction IV.4.

22. In other words, to doubt any given sensation by failing to distinguish between what is given in sensation proper and what is added by way of interpretation is to doubt all sensations and thereby forfeit the means of establishing truth. Contrari-

wise, blind acceptance of all interpreted sensations (such as a mirage) as true is equally unjustified, since "the whole question at issue"—the superimposed interpretation—is ignored. This important epistemological doctrine is discussed in detail in Introduction IV.4.

23. That is, if your moral choices (for or against something) are not based exclusively on *ataraxia* but on some other standard (such as expediency, duty, moderation, etc.), you are not a consistent Epicurean.

24. The desires under (1) are the only ones considered legitimate by the strict Epicurean, since the satisfying of them is all that is needed to end pain in the body or the mind. Those under (2) are characteristic of the looser or secular Epicurean. The satisfying of them makes for variety in diet, living, etc., but they do not remove pain and may actually invite disagreeable consequences (e.g., fancy foods vs. a plain diet); see note 16, above. Those under (3) are characteristic of the raw or naïve Cyrenaic; under this heading Epicurus would lump most of the gadgets and paraphernalia of the American way of life.

25. The student can easily apply this maxim in hundreds of cases for himself, e.g., the new washing machine that Ma wants, the high-speed camera that Dad wants, the fifteen-dollar bottle of Chanel No. 5 that Elaine wants for her birthday, and the white Jaguar that you want.

26. The desire "generated by idle fancy" is sometimes taken to refer to sexual passion (as by Bailey in his commentary). If so, this dictum is quite consistent with the narrow ascetic views expressed elsewhere; e.g., "If you subtract seeing, social contact, and sexual intercourse, the erotic passion dissolves" (*V.C.* 18) and "Sex never benefited any man, and it's a marvel if it hasn't injured him!" (*V.C.* 51). If this natural drive is unnecessary in the sense that it does not lead to physical pain when not satisfied, what about the immediate pains of frustration and the long-term psychological damage inflicted by abstinence? The Epicurean prohibition on sex is not the consequence of a pre-Freudian innocence; it is a piece of dogmatism that forces a basic human drive into a preconceived, negative, and "life-denying" pattern of the good life.

27. Far from being a disinterested virtue, friendship is part of the egocentric armament of the Epicurean in that it (1) is indispensable to one's personal happiness and (2) is a first-rate protection when one is attacked (e.g., prosecuted) by other individuals. Cf. *V.C.* 23: "Every friendship is desirable for itself, but it has its origin in personal advantage," and see the discussion in DeWitt, *op. cit.*, pp. 307–10.

28. See the discussion in Introduction VII.1.C.

29. "Nature's goal" is of course personal security and, beyond that, *ataraxia* in general. Justice is only secondarily a social value. Its primary value is to contribute to one's self-protection and peace of mind in a world full of potential aggressors and hostile individuals. Cf. also *L.D.* 6 and 7.

30. That is, the lower nonverbalizing and noncontracting animals are amoral. The second sentence contains the thesis elaborated by the seventeenth-century materialist Thomas Hobbes in his social contract theory: Primitive man in the "state of nature" is premoral and amoral. Morality is not natural to man but a purely utilitarian device to promote the general security and prosperity—values that cannot exist where every man is an uninhibited predator. By delegating most of their natural rights to a central authority or monarch (and here Hobbes goes beyond Epicurus), men agree to limit their rapacity, and this works to their common advantage. Furthermore, right and wrong come into existence for the first time, since only under the social contract are men able to obey or disobey the laws of the monarch. In the last analysis, morality or justice is a function of power and not a matter of mere agreement between individuals, as Epicurus saw it.

31. That is, justice is not an eternal archetype, as Plato would have it, but a social contract empirically arrived at in various times and places in human history.

32. Injustice is not a Platonic Form, any more than justice. Its only existence is empirical, i.e., in human relations. And here it is evil, not because of its effects on others but because it destroys the *agent's* happiness: If I am the wrongdoer, I may escape punishment for a time, but until the day I die I will have to worry about the law catching up with me, and that is bad (cf.

L.D. 35). This view of injustice is not only completely cynical but also quite consistent with Epicurus' egocentric ethics.

33. Whatever is just, whether it be an action or a law, works universally to the mutual advantage of the contracting parties. Nevertheless the justice of specific actions and laws is always relative to time, place, and culture. An empirical ethics must provide an inductive generalization or universal definition of justice, as it does here, and at the same time allow for a flexible application of that definition in particular instances, according to the requirements of experience.

34. This selection repeats the idea that justice is relative and emphasizes in addition the need for empirical testing of actions and laws. Mere legality is not necessarily a guarantee of utility. The last two sentences seem to mean that certain laws outlive their usefulness to society (e.g., the Sunday Blue Laws) and that the empirically minded person will not be fooled by "meaningless words" or clichés ("It's legal," "It's illegal") but will *look* and find out why such laws were once useful to society and whether they still are. This point is reinforced in *L.D.* 38 ff.

35. The Epicurean in his search for personal security in an uncertain and often hostile world (cf. *L.D.* 14) seeks to win like-minded persons to his way of life. Those he cannot win over he seeks to keep neutral. Failing this, he either avoids associating with them or forcibly ejects them from his life. There is a cult jargon in this passage that expresses a sectarian spirit of exclusiveness and separatism similar to certain ideas in the New Testament (e.g., "He that is not with me is against me" and "Pure religion and undefiled is this . . . to keep oneself unspotted from the world"). For the religious aspects of Epicureanism see Introduction VI.4.

36. The Epicurean may pity himself in his bereavement, but not his dead friend because "death is nothing" to him:

> "You who now slumber in death shall so continue for the residue of time, void of all ills and pains. It is we who bewailed you unappeasably as you became ash on the fearful pyre nearby, and this everlasting grief no day shall take

from our hearts." Of such an one we must ask, What is so
very bitter, if all comes to slumber and repose, that anyone
should languish in unending sorrow? [Lucr. 3.904–11]

The Vatican Collection of Aphorisms

1. So named because this collection of aphorisms is from a single
   MS discovered in the Vatican Library in 1888. Most of these
   moral observations are presumably from works of Epicurus
   that are now lost or from his personal letters to friends. Several
   are repetitions of sayings in *Leading Doctrines*; others are
   from disciples such as Metrodorus. The collection is put together haphazardly, is much less technical than *Leading Doctrines*, and has less importance. Only a selection of the eighty-
   one sayings is here presented.
2. For Epicurus' optimistic view of physical pain, see *L.D.* 4. By
   making out that the burden of physical pain is negligible he
   lets the reader infer that one variety of *ataraxia* is easily obtained—which is more propaganda than fact.
3. A Greek pun. The saying means, "We are free men, not the
   moral slaves of a compulsive determinism." See *Men.* 133–34
   and Introduction VII.2.
4. The Roman poet and Epicurean, Quintus Horatius Flaccus
   (Horace), put the idea more pungently: *Carpe diem quam
   minimum credula postero* ("Gather in today's harvest and put
   scant trust in tomorrow").
5. For Epicurean prejudices about sex see *L.D.* 30 and note, and
   especially Lucr. 4.1052–1120 (=L28).
6. Dreams, like everything else, have to be explained in materialistic terms. Epicurus rejected divination (i.e., reading the future by dreams and other means) as part of the paraphernalia
   of popular superstition. See Introduction V.2.b on direct perceptions of the mind.
7. Cf. *L.D.* 15.
8. A paradox easily understood when we remember that evil = pain
   and good = pleasure. Our natural drive to seek pleasure and
   avoid pain gives good the upper hand over evil in human nature.

9. See *V.C.* 9 and note, above.

10. The contrast here is between vulgar and aristocratic values, as Nietzsche later distinguished them. Self-pride, if justified (and it is in the case of the philosopher who has risen above mass values and opinions), was a virtue with the Greeks, not a vice.

11. This sounds like a piece of spiritual Rotarianism, coming as it does from the usually austere and matter-of-fact Epicurus. Actually the Epicurean gospel was widely disseminated in the ancient world, often by means of friendly contacts of person with person. See DeWitt, *op. cit.*, pp. 101–5, 307–10.

12. This cryptic saying seems to mean "How short is life and how little we have to show for it!"

13. I.e., the Epicurean's job is not to win popular acclaim but to get on with the serious business of healing his own spiritual wounds. See introduction VI.4.b on Epicureanism as a spiritual therapy.

14. I.e., what will be the consequences in pleasure and pain in each case?

Selected Bibliography

I. TEXTS AND TRANSLATIONS

Bailey, C. *Epicurus: The Extant Remains with Short Critical Apparatus, Translation and Notes*. Oxford: Clarendon Press, 1926.

_____. *Lucreti De Rerum Natura*. Oxford: Clarendon Press, 1947. Latin text and critical apparatus.

_____. *Lucretius: On the Nature of Things*. Oxford: Clarendon Press, 1924. English translation.

Diano, C. *Epicuri Ethica*. Florence: Sansoni, 1946. Greek text of Epicurus' writings on ethics, with Latin commentary.

Hicks, R. D. *Diogenes Laertius: Lives of Eminent Philosophers*. New York: G. P. Putnam's Sons, 1925. Loeb Classical Library. Book X contains the *Life of Epicurus*, in which Diogenes included the three extant letters and *Leading Doctrines*.

Latham, R. E. *Lucretius: The Nature of the Universe*. London: Penguin Books, 1951. English translation with introduction.

Rouse, W. H. D. *Lucretius, De Rerum Natura*. New York: G. P. Putnam's Sons, 1924. Standard text and translation in the Loeb Classical Library.

Usener, H. *Epicurea*. Leipzig: Teubner, 1887. A pioneer work, with Latin commentary, embracing all Epicurus' works and writings extant in 1887, together with excerpts from later Epicurean writers, culled from many sources.

II. GENERAL WORKS

Dewitt, N. W. *Epicurus and His Philosophy.* Minneapolis: University of Minnesota Press, 1954. By far the most comprehensive recent treatment of Epicurus and Epicureanism from a cultural and philosophical point of view. The author conducts a one-man crusade against all who have sought to vilify and pervert the teachings of Epicurus, and he sees Epicureanism as a preparation for the Christian gospel of love. Very valuable but somewhat tendentious in tone.

Festugière, A.-J. *Epicure et ses Dieux.* Paris: Presses Universitaires de France, 1946. Excellent for the Epicurean theology.

Fuller, B. A. G. *A History of Philosophy.* 3rd ed., revised by S. M. McMurrin. New York: Henry Holt & Co., 1955. Chap. XVI. A somewhat perfunctory and noncritical treatment, dutifully included in a standard encyclopedic history of Western philosophy.

Hadzsits, G. D. *Lucretius and Epicureanism.* Boston: Marshall Jones Co., 1926. A short informative account of the Roman poet and of the influence of the Epicurean tradition on later centuries.

Haringer, J. Von. *Epikur, Lebenskunst.* Zurich: Werner Classen, 1947. An attractive popularization.

Jones, W. T. *A History of Western Philosophy.* New York: Harcourt, Brace & Co., 1952. Vol. I, Chap. 3, "Atomism," and Chap. 8, esp. pp. 260–66 on Epicurus. A readable and critical account of atomism, Epicurus, and Lucretius; superior to Fuller.

Kahn, F. *Design of the Universe.* New York: Crown Publishers, Inc., 1954. Esp. Part Two, "The Atom." An excellent popularization of present-day physics and astronomy, recommended to those who wish to contrast ancient atomism with modern theory.

De Santillana, G. *The Origins of Scientific Thought, from*

Anaximander to Proclus, 600 B.C. to A.D. 500. Chicago: University of Chicago Press, 1961. Chapter 9 contains a semipopular treatment of Democritus, with various translated texts, by this eminent historian and philosopher of science.

Whyte, L. L. *Essay on Atomism: From Democritus to 1960.* Middletown, Connecticut: Wesleyan University Press, 1961. A compact account of the development of various atomic theories, written by a philosopher of science for those interested in the history of ideas.

Index

26 f., 76, 89, 194 (n. 49);
regarding sex, 236 (n. 26)
Dreams, 86, 97, 181 (*V.C.* 24)

Earthquakes, 144
Eclipses, lunar and solar, 140–141
Eidola, 20–22, 116 f.;
composite, 96; existence of,
21, 96; of the gods, 129–130
Empedocles, 5–6; theory of
perception, 211 (n. 6)
Empiricism: Epicurean, 27 ff.;
and ethics, 60 f., 235 (n. 20);
and verification of
judgments, 28–34
Epicureanism, viii–xi; ascetic,
61; dogmatic, 26, 76, 208
(n. 39); and empiricism,
27 ff., 176 (*L.D.* 22–25);
humanitarian, 27, 76; and
politics, 88; as a "salvation"
philosophy, 27; sectarian, 61,
74, 75, 179 (*L.D.* 39 f.);
secular, 62, 75; as a secular
religion, 53 ff.; as a spiritual
therapy, 54 f.
Epicurus: as anti-Platonist, 72,
74; ethics of, 56 ff.;
hedonism of, 58 ff.; mother
of, ix; personal life, 63; as
spiritual healer, 55; and state
religion, 88; his theory of
perception, x, 21–22;
veneration of, 53 f.; writings
of, 84–85

Epicurus's Garden, ix, viii, xi
Epistemology; *see* Knowledge,
theory of
Error, when it occurs, 97
Ethical goal, the; *see Ataraxia*
Evil; *see* Pain

Falsity, when it occurs, 97. *see
also* Truth
Feelings, the, as moral
criteria, 30
Films; *see* Atomic films
Form, Platonic, 26, 66, 209
(n. 2), 237 (n. 31 f.)
Freedom, moral, 18 f., 68–71
Free will; *see* Determinism
Friendship, 66, 89, 177
(*L.D.* 27 f.), 179 (*L.D.* 40),
183 (*V.C.* 52)
Frost, 145

Gods: blessed and impassive,
41 f.; do not control the
universe, 41 f.; existence of
the, 29, 39, 156; function of
the, 39–40; nature of the, 40–43, 156, 173 (*L.D.* 1); non-anthropomorphic, 40, 156
"Good judgment," 74, 160,
230 (n. 17)
Good life, the; *see* Hedonism
Greek science, 7 f.
Gymnosophists, ix

Hail, 144 f.
Happiness, two meanings of, 89
Health, spiritual: and

INDEX

Rain, 141 f.

Rainbow, the, 146

Rationalism, 27–28

Reality: consists of atoms and
space, 12 f., 93; infinite,
13 f., 94

Reason: ethical bearing of, 63–
65, 175 (*L.D.* 18–20); not a
primary test for truth, 205
(n. 24), 209 (n. 2); and the
selection of pleasures, 63–65;
and sensation, 28–29, 85

Reductio ad absurdum, 69, 188
(n. 11)

Relativity; *see* Pleasure and pain

Religion, popular: destroys
ataraxia, 43; Epicurean
attack on, ix, 43, 45 ff., 149;
evils of, 48 ff.; true
(Epicurean), 43

Responsibility, moral, 68, 160

"Salvation" philosophy,
Epicureanism as, 27, 203
(n. 19)

Science, natural, and the good
life, 110, 174 (*L.D.* 10–14)

Security, personal, and the
good life, 67, 174 (*L.D.* 6 f.),
179 (*L.D.* 40)

Self-sufficiency, 182 (*V.C.* 44),
183 (*V.C.* 77), 229 (n. 12)

Sensation: and atomic films,
20–22; cannot be refuted, 85;
impossible in death, 19 f.,
132 f.; product of interaction,
18–19; status of, 13; truth

and falsity of, 22–25, 176
(*L.D.* 24); validity of, 28–29

Sense data, infallible, 28, 191
(n. 32)

Sex, Epicurus on, 63, 87, 88,
160, 169–172, 181 (*V.C.* 18),
182 (*V.C.* 51)

Sight, 95 ff.

Size, of heavenly bodies, 151 f.

Skepticism, 24 f.

"Slow" and "fast," as
predicates of compound
bodies, 213 (n. 14)

Smell, 98

Snow, 145

Soul: bipartite, 118–119;
corporeal, 101 f., 121; and
death, 11, 57, 104; its atoms
indestructible, 10; mortality
of the, 57, 166; nature of the,
118–121; and sensation, 103 f.

Space, infinite, 13–14, 94; real,
7; "up" and "down" not
predicable of, 102–103

Stars, falling, 148; fixed stars,
147; slow moving, 148

Suicide, Epicurus on, 157, 182
(*V.C.* 38)

Superstition, and natural
causation, 149

Swerve, atomic, x, 16–18, 69–
71, 114–116

Theater of Dionysius, vii

Theological explanations, and
natural causation, 37–39

Theology, Epicurean, 40 ff.